THE BEDFORD SERII

MW00986364

Our Hearts Fell to the Ground

Plains Indian Views of How the West Was Lost

Edited with an Introduction by

Colin G. Calloway

Dartmouth College

Palgrave Macmillan

For Marcia who came to Wyoming, for Graeme who liked the fast wind, and for Megan, who slept in her crib beside me while I thought about this book.

For Bedford Books

President and Publisher: Charles H. Christensen
General Manager and Associate Publisher: Joan E. Feinberg
Associate History Editor: Richard Keaveny
Managing Editor: Elizabeth M. Schaaf
Production Editor: Heidi L. Hood
Production Assistant: Christina Smith
Copyeditor: Jane M. Zanichkowsky
Indexer: Steve Csipke
Text Design: Claire Seng-Niemoeller
Cover Design: Hannus Design Associates
Cover Art: William Cary (1840–1922) *The Fire Canoe, Fort Berthold,* ca. 1870 (0136.1834). Oil on canvas. From the Collection of Gilcrease Museum, Tulsa.

Library of Congress Catalog Card Number: 95–83531
Copyright © 1996 by BEDFORD BOOKS *of* St. Martin's Press

Softcover reprint of the hardcover 1st edition 1996 978-0-312-16050-0

Manufactured in the United States of America.

0 9 8 7 6
f e d c b a

For information, write: St. Martin's Press, Inc., 175 Fifth Avenue, New York, NY 10010
Editorial Offices: Bedford Books *of* St. Martin's Press, 75 Arlington Street, Boston, MA 02116

ISBN 978-1-349-61348-9   ISBN 978-1-137-07646-5 (eBook)
DOI 10.1007/978-1-137-07646-5

Acknowledgments

Arapooish, "Speech on Crow Country." From *The Adventures of Captain Bonneville U.S.A. in the Rocky Mountains and the Far West,* by Washington Irving, edited by Edgeley W. Todd. New edition copyright © 1961, 1986 by the University of Oklahoma Press.

Bear Head, "Account of the Massacre on the Marias." From *Blackfeet and Buffalo: Memories of Life Among the Indians,* by James Willard Schulz (Apikuni). Copyright © 1962 by the University of Oklahoma Press.

Jerome Big Eagle, "A Sioux Story of the War, ca. 1894." From *Collections of the Minnesota Historical Society* 6 (1894), pp. 382–400. Reprinted and edited in *Through Dakota Eyes: Narrative Accounts of the Minnesota Indian War of 1862,* edited by Gary Clayton Anderson and Alan R. Woolworth. St. Paul: Minnesota Historical Society Press, 1988, pp. 23–27, 55–56, 237.

"Kiowa Legend." From *American Indian Mythology,* by Alice Marriot and Carol K. Rachlin, pp. 169–70. Copyright © 1968 by Alice Marriot and Carol K. Rachlin. Reprinted with permission of HarperCollins Publishers, Inc.

Acknowledgments and copyrights are continued at the back of the book on pages 216–17, which constitute an extension of the copyright page. It is a violation of the law to reproduce these selections by any means whatsoever without the written permission of the copyright holder.

Foreword

The Bedford Series in History and Culture is designed so that readers can
study the past as historians do.
The historian's first task is finding the evidence. Documents, letters,
memoirs, interviews, pictures, movies, novels, or poems can provide
facts and clues. Then the historian questions and compares the sources.
There is more to do than in a courtroom, for hearsay evidence is welcome,
and the historian is usually looking for answers beyond act and motive.
Different views of an event may be as important as a single verdict. How
a story is told may yield as much information as what it says.
Along the way the historian seeks help from other historians and
perhaps from specialists in other disciplines. Finally, it is time to write, to
decide on an interpretation and how to arrange the evidence for readers.
Each book in this series contains an important historical document or
group of documents, each document a witness from the past and open to
interpretation in different ways. The documents are combined with some
element of historical narrative — an introduction or a biographical essay,
for example — that provides students with an analysis of the primary
source material and important background information about the world
in which it was produced.
Each book in the series focuses on a specific topic within a specific
historical period. Each provides a basis for lively thought and discussion
about several aspects of the topic and the historian's role. Each is short
enough (and inexpensive enough) to be a reasonable one-week assign-
ment in a college course. Whether as classroom or personal reading, each
book in the series provides firsthand experience of the challenge — and
fun — of discovering, recreating, and interpreting the past.

Natalie Zemon Davis
Ernest R. May

Preface

This book is designed both as a sequel to *The World Turned Upside Down: Indian Voices from Early America* (Bedford Books, 1994) and to stand on its own as a case study of Native American views of the changing world of the nineteenth century. The volume follows chronologically from my earlier book *The World Turned Upside Down* and *The Cherokee Removal: A Brief History with Documents*, edited by Michael Green and Theda Perdue (Bedford Books, 1995). As in *The World Turned Upside Down*, the selections in this volume do not tell the whole story. Rather, the episodes and statements are intended to illustrate larger trends and serve as springboards for fuller discussion of key issues in American Indian history.

Originally, this book was intended to present Indian perspectives from throughout the trans-Mississippi West and from first contacts with Spaniards in the Southwest in the 1540s to 1900. The sheer volume of materials demanded a more limited focus. Personal interest, the richness of the visual and documentary materials from the Great Plains, and the rapidity and dramatic nature of the changes that occurred there in the nineteenth century prompted this choice. Peter Nabokov's *Native American Testimony: A Chronicle of Indian-White Relations from Prophecy to the Present, 1492–1992* (Viking, 1991) provides an excellent collection of Indian statements from a broader area and over a longer time span; this book concentrates on one group of peoples during a particularly crucial era of their history. Numerous anthologies and coffee table books offer native statements on aspects of the old ways of life in a timeless past; this book concentrates on how Indian people perceived and experienced massive changes in their ways of life in the wake of contact with people of European origin or ancestry.

All the people in these pages had their own names for themselves. (Sometimes, the names by which they are best known stem from an enemy's characterization.) Nevertheless, I have retained the most widely known names for the various tribes rather than bombard students with a barrage of unfamiliar terms. Likewise, I recognize the limitations — and to some people the offensive nature — of terms such as *Indian, Native American,* and *white,* but have employed them in situations where some collective noun is necessary and none is entirely satisfactory.

I am grateful to Charles Christensen and the history staff at Bedford Books for their support and assistance on this project. Associate editor Richard Keaveny embraced the project with his usual enthusiasm, efficiency, and good humor; history intern Kate O'Sullivan provided able assistance; Heidi Hood steered the manuscript into publication; and Jane Zanichkowsky did a nice job of copyediting. I am also indebted to Gary Clayton Anderson, Peter Iverson, James P. Ronda, Michael L. Tate, and Robert M. Utley for their valuable and generous comments on the manuscript.

Colin G. Calloway

Contents

Illustrations

INTRODUCTION
How the West Was Lost

We did not think of the great open plains, the beautiful rolling hills, and the winding streams with tangled growth, as "wild." Only to the white man was nature a "wilderness" and only to him was the land "infested" with "wild" animals and "savage" people. To us it was tame. Earth was bountiful and we were surrounded with the blessings of the Great Mystery. Not until the hairy man from the east came and with brutal frenzy heaped injustices upon us and the families we loved was it "wild" for us. When the very animals of the forest began fleeing from his approach, then it was for us the "Wild West" began.

— Luther Standing Bear,
Land of the Spotted Eagle (1933)

The story of how the West was won holds a central place in American history, in popular imagination about the country's past, and even in America's sense of identity. Although there were many wests, and the struggle for the continent was fought many times in many different places, the era of American exploration, conquest, and settlement of the Great Plains in the nineteenth century is by far the most famous. The Lewis and Clark expedition, the fur trade, Manifest Destiny, wagon trains rolling across the plains to Oregon and California, Indian wars, cattle drives, and railroad-building all represent chapters in a story familiar, at least in its broad outlines and as popularized by Hollywood, to most Americans. Indians usually feature in the story as either savage opponents of civilization or helpless victims of an empire-building nation, depending on one's point of view. In either case, their history is a subplot in the national epic, and their actions and experiences usually receive minimal attention.

In this volume I attempt to allow some of the Indian people who lived through those times to speak for themselves. The nineteenth century was the time of most dramatic and traumatic change in the lives of Indian peoples on the plains: Their numbers dwindled under the onslaught of war and disease; their old ways of life were destroyed and new ones imposed; their lands passed into non-Indian hands; much of the world

1

they inhabited changed before their eyes as buffalo died and railroads and fences appeared. Indian people were catapulted from an ancient tribal world into a modern, industrializing society. The people who lived through, and sometimes participated in, these changes, saw things in their own way. Their views were sometimes very different from those held by white Americans at that time and from what white Americans today might expect them to have been. They varied according to time, tribe, place, gender, circumstance, and individual experience and character. But, taken together, their views give us some idea of what it meant to live on the other side of the frontier and to be subjected to "civilization." As Luther Standing Bear's words remind us, the same events can have radically different meanings for different people: One people's expansion usually entails another's dispossession, and extending one civilization usually means destroying another culture. The lives of the people in this volume remind us that "the Indian story" in the conquest of the American West was not simple and that the conquest was not complete.

THE INDIAN PEOPLES OF THE PLAINS

The arid grasslands of North America known as the Great Plains stretch from Texas to Saskatchewan, from the Missouri River to the Rocky Mountains. The plains are a hard and beautiful land of skies and distances, illuminated by strong sunlight, buffeted by seemingly constant winds, watered with little rain, and sheltered by few trees. Even today, in an age of modern conveniences, instant communication, and rapid travel, the plains can touch one's soul or break one's spirit. Some people think the high plains are a God-forsaken place; others see God's handiwork there more clearly than anywhere else. For thousands of years the plains have challenged the resilience of the people who have made them their home; their first inhabitants were pioneers just as much as those who came later.

The Indians of the Great Plains are the best known of all American Indian groups. Their ways of life, appearance, and experiences have come to be regarded as typical for all tribes, and Hollywood has helped to make the Plains Indian the stereotype for all Indians. In reality, however, Plains Indians were *a*typical. The culture they developed was unique to the region and their way of life as equestrian, buffalo-hunting nomads relatively short-lived. The forces that shaped their way of life also planted the seeds for its destruction.

American history books often begin the story of the trans-Mississippi West when Meriwether Lewis and William Clark explore the region in

1804–06: History begins when white Americans arrive; anything before that is *pre*history. In reality, human history on the Great Plains stretches back to a time beyond memory according to tribal legends and at least ten thousand years according to conservative scholarly estimates. During that time, Indians pioneered the land, adapted to environmental changes, and developed hundreds of communities and cultures. When Lewis and Clark crossed the continent they entered an Indian world with ancient roots but one that was already changed and continually changing as a result of contact with both Indian and non-Indian outsiders.

The Indian peoples living on the Great Plains by 1800 can be divided into two broad groups (see Figure 1). On the eastern edges of the plains, along the Missouri River, lived semisedentary farming tribes like the Mandans, the Hidatsas, the Arikaras, the Pawnees, and the Omahas. These peoples had lived in the region for hundreds of years. They inhabited earthen lodge villages, cultivated extensively, and practiced elaborate ceremonies that brought success in farming and hunting. Many of the buffalo-hunting Indians who lived deeper in the plains — the Blackfeet, the Sioux, the Cheyennes, the Arapahos, the Crows, the Kiowas, and the Comanches — were relatively recent arrivals.

Before the arrival of horses, small bands hunted buffalo and other game on foot. Horses transformed the life of the Plains Indians. Introduced by the Spaniards in the Southwest, horses quickly spread by trading and raiding from tribe to tribe on the plains. Most tribes were mounted by the early eighteenth century and were capable of traveling great distances and exploiting the rich resources of their environment to the full. The period between the acquisition of the horse and the coming of white settlers has been called the golden age of the Plains Indians, and people of the reservation era in the late nineteenth century looked back on those times with nostalgia. Horses, easily transportable skin tepees, and fluid band structures enabled Plains Indians to follow the buffalo herds at will. The buffalo provided the tribes with food, shelter, clothing, tools, and weapons. It became the economic and cultural base of the new societies that developed and, ironically, provided a key to their defeat in the second half of the nineteenth century, when white Americans slaughtered the herds and reduced mobile hunters to dependence on government rations.

From what is today Arizona and New Mexico, Plains Indians began to feel the influence of Spanish explorers, soldiers, and missionaries in the sixteenth century. Spaniards brought domesticated animals, new crops, new technology, and deadly new diseases. In the early 1540s, Francisco de Coronado led an expedition to the plains in search of the fabled seven cities of Cibola. He got as far north as Kansas, but found no cities of gold.

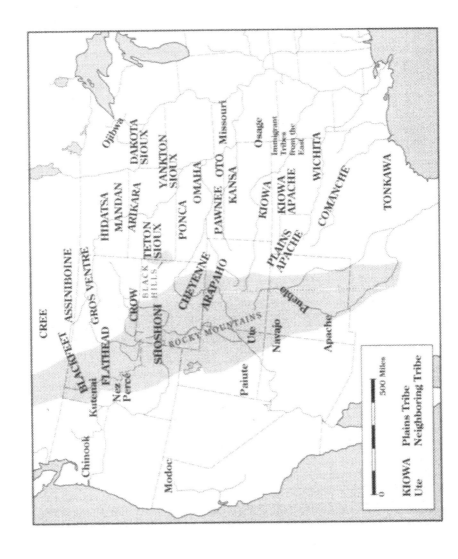

Horses appeared on the plains by the mid-seventeenth century, but a synchronized revolt by Pueblo peoples in the southwest in 1680 accelerated the diffusion of Spanish horses into Indian country. Spaniards in the early eighteenth century found themselves fighting with mounted Apache, Navajo, and Comanche warriors coming south from the plains. The tentative tentacles of Spanish and French ambitions collided on the plains as early as 1720, when Pedro de Villasur led an expedition from Santa Fe to reconnoiter French activities only to have his force all but exterminated by Indians and Frenchmen on the Platte River in Nebraska.[1]

French, British, Canadian, and Spanish traders preceded Lewis and Clark into Indian villages on the plains. With most of their needs supplied by buffalo, Plains Indians initially were able to maintain a measure of independence in their dealings with European traders. Northwest Company trader Charles Mackenzie, on the upper Missouri at about the time Lewis and Clark passed by, complained that beaver were plentiful there but the Indians refused to take the trouble of trapping them. They told him they would be happy to hunt beaver if they could do so in the same way they hunted buffalo, from horseback, "but they considered the operation of searching for them in the bowels of the earth, to satisfy the avarice of the Whites, not only troublesome, but very degrading." When Mackenzie pointed out that more northerly tribes were industrious and friendly to the whites, one chief responded angrily: "We are no Slaves!" Indians called the shots on the Great Plains in the early nineteenth century, and whites relied on them as allies and as traders; but, whether they trapped beaver or not, Indians were becoming tied into global trade networks as direct or indirect participants. The chief admitted that there were things the Indians had become dependent on, to their cost: "In my young days there were no white men, and we knew no wants," he said. "The white people came, they brought with them some good, but they brought the small pox, and they brought evil liquors; the Indians since diminish and they are no longer happy."[2] When Lewis and Clark crossed the continent in 1804–06, they met Indian people who wore woollen blankets, were accomplished traders, knew how to swear in French or English, drank alcohol, bore the marks of smallpox, and competed to secure or monopolize access to goods and guns.[3]

proved they could share the land w/ foreigners

Figure 1 (*opposite*). The Indian Peoples of the Great Plains in the Early to Mid-Nineteenth Century, Showing Neighboring Tribes Mentioned in the Text

The rich resources of the plains proved a magnet for Indian peoples at a time when other areas were feeling pressures generated by white invasion. In the eighteenth century the plains became a huge arena of competition between rival tribes jockeying for position and hunting territory. Cree Indians, armed with guns by Hudson Bay Company traders in the eastern woodlands, made alliances with Assiniboines and pushed west on to the northern plains.[4] Shoshonis expanded eastward on to the northern plains early in the century, but then other groups pushed them back into the Rocky Mountains.[5] The Crow Indians split from their Hidatsa relatives sometime before 1700, moved on to the plains, and eventually took up residence in the rich hunting territory of the Yellowstone region in southern Montana. The Cheyennes left Minnesota, crossed the Missouri River, and took up life as equestrian hunters on the plains. Comanches migrated southward from Wyoming, down through the central plains, and into the area of present-day Texas and Oklahoma by 1800. En route, they came into conflict with Apache bands, whom they pushed into the desert Southwest. The Apaches and Navajos had themselves migrated from the north hundreds of years before, coming into conflict with the Pueblo Indians of the Southwest and with the Spaniards at their northern frontier.

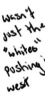

The Sioux, who once lived in present-day Minnesota and around the headwaters of the Mississippi, found themselves under increasing pressure from other tribes being edged west behind them. Late in the eighteenth century the Lakotas or Teton Sioux, moved on to the plains. The Lakotas — the Oglala, the Hunkpapa, the Sicangu or Brulé, the Miniconjou, the Sans Arc, the Two Kettle, and the Sihaspa or Blackfoot Sioux — were the western tribes of a huge nation that also included the Eastern Dakota and Middle Yankton divisions. They added to the turmoil on the plains as they pushed weaker tribes aside and seized hunting territories.[6]

Indian exiles from the East exacerbated the collision of cultures in the West. Cherokees, Shawnees, Potawatomis, and other groups who were expelled from their homelands and relocated into present-day Oklahoma and Arkansas under the Indian Removal Act of 1830 came into conflict with Osages and other indigenous tribes, pushing those peoples into further conflict with Comanches to the west of them and generating a series of chain reactions. Bitter conflicts erupted between the western tribes and the newcomers; armed with guns and firing in ranks, eastern Indians inflicted some costly defeats on mounted plains warriors. Competition between tribes increased further when the first white immigrants arrived and game stocks were depleted.

In these circumstances, the Great Plains became a battleground and war a way of life for the people who lived there. Young men sought visions that would guarantee success in battle and joined warrior societies that encouraged and sustained the martial spirit of the tribe. Success in war was the key to status and prestige for a Plains Indian male, and warriors endeavored to outdo each other in acts of bravery: Counting coup on an enemy without harming him or raiding for horses generally carried more prestige than killing an enemy. However, as warfare escalated on the plains, it also became more deadly; warriors now fought with guns introduced by European and American traders.

As horses spread across the plains from the Spanish Southwest, guns filtered into the area from the northeast via French and British traders. The two frontiers met in the second half of the eighteenth century at the Mandan, Hidatsa, and Arikara villages on the upper Missouri River in North Dakota where plains hunters went to trade meat and leather for corn, tobacco, and other crops grown by the women of those villages. Like other Indians in North America, Plains Indians were accustomed to trading over long distances. European traders recognized the pivotal importance of the upper Missouri rendezvous. Soon, Plains Indians found they could obtain manufactured goods and guns there, which they could then trade to neighbors who lived deeper in the plains. Crow traders often traveled to a rendezvous with Shoshonis in southwestern Wyoming; the Shoshonis in turn traded with Nez Percés, Flatheads, and other groups in the mountains. Many of those groups were in contact with Chinooks and other native traders who dealt with European and American maritime traders on the Pacific coast. The Cheyennes operated as middlemen, traveling between the Missouri and the plains. The Sioux held their own rendezvous with traders from the East.[7] The Blackfeet obtained guns from Canadian traders and tried to keep them out of the hands of rival tribes to their west. Blackfeet, Sioux, and other surrounding tribes laid siege to game-filled Crow territory in the Yellowstone valley. By mid-century the Crows faced extermination as the Sioux came to dominate the northern and central plains in alliance with the Cheyennes and the Arapahos. Horses, guns, and hunting territories were keys to survival.

Devastating epidemics of new diseases also threatened tribal survival. A massive smallpox epidemic killed thousands of people from Mexico to Canada between 1779 and 1783, largely following the routes by which horses were traded from tribe to tribe. Smallpox struck the Missouri River in 1801–02: When Lewis and Clark headed upstream from St. Louis in 1804, they passed abandoned villages, silent testimony to the ravages of a newly introduced disease.[8] In 1837 smallpox broke out in the Indian villages on the upper Missouri and wrought havoc across the northern plains. Smallpox struck the Comanches in 1816 and 1839–40. Unseen killers eroded the military power of Plains Indian societies long before the warriors turned to confront the American army.

THE CONQUEST OF THE PLAINS

Traditional histories of the United States portray American expansion westward as the advance of "civilization" and the winning of the continent. From an Indian perspective, of course, this was a story of invasion and dispossession.

The American explorers and traders who entered the Plains Indians' world in the early nineteenth century were just the latest in a series of white visitors and posed no immediate threat. The Great Plains was still Indian country, and most people in the East regarded it as the "Great American Desert." As American expansion gathered speed, however, and the doctrine of Manifest Destiny proclaimed Americans' right and duty to occupy all land westward to the Pacific, Indian peoples on the plains came under siege. In less than twenty years in the first half of the century, Americans colonized Texas and secured its independence from Mexico; conquered California, Arizona, New Mexico, parts of Utah, and Colorado during the war with Mexico (1846–48); discovered gold in California; and opened Oregon to settlement. Indians on the plains saw increasing numbers of white Americans crossing their lands.

Contrary to Hollywood's obsession with Plains Indian raids on wagon trains, emigrants traveling the overland trails to Oregon and California in the 1840s experienced relatively little hostility. In fact, Indians sometimes traded with the emigrants for food and other supplies and assisted them as guides and at river crossings.[9] But the pioneers brought more diseases: Cholera, measles, and scarlet fever soon added to the toll of deaths in Indian villages. Emigrants hunted and frightened away game and exhausted timber resources, while their stock wore out grazing lands along the trails. The Shoshonis felt the effects of game depletion as early as 1855. "This country was once covered with buffalo, elk, deer, and antelope, and we had plenty to eat," protested chief Washakie. "But now, since the white man has made a road across our land and has killed off our game, we are hungry, and there is nothing left for us to eat. Our women and children cry for food and we have no food to give them."[10] Tensions escalated: Indians regarded emigrants as trespassers, and the United States was determined to protect its citizens.

At the Treaty of Fort Laramie in 1851, Indians from all the major tribes on the northern plains accepted American proposals that they recognize and respect tribal boundaries. The United States hoped to reduce the level of conflict on the plains and restrict the tribes to designated areas in an effort to prevent confrontations, but fighting broke out only a few years later. A misunderstanding over the loss of an emigrant's cow erupted in the killing of Lieutenant John Grattan and his command by Brulé Sioux in 1854. General William S. Harney retaliated by attacking an Indian village at Ash Hollow the following year, and the stage was set for more than twenty years of open warfare between the Sioux and the United States Army.

The American Civil War (1861–65) slowed migration westward and called troops away from the frontiers, but conflicts with the Indians continued with little respite. After years of land loss and abuse, the Eastern Sioux rose up against settlers in Minnesota in 1862. American troops quelled the uprising, more than three hundred Indians were tried for murder, and thirty-eight were executed. Many Sioux fled to Canada or to their western relatives, and pursuing American forces came into conflict with Lakotas on the plains.

[handwritten margin note: this is what they get for trying to keep their land]

Two years later, amid white fears of an Indian war, John Chivington and the Colorado militia massacred Black Kettle's band of Cheyennes, and some Southern Arapahos, at Sand Creek, where the Indians had camped, supposedly under the protection of the U.S. government. A congressional investigation followed, but the damage was done. Cheyenne and Arapaho warriors bent on revenge joined their Sioux allies in the north.[11]

Industrializing America looked to westward expansion to help reunite the nation after the Civil War. National expansion mandated that Indians and buffalo herds be replaced with farmers and cattle herds. The government was determined to confine the nomadic tribes of the plains on reservations, where they could be segregated, supervised, and educated in "civilized" ways. The Army launched a series of campaigns to bring in the tribes.

[handwritten margin note: rude]

Plains Indians who counted on individual prowess and spiritual power to bring them victory now confronted the relentless discipline and superior firepower of American armies who waged total war (see Figure 2). The United States broke Indian resistance by slaughtering the buffalo herds, destroying Indian pony herds, and attacking Indian villages.

The Oglala chief Red Cloud fought the United States Army to a standstill in a war (1866–67) to protect Sioux lands against the building of the Bozeman Trail, which ran from Fort Laramie to the gold fields of Montana. In December 1866 — "the winter of one hundred slain" — the

Figure 2.   A Great Battle
Zotom, a Kiowa, participated in the attack on Adobe Walls in 1874 and fought in
the Red River War before he was exiled to Fort Marion as a prisoner. In this 1877
drawing he depicts two different concepts of warfare: Individualistic Plains Indian

Sioux lured the overconfident Captain William Fetterman into an ambush
and annihilated his command. At the Treaty of Fort Laramie in 1868, the
United States recognized Red Cloud's victory, agreed to abandon its forts
on the Bozeman Trail, and guaranteed the boundaries of Sioux territory,
including the Black Hills. But the final version of the treaty set aside lands
west of the Black Hills as hunting territory, with the intention that they
be ceded to the United States when the buffalo were gone. Having won
his victory, Red Cloud counseled peace and became the spokesman for
the people who tried to make a go of life on the reservations. Leadership
of those who resisted such a life passed to men like Crazy Horse and
Sitting Bull.
    On the southern plains, Kiowas, Comanches, and Southern Chey-
ennes found themselves compressed into a tightening circle of territory,
between Texans to the south and increasing numbers of settlers in
Kansas and along the Platte River to the north. Trader and agent William

warriors launching hit-and-run assaults on American soldiers standing and firing in ranks. The tails of the Indian ponies are tied up in preparation for battle and the flow of the action is from right to left, in keeping with traditional hide-painting conventions.

Bent warned in 1859 that the Indians would be forced into "a desperate war of starvation and extinction" if something was not done soon to prevent it.[12] The government tried to prevent it at the Treaty of Medicine Lodge in 1867. There the Kiowas, Comanches, Plains Apaches, Southern Cheyennes, and Southern Arapahos agreed to live on reservations established for them below the Kansas River. But the government failed to supply the tribes as promised; young men left the reservation to hunt, and peace was short-lived. In 1868 General Philip Sheridan conducted a winter campaign against the villages of the southern plains tribes. George Armstrong Custer attacked and destroyed Black Kettle's Southern Cheyenne village on the Washita River; Black Kettle and his wife died in the attack along with many of their people. In addition, Custer's command shot hundreds of Indian ponies. In 1874, hungry Indians, angered by the government's failure even to keep buffalo hunters out of the lands guaranteed to them by treaty, went to war to preserve what remained of their herds and their way of life. The Army launched a five-pronged invasion of the southern plains, during which Colonel Ranald Mackenzie attacked the camps of the Southern Cheyennes, Kiowas, and Comanches at Palo Duro Canyon, killing few warriors but burning four hundred lodges and slaughtering fourteen hundred horses. The following winter, the Indians began to come in from the snow-covered plains and submit to life on the reservations.[13] In 1875, seventy-two southern Plains Indian warriors, whom the government identified as ringleaders in the recent wars, were sent to exile in Florida, where they were imprisoned for three years in Fort Marion at Saint Augustine and used as experiments in a program of "civilization by immersion" conducted by Captain Richard H. Pratt.

Other forces, more powerful than Army bullets, were bringing an end to the world Plains Indians had created. The first transcontinental railroad was completed in 1869; other lines proliferated in the years that followed, bringing more emigrants to the West and facilitating the movement of troops and supplies. At the same time, the buffalo herds were systematically destroyed between 1867 and 1883. Early reports estimated the numbers of buffalo in millions; by the end of the century only a handful survived. With their food supply gone, and the buffalo-hunting culture in ruins, Indians faced a choice between starvation and the reservation.

Pressure to bring recalcitrant Indians to heel increased in the early 1870s, especially after George Custer led an expedition into the Black Hills that verified reports of gold in the region. Faced with a deep recession and unable to keep fortune hunters off Sioux lands, the United States tried to back out of the commitments it had made in the 1868 Treaty of Fort Laramie. The Black Hills were sacred to the Sioux. When U.S. commissioners offered to buy the land, Red Cloud responded: "My intention was that my children should depend on these hills for the future" and asked that "seven generations ahead . . . be fed." He gave the commissioners a long list of items to be provided in addition. Maybe the whites thought he was asking too much, "but I think those hills extend clear to the sky — maybe they go above the sky, and that is the reason I ask for so much."[14] The commissioners balked at the price, but Sitting Bull presented them with no such dilemma: The Black Hills, he said, were simply "not for sale."

Things came to a head in 1876. The government issued an ultimatum requiring all Sioux bands to report to their agencies by January 31. The Army then launched a three-pronged "pacification campaign" against the "hostiles" who refused to come in. Crow and Shoshoni warriors accompanied the American soldiers in the battle against their old Sioux enemies. The Oglala war chief Crazy Horse turned back one prong, led by

General George Crook, at the Battle of Rosebud Creek in June. Approaching from the east, Custer and the Seventh Cavalry attacked an unusually large Indian village in the valley of the Little Big Horn. "Long Hair" Custer and part of the regiment were promptly wiped out. But this was a hollow victory for the Indians, a final rally in a war already lost. The tribes had already seen their populations thinned by war and disease, the buffalo herds all but exterminated, and the old days of freedom rapidly disappearing. Humiliated by Custer's defeat, the Army would not now let them rest. The end would not be long in coming.

The great encampment split up, and the various bands were tracked down in the next year or so. In early September, the Army destroyed a Sioux village at Slim Buttes, inflicting a mortal stomach wound on the chief American Horse. "Wherever we went," said the Oglala holy man Black Elk, who was a youth at the time, "soldiers came to kill us."[15] On a bitter November morning, Mackenzie's American troops, together with Pawnee and Shoshoni allies, struck Dull Knife's Northern Cheyenne village on the Powder River in northeastern Wyoming. The destruction of the village continued through the afternoon and into the night. The soldiers burned 200 tepees, destroyed tons of buffalo meat, captured at least 1,000 buffalo robes and 750 ponies, and consigned blankets and sacred objects to the flames. That night the temperature fell to 30° below zero and a snowstorm began that lasted for almost two days. A dozen babies froze to death. Cheyenne warriors killed many of the horses they had saved so that the old people could place their freezing hands and feet into the dead animals' steaming entrails.[16] Other bands suffered similar defeats as the "Great Sioux War" degenerated into a series of sordid mopping-up operations. Sitting Bull fled to Canada; Crazy Horse surrendered in May 1877 and was dead within five months, bayoneted to death in a guardroom scuffle at Camp Robinson, Nebraska.

Beyond the Plains, Indian resistance crumbled in small-scale wars. In 1873, a group of Modocs fled their northern California reservation, took refuge in an area of lava beds, and fought off the Army for seven months before they were defeated and shipped to Indian Territory. After generations of peaceful relations with the Americans, the Nez Percé Indians of Oregon and Idaho fled for Canada rather than move to a reservation. Ably led by Chief Joseph and Looking Glass, they made an epic trek of fifteen hundred miles in 1877, fighting off pursuing American forces. But they were stopped just short of the border and shipped to Indian Territory. In Colorado, the White River Utes, who fought their last war against the United States Army in 1879, were forced to cede their reservation lands in Colorado and move west to Utah Territory. In the Southwest, the

Apaches fought the Americans for years — carrying "their lives on their finger nails" as the Chiricahua chief Cochise said[17] — but Geronimo and the last of the Apache holdouts surrendered in 1886. The government shipped all the Chiricahua Apaches — including many of the scouts who had helped bring the war to an end — to Florida. The Chiricahuas were held as prisoners of war for years in Florida and then in Alabama before being sent to Fort Sill, Oklahoma, where Geronimo died in 1909.

American military conquest of the West was complete. The Army and the destruction of the buffalo herds completed what disease, alcohol, and guns had begun. But fully defeating the Indians entailed imposing a new way of life as well as imposing military control. The government insisted that Indians live as white Americans lived. Those people who survived the wars for their lands now faced a battle for their minds and their souls.

THE RESERVATIONS AND THE ERA OF FORCED ACCULTURATION

As the United States extended its dominion over the Great Plains, it confined the Indian peoples living there to portions of their homelands. Treaty after treaty shrank the borders of these lands until the once-prosperous and free-ranging tribes were restricted to small reservations. As early as 1852, the Penateka band of Comanches in southern Texas found themselves pressed by the United States to relinquish their lands and their way of life and settle on a reservation. "Over this vast country, where for centuries our ancestors roamed in undisputed possession, free and happy, what have we left?" asked a Penateka chief named Ketumse. The Comanches' game had been killed or driven off, and the Penatekas were "forced into the most sterile and barren portions" of their land to starve. "Give us a country we can call our own, where we may bury our people in quiet," said Ketumse in resignation. Two years later, Ketumse and other Penateka chiefs agreed to accept a reservation for their people. They did so reluctantly, as one chief, Shanaco, explained to the Americans:

> You come into our country and select a small patch of ground, around which you run a line, and tell us the President will make us a present of this to live upon, when everybody knows that the whole of the entire country, from the Red River to the Colorado, is now and always has been ours from time immemorial. I suppose, however, if the President tells us to confine ourselves to these narrow limits, we shall be forced to do so, whether we desire it or not.

A Penateka chief named Buffalo Hump fled west with his followers rather than submit to the reservation, but Ketumse and his people embarked on the difficult new road. Most Plains Indians faced the same hard choices in the later nineteenth century, and most accepted life on the reservations with similar reluctance.[18]

The reservations functioned not only to deprive Indian tribes of valuable lands, but also as crucibles of change designed to break down tribal culture and society. As the first step in "civilizing" and assimilating Indians, American reformers felt it was necessary to eradicate Indianness, or as the contemporary saying went, "kill the Indian and save the man." Indians had to learn to lead sedentary lives on fixed plots of land, be self-supporting, and practice Christianity. Reservations were regarded as temporary, a stage in the process of incorporating Indians into mainstream American society.

The United States devoted enormous energy and resources to Americanizing the American Indians. It refined its system for dealing with Indians, creating a hierarchy of command that flowed from the secretary of the interior to the Bureau of Indian Affairs down through the individual agents on the reservations. United States military power backed up the system.

The agent was the key figure in implementing the government's policies on his reservation. As the new source of food and protection for Indian people, he usurped many of the traditional roles of Indian chiefs; meanwhile, the government further undermined the chiefs' authority by fomenting and exploiting divisions within Indian societies. The agent relied for assistance on the clerks, farmers, field matrons, and teachers who worked on the agency trying to transform Plains Indian societies into model American societies where men farmed while their wives worked in the home and their children attended school. Both the reservation police and the Courts of Indian Offenses were manned by Indians and charged with the suppression of polygamy, native dances, and other traditional customs. Indians complained frequently that agents behaved like dictators and lined their pockets at the expense of the people, but the government exploited existing divisions in Indian society and created new ones in a classic colonial strategy of divide and rule. Making Indians responsible for eradicating traditional customs and enforcing reservation regulations ensured that animosity against the changes was often directed at other Indians rather than at the government and its non-Indian agents.

At the same time, various organizations geared themselves for a reform of Indian policies that, they thought, was in the best interests of the Indians. President Grant had established a precedent by using churchmen as officials and agents as part of his "Peace Policy" in the 1860s, and many of the appointees had brought an element of humanitarianism to Indian affairs. In later years, groups calling themselves Friends of the Indian attempted to take things further. The Board of Indian Commissioners carried out investigations of conditions on reservations; the Indian Rights Association, founded in 1882, championed Indian causes; and reformers attended annual conferences at Lake Mohonk in New York, where, with Indians conspicuously absent, they discussed what was best for "the Indian."

Most believed that education was the key to saving the Indian. The Board of Indian Commissioners outlined its attitude toward the Indian in 1880: "As a savage we cannot tolerate him any more than as a half-civilized parasite, wanderer, or vagabond. The only alternative left is to fit him by education for civilized life."[19] Realizing that adults were likely to resist change, educators focused their attention on Indian children. Some children attended day schools on the reservations, but reformers preferred off-reservation boarding schools where children could be quarantined from the "contaminating" influences of their families. Parents who refused to send their children away to school were denied rations; many children were hauled off to school by soldiers or Indian police. Schools like Carlisle Industrial School in Pennsylvania, run by Captain Richard H. Pratt, became famous — or infamous — and served as a model for other educational facilities. By our standards, most schools a century ago seem inhuman and abusive: Students studied the three Rs, learned by rote, and endured strict discipline and corporal punishment. But schools for Indians were designed to function as agencies of forced acculturation and not primarily as places of academic learning. Like the children of immigrants from Europe who were streaming into the country at that time, the first Americans would have to learn to conform and to live like white Americans.

Plains Indian children in traditional times received their education from indulgent relatives in a supportive communal environment. The boarding schools came as a shock. When Indian children arrived at boarding schools, they received new names to replace their traditional ones, stiff uniforms in place of their native clothing, and a haircut. They ate a monotonous diet, endured harsh discipline, and followed daily routines designed to instill systematic habits. Teachers pushed "American" values on the children, taught patriotism and a version of American history that distorted or ignored the Indians' role, and punished those caught speaking their native language. Parents who had attended missionary and boarding schools often refrained from teaching their children their native tongue in order to save them from such punishment. Boys acquired vocational and manual skills, while girls tended to be trained for work as maids in the homes of middle-class white families. In fact, many students found themselves in a twilight world: They were not equipped or allowed to enter white society as equals, yet they had been subjected to sufficient change to make returning to the reservations a difficult and sometimes traumatic experience.

The government also launched a systematic attack on Indian religions. In their eyes, conversion to Christianity required that traditional rituals such as the Sun Dance be outlawed. Indians who continued to practice their religious ceremonies did so in secret. The government's policies of religious suppression were only partially successful, and they created tremendous hardship, undermining traditional spiritual supports at a time when people needed them most. Christian missionaries attempted to fill the void created by the suppression of traditional ceremonies, but in most cases they failed to eradicate traditional beliefs.

Even though government policies were intended to suppress tradi-tional ways of life, tribal culture and society proved more resilient than the reformers had imagined. In time, people managed to transform reservations from prisons into homelands where they preserved their own ways and values and defended their independence against outside interference.[20]

[margin handwriting: making the best out of the worst situation]

Originally envisioned as laboratories of change, reservations became bastions of the old ways so much so that the Friends of the Indian, who had originally supported the reservation system, now advocated breaking the reservations up, claiming they were "obstacles to progress." Congress responded by passing the Dawes, or the General Allotment, Act in 1887.[21]

Like Indian removal in the 1830s, allotment was a policy on which both pro- and anti-Indian groups could agree as a solution to what they perceived as the "Indian problem." Reformers believed that breaking up reservations and allotting lands to Indians as private property would end the poverty and dependency that existed on the reservations, push Indians into mainstream society, and transform them into independent farmers and productive members of society. Settlers and land speculators were eager to open "surplus" land for sale.

The Act, named after Senator Henry Dawes of Massachusetts, one of its prime instigators, contained the following provisions: (1) The presi-dent was authorized to designate allotments of 160 acres to heads of families, and lesser amounts to younger persons and orphans. (2) Indians were to select their own lands, but if they failed to do so, the agent would make the selection for them. Reservations were to be surveyed and rolls of tribal members prepared prior to allotment. (3) The government was to hold title to the land in trust for twenty-five years. (4) All allottees and all Indians who abandoned their tribal ways and became "civilized" were to be granted citizenship. (5) Surplus reservation lands could be sold.

The Allotment Act aimed to dismantle Indian societies that traditionally practiced communal ownership and reciprocal sharing. It was designed to instill white values concerning property among people who did not regard land as real estate to be bought and sold, and to promote nineteenth-century white American virtues of thrift, hard work, and ambition. As its supporters knew, allotment assaulted the very foundations — economic, social, and spiritual — of Indian life. Wooden Leg, a Cheyenne who had fought Custer at the Battle of the Little Big Horn, explained in later life: "All of our teachings and beliefs were that land was not made to be owned in separate pieces by persons and that the plowing up and destruction of vegetation placed by the Great Medicine and the planting of other vegetation according to the ideas of men was an interference with the plans of the Above."[22] The implications of allotment seem to have been understood all too well by the orchestrators of government policy. Theodore Roosevelt later described allotment as "a vast pulverizing engine to break up the tribal mass."[23]

In addition to undermining a way of life, allotment also proved economically impractical. One hundred and sixty acres per head of household was rarely sufficient for Indians to make a living by either herding or farming. The United States tried to transform Indians into farmers overnight on poor lands at the very time when white American farmers on good lands were struggling to make ends meet. Most Indians could not get loans to develop their allotments because they lacked collateral; they could not use their 160-acre plots as collateral because the government held the deed for twenty-five years. Moreover, the original acreage alloted to a family head was broken up into smaller parcels as it was divided among the heirs of the allottee. Many Indians were persuaded to lease their lands, and subsequent legislation relaxed the restrictions on sales of Indian lands. As white settlers bought up lands, many reservations assumed a checkerboard pattern of Indian and non-Indian property.

Allotment's main effect was to divest the Indians of more land. Tribal land holdings fell from almost 150 million acres in 1887 to about 50 million acres in 1934 when the allotment policy was terminated. As a result, Indians endured increasing poverty, despondency, and discrimination.

At the same time, Indians found themselves with less and less legal protection as the nineteenth century came to a close. For almost a century the United States dealt with Indian tribes through a series of negotiated treaties. In 1871, Congress declared that Indian tribes were no longer to be recognized as independent nations with whom the government would make treaties. Indians were now treated as "wards of the government" and found themselves subjected to increasing state and federal legislation. The Supreme Court decision in *Ex Parte Crow Dog* in 1881, arising from Crow Dog's murder of the Brulé Sioux chief Spotted Tail, deferred to tribal law and acknowledged the right of the Brulés to settle the matter in the customary way, with Crow Dog's family giving gifts to the family of Spotted Tail.[24] But Congress in 1885 passed the Major Crimes Act, which asserted congressional jurisdiction over Indian country for such crimes as rape, murder, and assault with a deadly weapon. In 1892, the Kiowas, Comanches, and Plains Apaches were pressured into agreeing to divide their lands under the terms of the Allotment Act. Lone Wolf, a Kiowa chief who had visited Washington, D.C., as part of a delegation protesting against passage of the act, sued to halt the land division as a blatant contravention of the Indians' treaty guarantees. In 1903, in *Lone Wolf v. Hitchcock,* the United States Supreme Court declared that Indians had no rights that Congress was bound to respect and that Congress had plenary power over the tribes. The United States could act unilaterally in violation of its own treaties, and Congress had the right to dispose of Indian lands as it saw fit.[25] Indians had virtually no legal status, and the reduction of their lands fit the prevailing philosophy that Indians were a "vanishing race." *went from bad to worse*

NATIVE RESPONSES AND
THE SEARCH FOR HOPE

By the end of the nineteenth century, many Plains Indians were in a state of shock. Once wealthy and powerful, they were now reduced to poverty and forced to rely on government annuities. Once free, they were now confined to nonproductive reservations, which they could not leave without permission. Warrior-hunters found themselves deprived of their traditional role in society and of traditional avenues of achievement. Even the environment and the ecology underwent great transformation as settlers pushed relentlessly to master and exploit the West. Pretty Shield, a Crow woman, found herself "trying to live a life that I do not understand."[26] Faced with a world of changes, Indians responded in a variety of ways. Some joined the Indian police as a means of attaining status; others sought escape in alcohol. Washakie of the Shoshonis and Plenty Coups of the Crows recognized that the survival of their people depended on dealing with the reality of American power and presence. Consequently, some chiefs attempted to cooperate with the government agents in the hope of securing better food, clothing, and shelter for their people.

Many realized that they must learn to cope with the new world that was being forced on them. "We have now entered upon this life, and there is no going back," Charles Eastman's Dakota father told him. "Besides, one would be like a hobbled pony without learning to live like those among whom we must live." Eastman went off to college, determined "to know all that the white man knows," and found himself "a stranger in a strange country, and deep in a strange life from which I could not retreat." He renounced "my bow and arrows for the spade and the pen," replaced soft moccasins with heavy shoes, practiced English every day, and "permitted myself to think and act as a white man." He went on to attend Dartmouth College and earn a medical degree from Boston University but insisted to the end, "I am an Indian." Eastman was one Indian who was able to change without surrendering his identity.[27]

Other Indians turned elsewhere in their efforts to cope with crisis. By the 1880s, as hunger, disease, and despondency plagued the reservations, the situation was ripe for new religions that promised better days or a return to the good days of old. The peyote religion spread from the Southwest across the plains. In 1887, a medicine man named Sword Bearer gained a following of frustrated young warriors on the Crow reservation in Montana and preached an apocalyptic vision that alarmed local whites. The Army went in, Sword Bearer was killed, and the potential rebellion was crushed. A larger tragedy was averted.[28] Three years later the Sioux were not so fortunate.

Many Sioux people listened attentively to reports of the Ghost Dance religion, which swept the plains at the end of the 1880s. The Ghost Dance originated in the Nevada region where a Paiute prophet named Wovoka promised a return of the old ways if Indians followed prescribed rituals. Not all Indians embraced the new religion, but reports of Indian warriors dancing in circles in expectation of the disappearance of white men and the return of the buffalo alarmed the authorities. Tensions intensified between the soldiers and the Sioux. The government regarded Sitting Bull as a troublemaker and in December 1890 dispatched Indian police to arrest him. Sitting Bull died in the ensuing mêlée. Two weeks later, the Seventh Cavalry massacred over two hundred men, women, and children of Big Foot's band of Miniconjou Sioux at Wounded Knee, South Dakota. Many wounded Indians died since they were left to lie on the battlefield in subzero temperatures. Wounded Knee brought the Indian wars of the West to a grisly end.

With most of their lands gone, their old ways of life destroyed, their ceremonies outlawed, their leaders killed or imprisoned, their children away in boarding schools, their numbers thinned by war, disease, and starvation, Indian people seemed to be on the verge of extinction by 1900. In the eyes of most white Americans, Indians were "vanishing Americans" who would survive into the twentieth century only if they stopped being Indians and submitted to complete assimilation. Plains Indians had long struggled to survive; the challenge of the new century was to survive as Indians. *they were just trying to co-habitat w/ the things they were given*

VOICES AND VISIONS

Many Indian voices from the nineteenth century and earlier are preserved not on printed pages in libraries and archives but in tribal, community, and family memories. Knowledge and traditions from the past, handed down from generation to generation, constitute a wealth of oral history on which ethnohistorians, anthropologists, and tribal historians can draw to provide a fuller and richer picture of Indian historical experiences.[29] Collecting and recording such oral histories is a major endeavor in itself as Indian and non-Indian scholars strive to preserve as much as they can of the oral memory into the twenty-first century.

The voices and visions presented in this volume, however, have been in print for some time. They were recorded from people who remembered firsthand the experiences they described. Most come from the following sources: (1) speeches made by Indian people and interpreted and recorded by white observers; (2) recollections of past events as told to white people; (3) autobiographies written by Indian people or compiled by white writers on the basis of their interviews with those Indians; and (4) visual documents in the form of winter counts, pictographic records, and ledger art — pencil and crayon drawings on paper produced by Plains Indians in the later part of the nineteenth century. As with any historical sources, students and scholars must critically evaluate these sources, recognizing the context and conditions in which they were produced, the audience for which they were intended, and the purpose they were intended to serve.

In the absence of written records, oral renditions and stories kept memory and history alive. Words had power. As the Crow warrior Two Leggings said, "Our breath is our wind and it is also our soul. Our words are our breath and they are sacred."[30] Solemn rituals and protocol governed treaty councils and other formal public meetings in which words were exchanged. For Indian people, what was said at these meetings was far more important than the written documents white participants produced. As the anthropologist Raymond DeMallie explains in analyzing Plains Indian treaty councils from an ethnohistorical perspective, whites and Indians alike understood the council as a diplomatic forum, but they differed in their understanding of the concept of the treaty. For Indians, the council was an end in itself. Coming together in peace, smoking the pipe to pledge the truthfulness of all statements made, and exchanging opinions and presents constituted an agreement, a meeting of hearts and minds. For white Americans, the council and its associated rituals were only a prelude to the real thing: a *written* agreement to which the requisite number of leaders "touched the pen" while the scribe placed an *X* after their names. Indian leaders who touched the pen believed they were validating what they had said in council, but, under white American law, their names on the treaty committed them only to those statements contained in the final document.[31]

Sometimes Indian leaders were induced, tricked, or coerced into signing documents that contained provisions to which they had not agreed. As in colonial times, the written record of treaty councils often departed sharply from what Indian people remembered as having taken place there. Interpreters sometimes were drunk, dishonest, or incompetent; where lands were being negotiated, cases of deliberate deception and distortion sometimes occurred; and the power and nuance of Indian statements often were lost in translation. At the Treaty of Medicine Lodge in 1867, seven languages were spoken and five interpreters used. One of the interpreters was Jesse Chisholm, a mixed-blood Cherokee; another was a well-traveled Delaware named Black Beaver. In addition to English, the participants spoke Comanche (an Uto-Aztecan language into which the Comanches had incorporated many words and phrases from the Southwest), Kiowa (which may be a Tanoan language, although linguists and anthropologists disagree), Cheyenne and Arapaho (both Algonkian languages), and Kiowa-Apache and Plains Apache (both Athapaskan dialects). Many of the Indians were fluent in Spanish, and several tribes spoke Comanche as a common trade language. Fisher-more, the Kiowas' council orator, spoke five languages. Nevertheless, the Plains Apaches' speeches had to be translated first into Arapaho and then into English. Newspaper reporters who covered the treaty recorded not what the Indians said, but what the interpreters said they said.[32]

Even Indian names suffered in translation: The Sioux warrior Tasun-kakokipapi, or Tashunkasaquipah, whose name translated as "Young Man of Whose Horses They Are Afraid," became known to the Americans as "Young Man Afraid of His Horses," which conveys a rather different impression of his prowess and character. It is hardly surprising that whites, who could not get Indians' names straight, faltered frequently in their attempts to produce an accurate translation of speeches that dealt with such complex concepts as human relationships with the land, with the animal world, and with future generations. When American peace commissioners in 1865 asked the Sioux chief Iron Nation where another Sioux chief lived, Iron Nation replied, "Everywhere; where he is." The commissioners had little use for or understanding of such an answer. As DeMallie explains, Indian treaty councils are the records of "dramatic conflict between mutually exclusive ways of life."[33] They are valuable historical documents, but they preserve Indian voices in a flawed and filtered form.

Despite cultural distances and errors in translation, Indians succeeded in conveying the point and the power of their words. American commissioners appointed to negotiate with the Sioux for the sale of the Black Hills in 1876 met Indian people who made their sentiments crystal clear:

> While the Indians received us as friends, and listened with kind attention to our propositions, we were painfully impressed with their lack of confidence in the pledges of the Government. At times they told their story of wrongs with such impassioned earnestness that our cheeks crimsoned with shame. In their speeches, the recital of the wrongs which their people had suffered at the hands of the whites, the arraignment of the Government for gross acts of injustice and fraud, and the description of treaties made only to be broken, the doubts and distrusts of present professions of friendship and goodwill, were portrayed in colors so vivid and language so terse, that admiration and surprise would have kept us silent had not shame and humiliation done so.[34]

The U.S. government continued the practice established in colonial times by the British, Spanish, and French of inviting Indian leaders to visit their capital cities in order to impress them with the wealth and power they saw there. The Americans hoped the visitors would return home convinced of the futility of resistance. Visiting Indians attracted considerable attention, especially if they were famous — and no longer "hostile" — chiefs like Red Cloud. Often they were invited to give speeches, and newspaper reporters were eager to take down their words. How much of the original speech survived the translation into English and transformation into print is difficult to gauge. In an age when many easterners were critical of government Indian policies and sympathetic to Indian visitors lamenting the plight of their people, some reporters were not above elaborating to cater to the tastes of their readers.

Indian statements recorded in less formal settings sometimes were closer to the original. Casual visitors in Indian country depended on translators to understand what was being said, but fur traders and others who lived with Indians needed no intermediaries. However, that is no guarantee that the speeches they recorded constitute a verbatim record of what was said: They might alter words and sentiments as they translated the speech into the written form in which it survives.

Then, as now, Indian words sometimes were appropriated for non-Indian purposes, and non-Indian writers sometimes felt few qualms about rewriting speeches supposedly given by Indian chiefs. For example, Seattle, or Seeathl, a chief of the Susquamish and Duwamish Indians on the Pacific northwest coast in the mid-nineteenth century, gave a speech that has become famous in America and Europe for its implicit criticisms of white society, its quiet dignity, and its ecological wisdom. The first published version of that speech, based on notes taken at the time, appeared more than thirty years after the speech was given. Later writers and editors added their own embellishments and modernized the language. The version of the speech accepted by many people today as an authentic Indian voice and frequently quoted for its environmental statements apparently was written by a college professor in Texas as part of a film script.[35]

As white Americans waged a relentless campaign to educate them, many Indians learned to read and write, both in English and in their native languages. They recognized that literacy was power. Red Cloud admitted that "the whites, who are civilized and educated, swindle me; and I am not hard to swindle because I do not know how to read and write."[36] In contrast, Wolf Chief, a Hidatsa who went to school, joined the Indian police, and ran a store on his reservation, wrote more than one hundred letters to the Office of Indian Affairs, articulating his people's concerns and complaints. "He has contracted the letter writing habit and cannot be suppressed," said one exasperated agent in 1886.[37]

Some Indians — Charles Eastman, Luther Standing Bear, and others — became quite prolific authors and wrote autobiographies. Others narrated their life stories to white journalists and social scientists who recognized the importance of preserving these life stories for posterity or who saw a market for literary sales. In both cases, the autobiographies were produced with a non-Indian audience in mind, and the structure, subject matter, and sentiments often reflect the tastes and interests of that audience.

As Indian people began to communicate their personal narratives to non-Indians, traditional narrative forms fell into other hands and were shaped for different audiences. Traditionally, lives had communal rather than individual significance, and people's doings and achievements reflected their society's values. Now, white America was interested in individual life stories but often assumed that those individual stories represented all Indian experiences. Some traditional aspects survived in the content and structure of the autobiography. Old warriors who were asked for their life stories would relate every heroic deed they had performed, "for coups were the essence of every warrior's life." Consequently, some autobiographies strike modern, non-Indian readers as a rather tedious list of war exploits. In addition, many autobiographies end with the beginning of life on the reservation, even though the narrator may have been young at the time. No traditional autobiographical form existed in which to give meaningful expression to the sedentary and inglorious new way of life. For many Indian people, what happened in the depressing early years of the reservation was too painful to discuss and "was not a story."[38] White readers tended to be interested in the dramatic and colorful days of old rather than in how Indian peoples adjusted to the drab monotony of reservation life, so editors had little reason to press their narrators for more.

But as-told-to autobiographies were collaborative projects, what Arnold Krupat calls bicultural composite compositions. Working through an interpreter, the Indian subject narrated the events of his or her life in response to questions posed by a white editor or writer, who then edited, revised, and polished the material into an autobiographical narrative. The interviewer posed questions that were of interest to white readers (such as "Who killed Custer?"), determined the shape of the book, and decided what was significant. Like the editor of this volume, these people looked at Indian life and history from a particular perspective and with their own sense of what was noteworthy. Their Indian informants may or may not have shared that view.[39]

Peter Nabokov's edition of the Crow warrior Two Leggings's life is a remarkable historical document, but as David Brumble reminds us, it is "a thoroughly reworked version of a transcription of an interpreter's on-the-spot translation of a long series of oral narratives and questions and answers."[40] Brumble adds that Indian narrators and white interviewers and editors left a valuable legacy, "affording us some sense of what it means to see the world and the self according to traditional tribal — perhaps even ancient — habits of mind," but it is a puzzling legacy: To understand the as-told-to Indian autobiography, we need to try and understand both the teller and the writer.[41] Working through interpreters, with their own conscious or unconscious agenda and with a white audience in mind, the social scientists who helped produce American Indian autobiographies generated historical documents that share some of the same limitations as Indian speeches translated and recorded in treaty councils: Frank Linderman, who interviewed the Crow chief Plenty Coups and the medicine woman Pretty Shield, employed sign language to better understand their stories but admitted that such life histories, "coming through an interpreter laboring to translate Crow thoughts into English words, must suffer some mutation, no matter how conscientious the interpreter may be."[42]

The writer and poet John G. Neihardt conducted extensive interviews with the Oglala Sioux holy man Black Elk in the 1930s and 1940s and from those interviews produced vivid accounts of Sioux life, religion, and history as related by the old man. Neihardt tended to embellish his informant's words for added poetic effect, and some scholars dismiss his books as unusable as an anthropological or historical record, arguing that they reveal far more about Neihardt than about Black Elk and that "Black Elk was for Neihardt merely a literary vehicle to express his own philosophy and around which to create his private fantasy world based on Lakota culture." However, as anthropologist Raymond DeMallie, a close scholar of Neihardt's interviews and of Sioux culture, explains, such a view fails to recognize "Neihardt's commitment to make the books speak for Black Elk faithfully, to represent what Black Elk would have said if he had understood the concept of literature and if he had been able to express himself in English." Neihardt saw himself as Black Elk's interpreter and literary spokesman. The poetry may be Neihardt's but the views, given added force by their interpreter, are Black Elk's.[43]

In addition, anyone relating his or her life story for posterity is liable to see the past in a certain light: Politicians who write their memoirs justify their conduct and decisions; people looking back on their lives feel nostalgia and often blame others for the way things have changed. Some Indians were hesitant to discuss certain things or anxious to justify their past actions to a white world they feared might be intent on punishing Indian wrongdoers. In short, all historical documents are cultural artifacts; many Indian autobiographies are bicultural artifacts. They merit the same scrutiny as other historical documents and should not always be accepted at face value as either an "authentic Indian voice" or an accurate record of past events.

Writing or narrating an autobiography was a new concept for Indian people, and one that involved tapering their life stories to fit what was essentially a nineteenth-century Western literary form. But recording the significant events of one's life was not new. Songs, oral narratives, and representational art conveyed and celebrated what was important in people's lives.[44] Plains Indian warriors depicted their heroic deeds on buffalo robes and tepee covers, almost as a kind of résumé, a public display of their achievements in a society where a man's career and standing depended on his military prowess. By the second half of the nineteenth century, Plains Indians obtained paper (often in the form of ledger books) and pencils, paints, and crayons from white Americans. Warrior-artists could now depict their deeds more easily and in more detail. The result was a new art form, grounded in traditional hide painting, but utilizing new materials. At first glance, these drawings appear simple, but they were not intended to be illustrations. Understanding the conventions the artists followed can allow one to decode these paintings, identifying individuals, following patterns of movement, and recognizing that the drawing might contain a sequence of events rather than a single frame in the action.

Plains Indians acquired new drawing materials when their lives and the world around them were undergoing unprecedented change, affording the artists new subject matter. Men who had been raised as warriors and buffalo hunters found they could no longer go to war, that there were no more buffalo to hunt, and that government pressures were forcing them to become sedentary farmers. Some visited the eastern United States and experienced at first hand the strange new world of the white man. Some of the most famous ledger art was produced by Southern Cheyenne and Kiowa Indians during their imprisonment at Fort Marion, Florida, from 1875 to 1878. Encouraged to draw and given access to drawing materials, they produced hundreds of drawings, selling many of them in books to tourists. Torn away from their families and homes and facing an uncertain future, the Fort Marion artists reflected on a way of life that seemed to be gone forever and depicted traditional buffalo hunts and war scenes. But they also tackled new subjects and experimented with new forms of composition. One Southern Cheyenne, Howling Wolf, who had produced pictographic representations of his war exploits before confinement, developed new styles at Fort Marion and continued to draw and paint once he was back on the reservation in Oklahoma. Men on the reservation had more time and more materials than ever before with which to produce visual records of the significant events in their lives, but, ironically, there was less reason or opportunity to record heroic deeds. Ledger art was a form of documentation unique to the late nineteenth century, exclusively done by males, and produced by members of only a few tribes. Nevertheless, the drawings of Howling Wolf and others constitute important visual documents reflecting the cultural attitudes of the artists and their societies during painful times of transition.[45]

These sources do not, of course, tell the whole story. There were many areas of life and experience about which Indian people preferred to remain silent. Their silence gives us clues as to how they felt but denies us their words. At a time when American policy aimed to suppress tribal religions and eradicate Indian culture, there were some things best not discussed, even with white friends. By 1900 the world of the Plains Indians was very different from what it had been in 1800: People lived in log cabins rather than in tepees; they farmed 160-acre plots of land instead of hunting across boundless plains; they wore white man's clothing and woollen blankets rather than buckskins and buffalo robes; they attended schools and churches whereas once they had learned and prayed only in the open; and they used manufactured goods instead of those crafted by hand from skin, stone, and bone. But these outward and visible changes sometimes concealed an inner world of continuity, where old clan ties, communal values, and traditional beliefs and meanings survived. Silence was a means of keeping some things alive by keeping them from view. It was a way to ensure that, contrary to the assumptions of their teachers and agents, Indians could continue to be Indians in twentieth-century America.

NOTES

[1] For the repercussions of such events see Elizabeth A. H. John, *Storms Brewed in Other Men's Worlds: The Confrontation of Indians, Spanish, and French in the Southwest, 1540–1795* (Lincoln: University of Nebraska Press, 1975).

[2] L. R. Masson, ed., *Les Bourgeois de la Compagnie du Nord-Ouest*, 2 vols. (New York: Antiquarian Press, 1960 reprint), 1:331–32.

[3] For an excellent survey of the Indian world Lewis and Clark encountered see James P. Ronda, *Lewis and Clark among the Indians* (Lincoln: University of Nebraska Press, 1984).

[4] Arthur J. Ray, *Indians in the Fur Trade: Their Role as Trappers, Hunters, and Middlemen in the Lands Southwest of Hudson Bay, 1660–1870* (Toronto: University of Toronto Press, 1974).

[5] Colin G. Calloway, "Snake Frontiers: The Eastern Shoshones in the Eighteenth Century," *Annals of Wyoming* 63 (1991), 82–92.

11111

11111

[6] Richard White, "The Winning of the West: The Expansion of the Western Sioux in the Eighteenth and Nineteenth Centuries," *Journal of American History* 65 (1978), 319–43.

[7] On the trade network that centered on the upper Missouri, see for example Joseph Jablow, "The Cheyenne in Plains Indian Trade Relations, 1795–1840," *Monographs of the American Ethnological Society* 19 (1966), and W. Raymond Wood and Thomas D. Thiessen, eds., *Early Fur Trade on the Northern Plains: Canadian Traders among the Mandan and Hidatsa Indians, 1738–1818* (Norman: University of Oklahoma Press, 1985); Gary Moulton, ed., *The Journals of the Lewis and Clark Expedition.* 9 vols. (Lincoln: University of Nebraska Press, 1983–), 3:386–445, passim.

[8] Moulton, ed., *The Journals of the Lewis and Clark Expedition*, 2:467, 479, 482n.

[9] John D. Unruh, Jr., *The Plains Across: The Overland Emigrants and the Trans-Mississippi West, 1840–1860* (Urbana: University of Illinois Press, 1970), chap. 5.

[10] W. C. Wanderwerth, comp., *Indian Oratory: Famous Speeches by Noted Indian Chieftains* (New York: Ballantine Books, 1971), 104; date of speech provided in Robert M. Utley, *The Indian Frontier of the American West 1846–1890* (Albuquerque: University of New Mexico Press, 1984), 47.

[11] For more information, see Stan Hoig, *The Sand Creek Massacre* (Norman: University of Oklahoma Press, 1961), which also includes extracts from the Congressional inquiry.

[12] LeRoy R. and Ann W. Hafen, eds., *Relations with the Indians of the Plains, 1857–1861: A Documentary Account of the Military Campaigns and Negotiations of Indian Agents* (Glendale, Cal.: The Arthur H. Clarke Co., 1959), 187.

[13] James L. Haley, *The Buffalo War: The History of the Red River Indian Uprising of 1874* (New York: Doubleday, 1976); Stan Hoig, *Tribal Wars of the Southern Plains* (Norman: University of Oklahoma Press, 1993), chap. 4; 296–99.

[14] Quoted in James C. Olson, *Red Cloud and the Sioux Problem* (Lincoln: University of Nebraska Press, 1965), 208–09.

[15] John G. Neihardt, *Black Elk Speaks: Being the Life Story of a Holy Man of the Oglala Sioux* (Lincoln: University of Nebraska Press, 1988 cd.), 134.

[16] Peter J. Powell, *Sweet Medicine: The Continuing Role of the Sacred Arrows, the Sun Dance, and the Buffalo Hat in Northern Cheyenne History.* 2 vols. (Norman: University of Oklahoma Press, 1969), 1:164–67.

[17] Wanderwerth, comp., *Indian Oratory*, 125.

[18] Jodye Lynn Dickson Schilz and Thomas F. Schilz, *Buffalo Hump and the Penateka Comanches* (El Paso: Texas Western Press, 1989), 38–40.

[19] Francis Paul Prucha, ed., *Americanizing the American Indians: Writings by the "Friends of the Indian" 1880–1900* (Lincoln: University of Nebraska Press, 1978), 194.

[20] Frederick E. Hoxie, "From Prison to Homeland: The Cheyenne River Reservation Before World War I," in Peter Iverson, ed., *The Plains Indians of the Twentieth Century* (Norman: University of Oklahoma Press, 1985), 55–75.

[21] For more information, see Wilcomb E. Washburn, *The Assault on Indian Tribalism: The General Allotment Law (Dawes Act) of 1887* (Philadelphia: J. B. Lippincott, 1975); Janet A. McDonnell, *The Dispossession of the American Indian, 1887–1934* (Bloomington: Indiana University Press, 1991).

[22] Thomas B. Marquis, interpreter, *Wooden Leg: A Warrior Who Fought Custer* (Minneapolis: The Midwest Co., 1931), 155.

[23] Virgil J. Vogel, *This Country Was Ours: A Documentary History of the American Indian* (New York: Harper and Row, 1972), 193.

[24] Sidney L. Harring, *Crow Dog's Case: American Indian Sovereignty, Tribal Law, and United States Law in the Nineteenth Century* (New York: Cambridge University Press, 1993).

[25] Blue Clark, *Lone Wolf v. Hitchcock: Treaty Rights and Indian Law at the End of the Nineteenth Century* (Lincoln: University of Nebraska Press, 1994).

[26] Frank B. Linderman, *Pretty-shield, Medicine Woman of the Crows* (Lincoln: University of Nebraska Press, 1972), 24.

[27] Charles Eastman, *From the Deep Woods to Civilization: Chapters in the Autobiography of an Indian* (Lincoln: University of Nebraska Press, 1977 ed.), 25, 48, 54, 58, 104.

[28] Colin G. Calloway, "Sword Bearer and the 'Crow Outbreak' of 1887," *Montana, The Magazine of Western History* 36 (Autumn 1986), 38–51.

[29] For example, Joseph Medicine Crow, *From the Heart of Crow Country: The Crow Indians' Own Stories* (New York: Orion Books, 1992).

[30] Peter Nabokov, *Two Leggings: The Making of a Crow Warrior* (New York: Thomas Y. Crowell, 1967), 25.

[31] Raymond J. DeMallie, "Touching the Pen: Plains Indian Treaty Councils in Ethnohistorical Perspective," in Fredrick C. Luebke, ed., *Ethnicity on the Great Plains* (Lincoln: University of Nebraska Press, 1980), 38–51.

[32] Douglas C. Jones, *The Treaty of Medicine Lodge: The Story of the Great Treaty Council as Told by Eyewitnesses* (Norman: University of Oklahoma Press, 1966), 104–09. Problems in translation were not unusual. When Lewis and Clark met the Salish-speaking Flatheads in western Montana they communicated with them via a chain of interpreters who translated the speeches from English to French, French to Hidatsa, Hidatsa to Shoshoni, and Shoshoni to Salish, and conveyed the responses along the same chain in reverse; Ronda, *Lewis and Clark among the Indians,* 156.

[33] DeMallie, "Touching the Pen," 38–51.

[34] *Eighth Annual Report of the Board of Indian Commissioners for 1876* (Washington, D.C.: U.S. Govt. Printing Office, 1877), 12.

[35] Rudolf Kaiser, "'A Fifth Gospel, Almost': Chief Seattle's Speech(es): American Origins and European Reception," in Christian F. Feest, ed., *Indians and Europe: An Interdisciplinary Collection of Essays* (Aachen, Germany: Edition Herodot Rader-Verl., 1987), 505–26.

[36] *Second Annual Report of the Board of Indian Commissioners to the Secretary of the Interior for the Year 1870* (Washington, D.C.: U.S. Govt. Printing Office, 1871), 42.

[37] Carolyn Gilman and Mary Jane Schneider, *The Way to Independence: Memories of a Hidatsa Indian Family, 1840–1920* (St. Paul: Minnesota Historical Society Press, 1987), 126.

[38] Lynne Woods O'Brien, *Plains Indian Autobiographies* (Boise: Idaho State College, 1973), 7–8.

[39] H. David Brumble, III, *American Indian Autobiography* (Berkeley: University of California Press, 1988); Hertha Dawn Wong, *Sending My Heart Back across the Years: Tradition and Innovation in Native American Autobiography* (New York: Oxford University Press, 1992); Arnold Krupat, ed., *Native American Autobiography: An Anthology* (Madison: University of Wisconsin Press, 1994).

[40] Brumble, *American Indian Autobiography,* 36.

[41] Ibid., 98.

[42] Frank B. Linderman, *Pretty-shield: Medicine Woman of the Crows* (Lincoln: University of Nebraska Press, 1972), 11.

[43] Raymond J. DeMallie, ed., *The Sixth Grandfather: Black Elk's Teachings Given to John G. Neihardt* (Lincoln: University of Nebraska Press, 1984), xxi–xxii. Interested students should compare the documents from *Black Elk Speaks,* reprinted in this volume, with those closer to the original, reprinted in *The Sixth Grandfather.*

[44] Evan M. Maurer, et al., *Visions of the People: A Pictorial History of Plains Indian Life* (Minneapolis Institute of Arts, 1992); Wong, *Sending My Heart Back across the Years.*

[45] Joyce M. Szabo, *Howling Wolf and the History of Ledger Art* (Albuquerque: University of New Mexico Press, 1994), and "Shields and Lodges, Warriors and Chiefs: Kiowa Drawings as Historical Records," *Ethnohistory* 41 (1994), 1–24; Karen Daniels Peterson, *Howling Wolf: A Cheyenne Warrior's Graphic Interpretation of His People* (Palo Alto, Cal.: American West Publishing, 1968), and *Plains Indian Art from Fort Marion* (Norman: University of Oklahoma Press, 1971). The latter work contains a "pictographic dictionary" to aid in the interpretation of these drawings.

1

Lone Dog's Winter Count

Like many other native societies, American Indians often have been regarded as "people without history" before Europeans arrived to record what was going on.[1] In reality, of course, all peoples, whether literate or not, devise ways of recording their history and preserving for posterity the events that give meaning to their collective lives. In oral cultures like those of the Plains Indians, the memories of the elders served as repositories of tribal histories, and songs, stories, dances, and other public performances fastened traditions in the lives of successive generations. But Indian people also made visual records of noteworthy events: Individual warriors recorded their own heroic deeds; tribal historians compiled winter counts or calendars of events significant to the community as a whole.

Winter counts are historical records unique to the plains. Usually painted on a buffalo robe in a spiral of years, they chronicle the people's history, with each year marked by a pictographic device symbolizing a memorable event. These symbols functioned as mnemonic devices, allowing the keeper of the winter count to recall each year in full at some future date. Sometimes a single individual would compile a winter count, recording the years of his own life; at other times the winter count would be made over two or three generations or compiled by one person in consultation with elders who remembered the events or who had received knowledge of them from people long since dead.

Winter counts served the purposes of tribal historians; they are also of great value to modern ethnohistorians when used in conjunction with documentary evidence. Most plains winter counts record outbreaks of smallpox and measles and other epidemics, and most note "the winter when the stars fell," the meteor shower visible throughout the western United States in November 1833. But winter counts sometimes make no reference to things outsiders might assume would be significant: Some Sioux counts say nothing about the defeat of George Custer in 1876. Instead, the calendars contain numerous references to individual com-

31

Figure 3.   Lone Dog's Buffalo Robe

bats, remarkable incidents, and other things that would jog the memory
of the keeper.[2]

Like other historical sources, winter counts have limitations: Their
chronology usually cannot be established without cross-referencing to
other sources; interpretation of the mnemonic devices can vary consid-
erably, and it is not always clear how much of the interpretation came
from the keeper of the winter count, how much from the translator, and
how much from the ethnologist or other scholar who then transferred
this information into a written chronology of events. Nevertheless, they
provide scholars with a research tool not available anywhere else and,
properly analyzed, offer the opportunity to integrate Indian and non-Indian records to create a richer story of the past.[3]

This collection reproduces Lone Dog's winter count because it pro-
vides an Indian record of events for most of the nineteenth century. Lone
Dog was a Yanktonai Sioux from North Dakota. According to Colonel
Garrick Mallery, who first published the calendar in 1877, Lone Dog was

not old enough to remember the earliest events; either he received the earlier records from a predecessor or gathered the traditions from the elders and worked backward, the object being "to establish some system of chronology for the use of the tribe or more probably in the first instance for the use of his own band." Lone Dog claimed that "with the counsel of the old men of his tribe, he decided upon some event or circumstance which should distinguish each year as it passed, and marked what was considered to be its appropriate symbol or device upon a buffalo robe kept for the purpose." From time to time the robe was displayed to other Indians in the tribe, "who were thus taught the meaning and use of the signs as designating the several years."[4]

Read from the center outward, counterclockwise, the winter count in Figure 3 provides a picture or symbol for each year of the major period of white invasion, yet whites play but a small role in this chronicle. There are seven references to trade with whites and four references to diseases introduced by whites. Twenty-four years are marked by memorable episodes of intertribal conflict, but there are no direct references to battles with whites and there is no indication of the Great Sioux Uprising in Minnesota in 1862. The selected symbols from the winter count and their interpretations are taken from the version recorded by Mallery in his report to the Smithsonian Institution's Bureau of American Ethnology in 1888 and 1889.[5]

1800–01. — Thirty Dakotas were killed by Crow Indians. The device consists of thirty parallel black lines in three columns, the outer lines being united. In this chart, such black lines always signify the death of Dakotas killed by their enemies. . . .

1801–02. — Many died of smallpox. The smallpox broke out in the tribe. The device is the head and body of a man covered with red blotches. . . .

1802–03. — A Dakota stole horses with shoes on, i.e., stole them either directly from the whites or from some other Indians who had before obtained them from whites, as the Indians never shoe their horses. The device is a horseshoe.

1813–14. — The whooping-cough was very prevalent and fatal. The sign is suggestive of a blast of air coughed out by the man-figure.

1818–19. — The measles broke out and many died. . . .

1821–22. — The character represents the falling to earth of a very brilliant meteor.

1823–24. — White soldiers made their first appearance in the region. So said the interpreter, Clement, but from the unanimous interpretation of others the event portrayed is the attack of the United States forces accompanied by Dakotas upon the Arikara villages. . . .[6]

1833–34. — "The stars fell," as the Indians all agreed. This was the great meteor shower observed all over the United States on the night of November 12 of that year. In this chart the moon is black and the stars are red.

1839–40. — The Dakotas killed an entire village of Snake or Shoshoni Indians. The character is the ordinary tipi pierced by arrows.

1840–41. — The Dakotas made peace with the Cheyennes. The symbol of peace is the common one of the approaching hands of two persons. The different coloration of the two hands and arms shows that they belonged to two different persons, and in fact to different tribes. The mere unceremonial hand grasp or "shake" of friendship was not used by the Indians before it was introduced by Europeans.

1849–50. — The Crows stole a large drove of horses (it is said eight hundred) from the Brulés. The circle is a design for a camp or corral from which a number of horse-tracks are departing.

1851–52. — Peace with the Crows. Two Indians, with differing arrangement of hair, showing two tribes, are exchanging pipes for a peace smoke.[7]

1855–56. — Gen. Harney, called by the Dakota Putinska ("white beard" or "white mustache"), made peace with a number of the tribes or bands of the Dakotas. The figure shows an officer in uniform shaking hands with an Indian.[8]

1863–64. — Eight Dakotas were killed. Again the short, parallel black lines united by a long stroke. In this year Sitting-Bull fought General Sully in the Black Hills.[9]

1867 68. Many flags were given them by the Peace Commission. The flag refers to the visit of the Peace Commissioners, among whom were Generals Sherman, Terry, and other prominent military and civil officers. . . .

1868–69. — Texas cattle were brought into the country. . . .

1869–70. — An eclipse of the sun. This was the solar eclipse of August 7, 1869. . . .

1870–71. — The Uncpapas had a battle with the Crows, the former losing, it is said, 14, and killing 29 out of 30 of the latter, though nothing appears to show those numbers. The central object is not a circle denoting multitude, but an irregularly rounded object, perhaps intended for one of the wooden inclosures or forts frequently created by the Indians, and especially the Crows.[10] The Crow fort is shown as nearly surrounded, and bullets, not arrows or lances, are flying.

NOTES

[1] Eric R. Wolf, *Europe and the People without History* (Berkeley: University of California Press, 1982).

[2] See, for example, Garrick Mallery, "Picture-Writing of the American Indians," *10th Annual Report of the Bureau of American Ethnology, 1888–89* (Washington, D.C.: U.S. Govt. Printing Office, 1893), 266–328; James Mooney, "Calendar History of the Kiowa Indians," *17th Annual Report of the Bureau of American Ethnology, 1895–96,* part 1 (Washington, D.C.: U.S. Govt. Printing Office, 1898), 129–445; N. A. Higgingbotham, "The Wind-Roan Bear Winter Count," *Plains Anthropologist* 26 (1981), 1–42.

[3] Melburn D. Thurman, "Plains Indian Winter Counts and the New Ethnohistory," *Plains Anthropologist* 27 (1982), 173–75.

[4] Mallery, "Picture-Writing," 266–67.

[5] Ibid., 266–328.

[6] Roger L. Nichols, "Backdrop for Disaster: Causes of the Arikara War of 1823," *South Dakota History* 14 (Summer 1984), 93–113, discusses these events.

[7] At the Treaty of Fort Laramie in 1851, the tribes of the northern plains agreed to refrain from hostilities against their neighbors and to recognize boundaries between tribal lands established by the United States. The truce between the Sioux and the Crows did not last. See Kingsley M. Bray, "Lone Horn's Peace: A New View of Sioux-Crow Relations," *Nebraska History* 66 (Spring 1985), 28–47.

[8] The minutes of a council held March 1, 1856, between General William S. Harney and delegates from nine Sioux bands are in 34th Congress, 1st session, Senate Executive Document No. 94.

[9] The Battle of Killdeer Mountain, July 28, 1864, was one of several conflicts with Sully that year. Sioux casualties at Killdeer Mountain were higher than the winter count suggests, so the entry may refer to another fight.

[10] Or it may simply mean that the Crows fought from cover.

2

Horses, Guns, and Smallpox

In the century before Lewis and Clark, Indian peoples dealt with the triple impact on their lives of newly introduced horses, firearms, and epidemic diseases, which penetrated the plains far in advance of white traders and settlers and generated dramatic changes in Indian culture, social organization, trade, warfare, and tribal location. The equestrian hunting peoples enjoyed unprecedented freedom and prosperity in this era, but their new way of life was already being undermined as killer diseases followed horses and trade goods through Indian country and European guns injected a deadly new element into intertribal relations. Biological disasters and escalating warfare with powerful new weapons eroded the Plains Indians' capacity for resistance to American expansion long before American soldiers and settlers invaded their lands.

As horses passed from tribe to tribe through the plains and mountains, they made the Indians vastly more mobile, increased their ability to pursue the buffalo herds, and broadened their horizons. They also transformed the quality of life on the open plains. Pretty Shield, a Crow woman, said her grandmothers recalled how in the old days they used to travel on foot and load packs onto dogs and that old women who were worn out had to be left behind to die. "All this was changed by the horse," Pretty Shield said. "Even the old people could ride. Ahh, I came into a happy world. There was always fat meat, glad singing, and much dancing in our villages. Our people's hearts were then as light as breath-feathers."[1] In fact, horses became so central to the Indians' way of life that some tribal legends regarded their arrival as a gift from the gods rather than a by-product of Europe's invasion of America.[2]

In addition to making daily life easier, horses also made Plains Indian warriors more formidable and created a new world of intertribal competition. Newcomers to the plains, like the Cheyennes, migrated westward and embraced the new culture of horse riding and buffalo hunting. New arrivals and old inhabitants began to jockey for position on the rich buffalo grounds; mounted hunters trespassed on enemy territory in pursuit of

37

the buffalo herds. Warriors traveled vast distances to trade or raid for horses; stealing horses from one's enemies ranked as a major coup, and pony herds became a measure of individual and tribal wealth. Some tribes specialized in horse breeding; others became horse traders. Horses were a form of transportation, a medium of trade, a means of production, a reason for going to war, a vital weapon of warfare, and, in hard times, a source of food.[3]

At about the same time as horses entered the Plains Indian world, European trade goods, and especially guns, began to appear. Like horses, guns transformed and increased intertribal conflicts. A people's chances of success and even survival in the new world that was evolving on the plains depended on whether, and in what amounts, they were able to obtain horses and guns.[4] People fighting with traditional weapons, and on foot, could not compete with others who had access to both guns and horses.

As a result, guns and horses meant power and prosperity. Possession of firearms allowed a tribe to expand at the expense of unarmed neighbors. For example, in the eighteenth century, Crees expanded westward, coming into conflict with the Blackfeet; Ojibwas pushed against the Sioux on the western edges of the Great Lakes. In 1719, Comanches, Utes, Wichitas, and Pawnees armed with muskets from the French defeated the Apaches on the southern plains. The southward-moving Comanches, who were better mounted than the Apaches, secured regular supplies of guns and ammunition from French traders via Osage and Wichita intermediaries. The Apaches were denied guns by Spanish Indian policy, which sought to keep firearms out of Indian hands. By the mid-eighteenth century, the Comanches had driven out the Apaches and achieved dominance as "lords of the south plains." On the northern plains, the Snake, or Shoshoni, Indians acquired horses, expanded their range, and inflicted defeats on the Blackfeet. Then the Blackfeet acquired both horses and guns and turned the tables.

Quickly appreciating the value and danger of firearms, Indian peoples endeavored to secure and maintain favorable positions in the trade networks that crossed the plains. Bands shifted location and conducted their foreign policies in such a way as to tap into the trade networks that conveyed such vital commodities as horses and guns (see Figure 4). The Cheyennes traded horses at the Arikara villages to their northeast and

Figure 4 (*opposite*).   The Diffusion of Horses and Guns onto the Great Plains

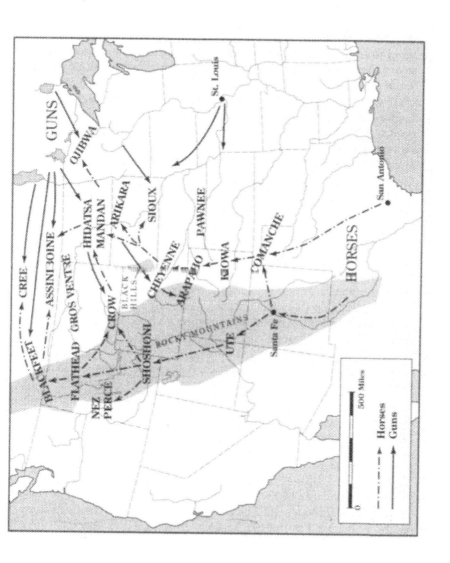

GUNS

HORSES

St. Louis

San Antonio

OJIBWA

CREE

ASSINIBOINE

GROS VENTRE

BLACKFEET

FLATHEAD

NEZ PERCE

SHOSHONI

CROW

HIDATSA

MANDAN

ARIKARA

BLACK HILLS

CHEYENNE

ARAPAHO

SIOUX

PAWNEE

IOWA

COMANCHE

UTE

Santa Fe

ROCKY MOUNTAINS

Horses

Guns

500 Miles

0

39

then sold the guns they acquired there to Arapahos, Kiowas, and other tribes to their south and west, acquiring more horses in return.[5] Crows traveled between the Hidatsas on the Missouri and the Flatheads in the Rockies. Tribes with guns usually tried to keep them out of the hands of those without, which explains both the hostility Lewis and Clark encountered from Brulé Sioux on the Missouri River as the explorers started west and their clash with the Blackfeet on the way home: Both the Sioux and the Blackfeet feared the Americans would threaten their favorable trading position by trading guns to other tribes.[6] Blackfeet fears were well founded. They got their guns from British traders east of the Rockies and tried to prevent guns from reaching the Kutenais, the Flatheads, and other tribes to their south and west. During the first decade of the nineteenth century, British and American traders managed to circumvent the Blackfeet and supply their enemies. In 1810, armed with guns, the Flatheads and the Kutenais defeated the Blackfeet for the first time.[7]

As Indian peoples welcomed horses into their cultures and incorporated firearms into their arsenals, they also became exposed to unseen forces of destruction. Epidemic diseases, introduced to America by European invaders, traveled silently along the same trade routes and war trails by which horses and guns spread to the different tribes. Smallpox, measles, cholera, and other new diseases wrought havoc in Indian villages, scything down populations at an alarming rate. Mortality rates of between 50 and 90 percent were common whenever new epidemics struck. Indians in Texas suffered epidemics as early as the sixteenth century, and outbreaks of smallpox occurred time and again in the seventeenth and eighteenth centuries. A smallpox epidemic that broke out in Mexico spread to Spanish settlements in the Southwest in 1779. Indians who raided and traded for horses in the area carried the deadly disease with them when they returned home. For four years it swept western America, spreading to the forests of Canada and killing between one-third and one-half of the people it attacked. Recurrent outbreaks of disease and Sioux attacks reduced the Arikaras from the eighteen, or even thirty-two, villages they told French traders they once inhabited to two or three villages by the time Lewis and Clark arrived; the Mandans suffered similar reductions. The Omaha Indians, who numbered as many as three thousand in the late 1700s, were reduced to less than three hundred by 1802, losing more than fifteen hundred to the 1801–02 smallpox epidemic, a mortality rate of 75 percent. The same epidemic spread north to the Saskatchewan River in Canada via the Arapahos and the Gros Ventres. Smallpox struck the central plains in the early 1830s and erupted on the upper Missouri in 1837. Immigrant wagon trains on the trails to Oregon and California brought cholera in the 1840s. Cholera may have killed as many as one-quarter of the Comanches in 1849–50. Smallpox hit the Comanches again in 1861–62, the Blackfeet again in 1869. Disease killed far more Indians than did American soldiers' bullets. A Cheyenne named Little Wolf said simply: "Many have died of diseases we have no name for."[8]

The Indian peoples that American explorers, soldiers, and settlers encountered on the Great Plains in the nineteenth century were peoples very much in flux. They lived in a world that was very different from the one their ancestors inhabited one hundred years before, and they were still adjusting to its challenges and opportunities. Plains Indians who sat on horseback holding guns as they watched Americans edge into their territory were veterans of recurrent intertribal wars and survivors of recurrent epidemics. The documents in this chapter illustrate the impact on Indian peoples of the three forces — horses, firearms, and disease — that so dramatically altered their lives.

HOW THE BLACKFEET GOT HORSES, GUNS, AND SMALLPOX

By 1800, all the peoples of the Great Plains had acquired horses and experienced smallpox. Most had some firearms; those who did not were anxious to get them. The experience of the Piegans in present-day Montana (the southernmost tribe of the Blackfoot Confederacy, which also comprised the Siksika, or Northern, Blackfeet and the Blood Indians) and their Shoshoni enemies illustrates the changes in warfare and shifting balances of power that arose from the introduction of horses, guns, and epidemic diseases.

In the winter of 1787–88, a Cree named Saukamappee, who was living among the Blackfeet, gave fur trader David Thompson the following account of how his adopted people first encountered horses sometime around 1730, first employed firearms against their enemies, and caught smallpox in 1781.[9] Thompson was a Welshman working for the Canadian Northwest Company. He described Saukamappee as "an old man of at least 75 to 80 years of age, . . . his face slightly marked with the smallpox."

In the eighteenth century the Blackfeet and other tribes referred to the Shoshonis as Snakes and designated them as such in sign language. The Shoshonis originated in the Great Basin area of Nevada, but a great drought in the area, more than five hundred years before Lewis and Clark, triggered a series of population movements. Groups of Shoshoni speakers drifted across the Rocky Mountains in the early sixteenth century. While their Comanche relatives moved south, the Shoshonis moved north and east. They obtained horses from Utes and Comanches by about 1700 and moved onto the buffalo-rich plains of Wyoming and Montana in increasing numbers. They appear to have extended as far north as the Saskatchewan River, where they came into conflict with the Blackfeet by the third decade of the eighteenth century. As Saukamappee's narrative shows, the Shoshoni cavalry brought a new form of warfare to the northern plains.

However, firearms soon offset Shoshoni wealth in horses. The Blackfeet enlisted the help of the Cree (Nahathaway) and Assiniboine (Stone) Indians, who came to their aid with guns. As the Blackfeet began to close the gap on the Shoshonis in terms of horse power, they built up their arsenals of firearms and steel weapons, either by trading with Cree and Assiniboine middlemen or by dealing directly with the French, British, and Canadian traders who came to their country in growing numbers. The Blackfeet halted the spread of guns westward by controlling the trade routes, and only a few firearms made it to the Shoshonis via other routes. Shoshoni tradition recalled that before Lewis and Clark, "we knew nothing about guns except their effects." Smallpox hit both the Blackfeet and the Shoshonis in 1781, killing between one-third and one-half of the people and interrupting hostilities for several years. However, by 1805, when Lewis and Clark encountered the Shoshonis for the first time, the Blackfeet and their allies had succeeded in pushing the Shoshonis off the plains and into the Rocky Mountain ranges of western Wyoming and Idaho. The Shoshonis welcomed American traders into their country; the new source of firearms allowed them to confront Blackfeet and other enemies on equal terms again in the nineteenth century.[10]

SAUKAMAPPEE

Memories of War and Smallpox
1787–1788

The Peeagans [Piegans] were always the frontier Tribe, and upon whom the Snake Indians made their attacks, these latter were very numerous, even without their allies; and the Peeagans had to send messengers among us to procure help. Two of them came to the camp of my father, and I was then about his age (pointing to a Lad of about sixteen years) he promised to come and bring some of his people, the Nahathaways with him, for I am myself of that people, and not of those with whom I am. My father brought about twenty warriors with him. There were a few guns amongst us, but very little ammunition, and they were left to hunt for the · families; Our weapons was a Lance, mostly pointed with iron, some few of stone, A Bow and a quiver of Arrows; the Bows were of Larch, the length came to the chin; the quiver had about fifty arrows, of which ten had iron points, the others were headed with stone. He carried his knife on his breast and his axe in his belt. Such was my father's weapons, and those with him had much the same weapons. I had a Bow and Arrows and a knife, of which I was very proud. We came to the Peeagans and their allies. They were camped in the Plains on the left bank of the River (the north side) and were a great many. We were feasted, a great War Tent was made, and a few days passed in speeches, feasting, and dances. A war chief was elected by the chiefs, and we got ready to march. Our spies had been out and had seen a large camp of the Snake Indians on the Plains of the Eagle Hill, and we had to cross the River in canoes, and on rafts, which we carefully secured for our retreat. When we had crossed and numbered our men, we were about 350 warriors (this he showed by counting every finger to be ten, and holding up both hands three times and then one hand) they had their scouts out, and came to meet us. Both parties made a great show of their numbers, and I thought that they were more numerous than ourselves.

After some singing and dancing, they sat down on the ground, and placed their large shields before them, which covered them: We did the same, but our shields were not so many, and some of our shields had to shelter two men. Theirs were all placed touching each other; their Bows

Richard Glover, ed., *David Thompson's Narrative, 1784–1812* (Toronto: The Champlain Society, 1962), 240–47.

were not so long as ours, but of better wood, and the back covered with the sinews of the Bisons which made them very elastic, and their arrows went a long way and whizzed about us as balls do from guns. They were all headed with a sharp, smooth, black stone (flint) which broke when it struck anything. Our iron headed arrows did not go through their shields, but stuck in them; On both sides several were wounded, but none lay on the ground; and night put an end to the battle, without a scalp being taken on either side, and in those days such was the result, unless one party was more numerous than the other. The great mischief of war then, was as now, by attacking and destroying small camps of ten to thirty tents, which are obliged to separate for hunting: I grew to be a man, became a skilfull and fortunate hunter, and my relations procured me a Wife. She was young and handsome and we were fond of each other. We had passed a winter together, when Messengers came from our allies to claim assistance.

By this time the affairs of both parties had much changed; we had more guns and iron headed arrows than before; but our enemies the Snake Indians and their allies had Misstutim (Big Dogs, that is Horses) on which they rode, swift as the Deer, on which they dashed at the Peeagans, and with their stone Pukamoggan[11] knocked them on the head, and they had thus lost several of their best men. This news we did not well comprehend and it alarmed us, for we had no idea of Horses and could not make out what they were. Only three of us went and I should not have gone, had not my wife's relations frequently intimated, that her father's medicine bag would be honored by the scalp of a Snake Indian. When we came to our allies, the great War Tent [was made] with speeches, feasting, and dances as before; and when the War Chief had viewed us all it was found between us and the Stone Indians we had ten guns and each of us about thirty balls, and powder for the war, and we were considered the strength of the battle. After a few days march our scouts brought us word that the enemy was near in a large war party, but had no Horses with them, for at that time they had very few of them. When we came to meet each other, as usual, each displayed their numbers, weapons and shiel[d]s, in all which they were superior to us, except our guns which were not shown, but kept in their leathern cases, and if we had shown [them], they would have taken them for long clubs. For a long time they held us in suspense; a tall Chief was forming a strong party to make an attack on our centre, and the others to enter into combat with those opposite to them; We prepared for the battle the best we could. Those of us who had guns stood in the front line, and each of us [had] two balls in his mouth, and a load of powder in his left hand to reload.

We noticed they had a great many short stone clubs for close combat, which is a dangerous weapon, and had they made a bold attack on us, we must have been defeated as they were more numerous and better armed than we were, for we could have fired our guns no more than twice; and were at a loss what to do on the wide plain, and each Chief encouraged his men to stand firm. Our eyes were all on the tall Chief and his motions, which appeared to be contrary to the advice of several old Chiefs, all this time we were about the strong flight of an arrow from each other. At length the tall chief retired and they formed their long usual line by placing their shields on the ground to touch each other, the shield having a breadth of full three feet or more. We sat down opposite to them and most of us waited for the night to make a hasty retreat. The War Chief was close to us, anxious to see the effect of our guns. The lines were too far asunder for us to make a sure shot, and we requested him to close the line to about sixty yards, which was gradually done, and lying flat on the ground behind the shields, we watched our opportunity when they drew their bows to shoot at us, their bodies were then exposed and each of us, as opportunity offered, fired with deadly aim, and either killed, or severely wounded, every one we aimed at.

The War Chief was highly pleased, and the Snake Indians finding so many killed and wounded kept themselves behind their shields; the War Chief then desired we would spread ourselves by two's throughout the line, which we did, and our shots caused consternation and dismay along their whole line. The battle had begun about Noon, and the Sun was not yet half down, when we perceived some of them had crawled away from their shields, and were taking to flight. The War Chief seeing this went along the line and spoke to every Chief to keep his Men ready for a charge of the whole line of the enemy, of which he would give the signal; this was done by himself stepping in front with his Spear, and calling on them to follow him as he rushed on their line, and in an instant the whole of us followed him, the greater part of the enemy took to flight, but some fought bravely and we lost more than ten killed and many wounded; Part of us pursued, and killed a few, but the chase had soon to be given over, for at the body of every Snake Indian killed, there were five or six of us trying to get his scalp, or part of his clothing, his weapons, or something as a trophy of the battle. As there were only three of us, and seven of our friends, the Stone Indians, we did not interfere, and got nothing. . . .

The terror of that battle and of our guns has prevented any more general battles, and our wars have since been carried by ambuscade and surprize, of small camps, in which we have greatly the advantage, from the Guns, arrow shods of iron, long knives, flat bayonets, and axes from the Traders. While we have these weapons, the Snake Indians have none, but what few they sometimes take from one of our small camps which they have destroyed, and they have no Traders among them. We thus continued to advance through the fine plains to the Stag River[12] when death came over us all, and swept away more than half of us by the Small pox, of which we knew nothing until it brought death among us. We caught it from the Snake Indians. Our Scouts were out for our security, when some returned and informed us of a considerable camp which was too large to attack and something very suspicious about it; from a high knowl they had a good view of the camp, but saw none of the men hunting, or going about; there were a few Horses, but no one came to them, and a herd of Bisons [were] feeding close to the camp with other herds near. This somewhat alarmed us as a stratagem of War; and our Warriors thought this camp had a larger not far off; so that if this camp was attacked which was strong enough to offer a desperate resistance, the other would come to their assistance and overpower us as had been once done by them, and in which we lost many of our men.

The council ordered the Scouts to return and go beyond this camp, and be sure there was no other. In the mean time we advanced our camp; The scouts returned and said no other tents were near, and the camp appeared in the same state as before. Our Scouts had been going too much about their camp and were seen; they expected what would follow, and all those that could walk, as soon as night came on, went away. Next morning at the dawn of day, we attacked the Tents, and with our sharp flat daggers and knives, cut through the tents and entered for the fight; but our war whoop instantly stopt, our eyes were appalled with terror; there was no one to fight with but the dead and the dying, each a mass of corruption. We did not touch them, but left the tents, and held a council on what was to be done. We all thought the Bad Spirit had made himself master of the camp and destroyed them. It was agreed to take some of the best of the tents, and any other plunder that was clean and good, which we did, and also took away the few Horses they had, and returned to our camp.

The second day after this dreadful disease broke out in our camp, and spread from one tent to another as if the Bad Spirit carried it. We had no belief that one Man could give it to another, any more than a wounded Man could give his wound to another. We did not suffer so much as those that were near the river, into which they rushed and died.[13] We had only a little brook, and about one third of us died, but in some of the other camps there were tents in which every one died. When at length it left us, and we moved about to find our people, it was no longer with the song and the dance; but with tears, shrieks, and howlings of despair for those who would never return to us. War was no longer thought of, and we had enough to do to hunt and make provision for our families, for in our sickness we had consumed all our dried provisions; but the Bisons and Red Deer were also gone, we did not see one half of what was before, whither they had gone we could not tell, we believed the Good Spirit had forsaken us, and allowed the Bad Spirit to become our Master. What little we could spare we offered to the Bad Spirit to let us alone and go to our enemies. To the Good Spirit we offered feathers, branches of trees, and sweet smelling grass. Our hearts were low and dejected, and we shall never be again the same people.

HOWLING WOLF: TRADING GUNS FOR HORSES

Howling Wolf was a Southern Cheyenne who hunted buffalo and fought Indian and white enemies on the southern plains before the Army incarcerated him. Although a great hunter and warrior, he is best known for his skill in portraying the history and customs of his people in pictures. One of the "ringleaders" sent into captivity at Fort Marion, Florida, in 1875, Howling Wolf became, for a time, a convert to the white man's ways as advocated by his jailer/teacher, Richard H. Pratt. Like many of the other prisoners at Fort Marion, he applied traditional Plains Indian art to a new medium, producing drawings of Indian life on paper with ink, watercolor, and colored pencils. He continued to draw after he returned to the reservation, leaving a valuable visual record of Plains Indian life in the old days, of their wars, and of their transition to a new world. In his later years, Howling Wolf returned to many of his more traditional Indian ways. He died in a car accident in 1927 at age seventy-seven. His life "spanned the transitional years between the era of the equestrian nomad shown in his drawings and the age of the automobile, which was instrumental in his death."[14]

Figure 5 is taken from a sketchbook of a dozen drawings done by Howling Wolf sometime between 1878 and 1881, after he returned from Florida to Oklahoma. Like other pictographic drawings, it shows not a single event at a single moment, but rather a sequence of events. The Cheyennes on the right and Kiowas on the left are trading guns for horses. The Cheyenne in the center foreground clasps hands with the Kiowa chief, Satank, or Sitting Bear, who is identified by the name-symbol above his head. Satank leads a horse with a brand, indicating that it has

Figure 5. Trading Guns for Horses
Painted by Howling Wolf (ca. 1878–81).

been obtained from whites. He is about to trade it for the pack, carried on a travois pulled by a dog, to which the Cheyenne points. Behind the dog, another Cheyenne holds out a powder horn for trade. Another, holding a gun, remains in the background, partially hidden by a tree and a hillock.

The X in the center of the picture symbolizes exchange and shows that a trade has taken place. The Kiowa on the left has led his horse from the Kiowa camp toward the Cheyennes, as indicated by the hoofprints. The Cheyenne chief in the foreground (identified by the pipe-tomahawk he holds) calls his wife to lead the horse away. As she does so (again signified by the hoofprints), the horse appears to become skittish, and the lines issuing from her mouth indicate she is speaking to the animal, presumably to try to calm it down. The woman's sex is indicated by her plain leggings and dress with fringed side-panels. Other Kiowas wait to trade in the upper left. A small boy, oblivious to the events around him, lies on the riverbank, taking aim at a bird in a tree.[15]

The original sketchbook contained captions written by Ben Clark, a scout and interpreter at Fort Reno, near the reservation where Howling Wolf lived. The caption for this picture reads: "The first horses owned by Cheyennes which they are trading for from the Kiowas on the Arkansas or what the Indians call Flint River the arrow indicating its name from its flint head. Supposed to be over 150 years ago. Cheyennes on right with dog travois, Kiowas on left." Although Captain John Bourke, who knew Clark, described him as "a man of clear intellect, expressing himself in good language, honest and truthful in his statements and accurate in his deductions," there are problems with Clark's interpretation. The Cheyennes obtained horses by about 1750, when they were living in North Dakota and still practicing horticulture. Here, they are shown hundreds of miles to the south, dealing with a Kiowa chief, Satank, who lived in the nineteenth century. It is possible that an earlier chief had the same name and that Howling Wolf used artistic license in depicting country with which he was familiar, but Cheyennes themselves offer a more plausible explanation. Anthropologist John Moore tells how elders of the Kiowas, Comanches, Plains Apaches, Cheyennes, and Arapahos identified the picture as depicting the Great Peace made between the tribes in 1840 and "had a fine time naming the people and events in the picture, which shows the activities of the second day of the alliance, when the Kiowas gave horses to the Cheyennes."[16] The Cheyennes and the Arapahos needed horses, and the Kiowas and Comanches needed guns with which to resist growing Indian and white pressure on their eastern frontiers. The Great Peace guaranteed the necessary exchanges by regular trade rather than

sporadic raiding. Historians are often suspicious of oral tradition, prefer-
ring written sources, but in this case oral tradition provides clarification
and the documentary sources are misleading.

"I BRING DEATH": THE KIOWAS MEET SMALLPOX

Deadly new diseases left a searing impression on the minds of survivors.
Winter counts from throughout the plains record outbreaks of smallpox,
measles, and other diseases as the most memorable event of many years;
taken together these winter counts confirm that many epidemics were in
fact pandemics — the same disease struck virtually everywhere. Experiences of smallpox became entrenched in tribal and individual memory,
but not all Indian peoples possess strong oral traditions relating to the
new diseases. For some, the impact of smallpox may have been so
devastating that it became something that one did not talk about. Pretty
Shield indicated this kind of reaction when talking to Frank Linderman
in the twentieth century. She remembered how the Crows caught smallpox from the Shoshonis when she was sixteen. It killed her father "and
more than a hundred others, in one moon," she said. "I had it myself."
She recalled how her people "became terrified and died," but she refused
to dwell on the memory. "When a woman sees whole families wiped out,
even whole clans, and cannot help, cannot even hope, her heart falls down
and she wishes that she could die. . . . I do not like to think
about it."[17]

In this legend, Saynday, the trickster hero of the Kiowas,
protects his people against smallpox and turns the deadly
disease against their Pawnee enemies. Although the legend
refers to the first encounter with smallpox, it is clearly a
creation of the late nineteenth century, by which time the
Kiowas had had plenty of experience with the disease: As
far-ranging horse traders they could not have escaped the
epidemic of 1779–81 on the plains, and they certainly suffered
from outbreaks in 1801–02, 1816, 1839–40, and 1861–62.
Kiowa winter counts record 1839–40 as "smallpox winter"[18]
(see Figure 6). Smallpox continued to plague the Kiowas as
late as 1899–1901.

Figure 6.   The Smallpox Winter
The Kiowa winter count record of 1839–40.

Kiowa Legend

Saynday was coming along, and as he came he saw that all his world had changed. Where the buffalo herds used to graze, he saw white-faced cattle. The Washita River, which once ran bankful with clear water, was soggy with red mud. There were no deer or antelope in the brush or skittering across the high plains. No white tipis rose proudly against the blue sky; settlers' soddies dented the hillsides and the creek banks. My time has come, Saynday thought to himself. The world I lived in is dead. Soon the Kiowa people will be fenced like the white man's cattle, and they cannot break out of the fences because the barbed wire will tear their flesh. I can't help my people any longer by staying with them. My time has come, and I will have to go away from this changed world.

Off across the prairie, Saynday saw a dark spot coming toward him from the east, moving very slowly.

That's strange, too, Saynday thought to himself. The East is the place of birth and of new life. The things that come from the East come quickly; they come dancing and alive. This thing comes as slowly as death to an old man. I wonder what it is?

Almost absent-mindedly, Saynday started walking eastward. As he went the spot grew larger, and after a while Saynday saw that it was a man on a horse.

The horse was black, but it had been powdered to roan with the red dust that the plows had stirred up when they slashed open the plains. Red dust spotted the man's clothing — a black suit and a high hat, like a missionary's. Red dust blurred his features, but behind the dust Saynday could see that the man's face was pitted with terrible scars.

The stranger drew rein, and sat looking at Saynday. The black roan horse lifted one sore hoof and drooped its head as if it were too weary to carry its burden any further.

"Who are you?" the stranger asked.

"I'm Saynday. I'm the Kiowas' Old Uncle Saynday. I'm the one who's always coming along."

"I never heard of you," the stranger said, "and I never heard of the Kiowas. Who are they?"

"The Kiowas are my people," Saynday said, and even in that hard time he stood up proudly, like a man. "Who are you?"

Alice Marriott and Carol K. Rachlin, *American Indian Mythology* (New York: Thomas Y. Crowell, 1968), 173–77.

"I'm Smallpox," the man answered.

"And I never heard of *you*," said Saynday. "Where do you come from and what do you do and why are you here?"

"I come from far away, across the Eastern Ocean," Smallpox answered. "I am one with the white men — they are my people as the Kiowas are yours. Sometimes I travel ahead of them, and sometimes I lurk behind. But I am always their companion and you will find me in their camps and in their houses."

"What do you do?" Saynday repeated.

"I bring death," Smallpox replied. "My breath causes children to wither like young plants in spring snow. I bring destruction. No matter how beautiful a woman is, once she has looked at me she becomes as ugly as death. And to men I bring not death alone, but the destruction of their children and the blighting of their wives. The strongest warriors go down before me. No people who have looked on me will ever be the same." And he chuckled low and hideously. With his raised forearm, Smallpox pushed the dust off his face, and Saynday saw the scars that disfigured it.

For a moment Saynday shut his eyes against the sight, and then he opened them again. "Does that happen to all the people you visit?" he inquired.

"Every one of them," said Smallpox. "It will happen to your Kiowa people, too. Where do they live? Take me to them, and then I will spare you, although you have seen my face. If you do not lead me to your people, I will breathe on you and you will die, no matter whose Old Uncle you are." And although he did not breathe on Saynday, Saynday smelled the reek of death that surrounded him.

"My Kiowa people are few and poor already," Saynday said, thinking fast as he talked. "They aren't worth your time and trouble."

"I have time and I don't have to take any trouble," Smallpox told him. "Even one person whom I blot out, I can count."

"Oh," said Saynday. "Some of your ways are like the Kiowas', then. You count the enemies that you touch."

"I have no enemies," said Smallpox. "Man, woman, or child — humanity is all alike to me. I was brought here to kill. But, yes, I count those I destroy. White men always count: cattle, sheep, chickens, children, the living and the dead. You say the Kiowas do the same thing?"

"Only the enemies they touch," Saynday insisted. "They never count living people — men are not cattle, any more than women and children are."

"Then how do you know the Kiowas are so few and poor?" Smallpox demanded.

"Oh, anybody can see that for himself," Saynday said. "You can look at a Kiowa camp and tell how small it is. We're not like the Pawnees. They have great houses, half underground, in big villages by the rivers, and every house is full of people."

"I like that," Smallpox observed. "I can do my best work when people are crowded together."

"Then you'd like the Pawnees," Saynday assured him. "They're the ones that almost wiped out the Kiowas; that's why we're so few and so poor. Now we run away whenever we see a stranger coming, because he might be a Pawnee."

"I suppose the Pawnees never run away," Smallpox sneered.

"They couldn't if they wanted to," Saynday replied. "The Pawnees are rich. They have piles of robes, they have lots of cooking pots and plenty of bedding — they keep all kinds of things in those underground houses of theirs. The Pawnees can't run away and leave all their wealth."

"Where did you say they live?" Smallpox asked thoughtfully.

"Oh, over there," Saynday said, jerking his chin to the north.

"And they are rich, and live in houses, with piles of robes to creep into and hide?"

"That's the Pawnees," Saynday said jauntily. He began to feel better. The deathly smell was not so strong now. "I think I'll go and visit the Pawnees first," Smallpox remarked. "Later on, perhaps, I can get back to the Kiowas."

"You do that," directed Saynday. "Go and visit the Pawnees, and when you grow tired there from all the work you have to do, come back and visit my poor people. They'll do all they can for you."

"Good," said Smallpox. He picked up his reins and jerked his weary horse awake. "Tell your people when I come to be ready for me. Tell them to put out all their fires. Fire is the only thing in the whole world that I'm afraid of. It's the only thing in God's world that can destroy me."

Saynday watched Smallpox and his death horse traveling north, away from the Kiowas. Then he took out his flint and steel, and set fire to the spindly prairie grass at his feet. The winds came and picked up the fire, and carried it to make a ring of safety around the Kiowas' camps.

"Perhaps I can still be some good to my people after all," Saynday said to himself, feeling better.

And that's the way it was, and that's the way it is, to this good day.

NOTES

[1] Frank B. Linderman, *Pretty-shield, Medicine Woman of the Crows* (Lincoln: University of Nebraska Press, 1972), 83.

[2] See, for example, LaVerne Harel Clark, *They Sang for Horses: The Impact of the Horse on Navajo and Apache Folklore* (Tucson: University of Arizona Press, 1966).

[3] Frank Gilbert Roe, *The Indian and the Horse* (Norman: University of Oklahoma Press, 1955); John C. Ewers, "The Horse in Blackfoot Indian Culture, with Comparative Material from Other Western Tribes," Smithsonian Institution, Bureau of American Ethnology *Bulletin* 159 (1955).

[4] Frank R. Secoy, "Changing Military Patterns on the Great Plains," *Monographs of the American Ethnological Society* 21 (1953), 92. (Reprinted, Lincoln: University of Nebraska Press, 1992).

[5] Joseph Jablow, "The Cheyenne in Plains Indian Trade Relations, 1795–1840," *Monographs of the American Ethnological Society* 19 (1966). (Reprinted, Lincoln: University of Nebraska Press, 1994).

[6] For analysis of both encounters see James P. Ronda, *Lewis and Clark among the Indians* (Lincoln: University of Nebraska Press, 1984).

[7] The relationship between war and trade is discussed in more detail in Colin G. Calloway, "The Intertribal Balance of Power on the Great Plains, 1760–1850," *Journal of American Studies* 16 (1982), 25–47.

[8] A. P. Nasatir, ed., *Before Lewis and Clark: Documents Illustrating the History of the Missouri, 1785–1804.* 2 vols. (Lincoln: University of Nebraska Press, 1990 ed.) 1:299; Gary Moulton, ed., *The Journals of the Lewis and Clark Expedition.* 9 vols. (Lincoln: University of Nebraska Press, 1983), 2:482n, 3:401–02; Annie Heloise Abel, ed., *Tabeau's Narrative of Loisel's Expedition to the Upper Missouri* (Norman: University of Oklahoma Press, 1968), 123; Alice M. Johnson, ed., *Saskatchewan Journals and Correspondence* (London: Hudson's Bay Record Society, 1967), 294; Russell Thornton, *American Indian Holocaust and Survival: A Population History since 1492* (Norman: University of Oklahoma Press, 1987), 91–94; William R. Brown, Jr., "Comancheria Demography, 1805–1830," *Panhandle Plains Historical Review* 59 (1986), 1–17; Ernest Wallace and E. Adamson Hoebel, *The Comanches* (Norman: University of Oklahoma Press, 1952), 149.

[9] For another Indian account of how the Blackfeet obtained their first horses and guns, see James Willard Schultz (Apikuni), *Why Gone Those Times: Blackfoot Tales* (Norman: University of Oklahoma Press, 1974), 129–40. In the winter of 1877–78, Red Eagle told Schultz how the Blackfeet got their first guns from the Crees and then turned them against the Crows and other enemies. Red Eagle said, "This is the story of the gun as my grandfather told it to me — and as his father told it to him."

[10] Colin G. Calloway, "Snake Frontiers: The Eastern Shoshones in the Eighteenth Century," *Annals of Wyoming* 63 (1991), 82–92.

[11] War clubs.

[12] Probably the Red Deer River, which joins the Bow River to form the South Saskatchewan.

[13] Taking a sweat bath and then immersing the body in a cold stream was a common practice in treating ailments; in the case of smallpox, it only made things worse.

[14] For more information, see Karen Daniels Peterson, *Howling Wolf: A Cheyenne Warrior's Graphic Interpretation of His People* (Palo Alto, Cal: American West Publishing Co., 1968); Joyce M. Szabo, *Howling Wolf and the History of Ledger Art* (Albuquerque: University of New Mexico Press, 1994).

[15] Peterson, *Howling Wolf,* plate 2.

[16] Ibid.; John H. Moore, *The Cheyenne Nation: A Social and Demographic History* (Lincoln: University of Nebraska Press, 1987), 6–7.

[17] Linderman, *Pretty-shield, Medicine Woman of the Crows*, 45.

[18] James Mooney, "Calendar History of the Kiowa Indians," *17th Annual Report of the Bureau of American Ethnology, 1895–96*, part 1 (Washington, D.C.: U.S. Govt. Printing Office, 1898), 274; Thornton, *American Indian Holocaust and Survival*, 128–31.

3

A Pawnee Vision of the Future

Hollywood has treated the Pawnee Indians of Nebraska badly. In both *Little Big Man* (1970) and *Dances with Wolves* (1990), films that generally present Indians in a favorable light, the Pawnees are portrayed as villains. The Pawnees in *Dances with Wolves* are one-dimensional stereotypes, playing violent villains to Kevin Costner's Lakota heroes; ironically, the Pawnees are playing roles identical to those the Lakotas used to play when the heroes were all white. In reality, the Pawnees were a sophisticated people who sought to order their universe and renew their world through complex rituals.

Pawnee life followed a regular and precise seasonal cycle in which the tribe planted crops, gathered wild food, and hunted buffalo. Pawnee priests observed the positions of the stars to learn exactly when to plant, when to hunt, and when to begin the ceremonies that ensured the continuation of the whole cycle. Pawnee people traced their origins to the nighttime sky, and in Pawnee cosmology the stars acted as intermediaries between heaven and earth. The Pawnees drew charts of the stars on elk skins and even arranged their villages so that their earth lodges reflected the positions of the stars.[1]

The nineteenth century brought disaster and chaos to the Pawnee world. Epidemic diseases wrought havoc in their villages: A smallpox epidemic in the early 1830s killed about half the tribe. As the Lakota, or Teton, Sioux expanded westward they encroached on Pawnee hunting territory, attacked Pawnee villages, and eventually drove the Pawnees into Oklahoma in 1875. Meanwhile, white Americans sought to "civilize" the Pawnees and reorder the Pawnee universe. Quaker missionaries tried to make them give up hunting and become farmers, ignoring the fact that the Pawnees had been farmers for hundreds of years — they grew ten varieties of corn, eight types of beans, and seven kinds of squash and pumpkins — and failing to understand the integral relationship between buffalo hunting and horticulture in Pawnee economic and spiritual life. Pawnees hunted buffalo not only to feed and clothe themselves but also to dedicate meat to Tirawa, the Great Spirit, and thereby maintain the sacred order of things. The Quakers and other nineteenth-century missionaries saw themselves as offering the Pawnees the chance to abandon "savage" ways, embrace "civilization," and survive the future. In reality, they destroyed more than they ever could have imagined.

By the 1820s, the Pawnees were a people under assault on several fronts. As the following speech suggests, they could see the writing on the wall. But they were not ready to capitulate, to stop being Pawnees. The sentiments expressed here by the Pawnees as they confronted their future were echoed time and again by other peoples at other times in response to white American demands that they give up buffalo hunting and settle down as farmers: Let us continue as we are until the buffalo are gone; then we'll talk about becoming farmers.

The following speech was delivered to President James Monroe during a visit to Washington, D.C., in 1822 by a delegation of sixteen Pawnee, Omaha, Oto, Missouri, and Kansa Indians. The speaker was the Pawnee chief Sharitarish, not the younger Petalesharo, who accompanied the delegation and to whom it is sometimes attributed.

SHARITARISH

"We Are Not Starving Yet"

1822

My Great Father. — I have travelled a great distance to see you. I have seen you, and my heart rejoices; I have heard your words; they have entered one ear, and shall not escape the other; and I will carry them to my people as pure, as they came from your mouth.

My Great Father. — I am going to speak the truth. The Great Spirit looks down upon us, and I call Him to witness all that may pass between us on this occasion. If I am here now, and have seen your people, your houses, your vessels on the big lake, and a great many wonderful things, far beyond my comprehension, which appear to have been made by the Great Spirit, and placed in your hands, I am indebted to my father here,

Jedediah Morse, *A Report to the Secretary of War of the United States on Indian Affairs* (New Haven: S. Converse, 1822), 242–45.

who invited me from home, under whose wings I have been protected.[2] Yes, my Great Father, I have travelled with your chief. I have followed him, and trod in his tracks; but there is still another Great Father, to whom I am much indebted — it is the Father of us all. Him who made us and placed us on this earth. I feel grateful to the Great Spirit for strengthening my heart for such an undertaking, and for preserving the life which he gave me. The Great Spirit made us all — he made my skin red, and yours white. He placed us on this earth, and intended that we should live differently from each other. He made the whites to cultivate the earth, and feed on domestic animals; but he made us red skins, to rove through the uncultivated woods and plains, to feed on wild animals, and to dress in their skins. He also intended that we should go to war to take scalps — steal horses, and triumph over our enemies — cultivate peace at home, and promote the happiness of each other. I believe there are no people, of any color, on this earth, who do not believe in the Great Spirit — in rewards and in punishments. We worship him, but we worship him not as you do. We differ from you in appearance and manners, as well as in our customs; and we differ from you in our religion. We have no large houses, as you have, to worship the Great Spirit in; if we had them to day, we should want others to morrow, for we have not, like you, a fixed habitation — we have no settled home, except our villages, where we remain but two moons in twelve; we, like animals, rove through the country, whilst you whites reside between us and heaven; but still my Great Father, we love the Great Spirit — we acknowledge his supreme power — our peace, our health, and our happiness depend upon him; and our lives belong to him — he made us, and he can destroy us.

My Great Father. — Some of your good chiefs, or, as they are called, *Missionaries,* have proposed to send of their good people among us to change our habits, to make us work, and live like the white people. I will not tell a lie, I am going tell the truth. You love your country; you love your people; you love the manner in which they live, and you think your people brave. I am like you, my Great Father, I love my country; I love my people; I love the manner in which we live, and think myself and warriors brave; spare me then, my Father, let me enjoy my country, and pursue the buffaloe, and the beaver, and the other wild animals of our wilderness, and I will trade the skins with your people. I have grown up and lived thus long without work; I am in hopes you will suffer me to die without it. We have yet plenty of buffaloe, beaver, deer, and other wild animals; we have also an abundance of horses. We have every thing we want. We have plenty of land, *if you will keep your people off of it.*

[handwritten margin note, left: "how God made them equally"]

[handwritten note, bottom: "Even after already being pushed away, they still say they have enough just to keep what they still have"]

My Father has a piece on which he lives (Council Bluffs) and we wish him to enjoy it. We have enough without it; but we wish him to live near us to give us good counsel; to keep our ears and eyes open, that we may continue to pursue the right road; the road to happiness. He settles all differences between us and the whites, and between the red skins themselves — He makes the whites do justice to the red skins, and he makes the red skins do justice to the whites. He saves the effusion of human blood, and restores peace and happiness in the land. You have already sent us a father; it is enough, he knows us, and we know him. We have confidence in him. We keep our eye constantly upon him, and since we have heard *your* words, we will listen more attentively to *his.*

It is too soon, my Great Father, to send those good men among us. We are not starving yet. We wish you to permit us to enjoy the chase, until the game of our country is exhausted; until the wild animals become extinct. Let us exhaust our present resources, before you make us toil, and interrupt our happiness. Let me continue to live as I have done, and after I have passed to the Good or Evil Spirit from the wilderness of my present life, the subsistence of *my children* may become so precarious, as to need and embrace the offered assistance of those good people.

There was a time when we did not know the whites. Our wants were then fewer than they are now. They were always within our control. We had then seen nothing which we could not get. But since our intercourse with the *whites,* who have caused such a destruction of our game, our situation is changed. We could lie down to sleep, and when we awoke, we found the buffaloe feeding around our camp; but now we are killing them for their skins, and feeding the wolves with their flesh, to make our children cry over their bones.

Here my Great Father, is a pipe which I present you, as I am accustomed to present pipes to all red skins in peace with us. It is filled with such tobacco as we were accustomed to smoke, before we knew the white people. I know that the robes, leggins, moccasins, bear's claws, &c. are of little value to you, but we wish you to have them deposited and preserved in some conspicuous part of your lodge, so that when we are gone, and the sod turned over our bones, if our children should visit this place, as we do now, they may see and recognize with pleasure the deposites of their fathers, and reflect on the times that are past.

Fifty years after Sharitarish made his plea for time, the Pawnees were still endeavoring to go on buffalo hunts because "we are afraid when we have no meat to offer the Great Spirit he will be angry and punish us." By the 1870s the herds were depleted, the Pawnees were living on a reservation, and they had to ask permission of their Indian agent before they went hunting; he, not their religious leaders, decided the time and duration of the hunt, as well as who should go. The great, communal, semiannual hunts of the past were replaced by smaller hunting parties seeking out diminished herds at the sufferance of the government. On one occasion when permission was denied, some men went out hunting anyway "but returned without meat or robes."[3] With their old way of life disappearing before their eyes, the Pawnees had to be more receptive to the missionaries and the way of life they offered.[4]

NOTES

[1] Gene Weltfish, *The Lost Universe: The Way of Life of the Pawnee* (New York: Ballantine Books, 1971), 97–98, 200, 207, 243; Douglas R. Parks, ed., *Ceremonies of the Pawnee* by James R. Murie (Lincoln: University of Nebraska Press, 1989), 39–42; Douglas R. Parks and Waldo R. Wedel, "Pawnee Geography: Historical and Sacred," *Great Plains Quarterly* 5 (1985), 143–76; Richard White, "The Cultural Landscape of the Pawnees," *Great Plains Quarterly* 2 (1982), 31–40; and *The Roots of Dependency: Subsistence, Environment and Social Change among the Choctaw, Pawnee and Navajo* (Lincoln: University of Nebraska Press, 1983), 171–73.

[2] Major Benjamin O'Fallon, the U.S. Indian agent for the Upper Missouri, headquartered at Council Bluffs. He accompanied the Pawnee delegation on their tour of the eastern United States.

[3] Martha Royce Blaine, *Pawnee Passage: 1870–1875* (Norman: University of Oklahoma Press, 1990), 66, 84–86, 94; *Sixth Annual Report of the Board of Indian Commissioners for the Year 1874* (Washington, D.C.: U.S. Govt. Printing Office, 1875), 102; *Ninth Annual Report of the Board of Indian Commissioners for 1877* (Washington, D.C.: U.S. Govt. Printing Office, 1878), 56.

[4] On the Quaker missionaries' "record of failure and frustration" among the Pawnees and their neighbors, see Clyde A. Milner, II, *With Good Intentions: Quaker Work among the Pawnees, Otos, and Omahas in the 1870s* (Lincoln: University of Nebraska Press, 1982).

4

The Life and Death
of Four Bears

By any standard, Mato Topé, second chief of the Mandans, was a remarkable man. Known to the whites as Four Bears, he was the most prominent Indian of his day on the upper Missouri River. He was without peer as a warrior, but he was also a husband, father, artist, and ceremonial leader. The American artist George Catlin described him as an "extraordinary man," handsome, generous, and brave, "the most popular man in the nation."[1] The life of Four Bears, as recorded by himself and by visiting artists, and his death, as recorded by fur trader Francis Chardon, illustrate the warrior culture of the Plains Indians and the sudden collapse of an entire society amid the horrors of a smallpox epidemic.

The Mandan Indians inhabited earthen lodge villages on the banks of the Missouri River in what is now North Dakota. For hundreds of years before whites (and even before many other Indian peoples) arrived on the northern plains they grew corn (maize), beans, squash, and tobacco, hunted buffalo, and developed a rich ceremonial life. The villages of the Mandans and their Hidatsa and Arikara neighbors developed into a thriving trade center, a natural market for the exchange of agricultural surpluses produced by the village women and of horses, buffalo meat, and hides brought in from the plains by equestrian hunters. Lewis and Clark spent their first winter at this major rendezvous, gathering information about the tribes they could expect to meet when they headed west in the spring. The Mandans' strategic position at the hub of a far-reaching trade network, which transmitted disease as easily as merchandise, had already cost them dearly, however: In precontact times they may have occupied as many as nine villages; when French explorers met them in the 1730s they were living in half a dozen villages; by the time Lewis and Clark arrived they were down to two.[2]

For Mandan males, as for others in the world of escalating conflict on the northern plains in the early nineteenth century, war was the path to status, and a warrior was expected to display his war record publicly and

61

truthfully. Warriors recounted their coups before the people, depicted their achievements on buffalo hides, and displayed their prowess in the body paint, feathers, and accoutrements of war that they wore. George Catlin visited the Mandans in the summer of 1832; the Swiss artist Karl Bodmer, accompanying the expedition of the German scientist Prince Maximilian of Wied, arrived in the winter of 1833–34. Both artists painted two portraits of Four Bears. He impressed them as had no other Indian they met. Catlin devoted a whole chapter of his book, *Letters and Notes on the Manners, Customs, and Conditions of North American Indians,* to Four Bears and his exploits. Four Bears visited the artists and watched them at work frequently and incorporated some of their techniques into his own art.[3]

Four Bears was a man of many talents and accomplishments, but in the Plains Indian culture of the 1830s what mattered most were his military exploits. His war record was his résumé, and he displayed it regularly. On one occasion, wrote Prince Maximilian, Four Bears returned from the other Mandan village "and told us, with great satisfaction and self-complacency, that he had enumerated all his exploits and that no one had been able to surpass him."[4]

Both Catlin and Bodmer did full-length portraits of Four Bears, regaled in a buffalo robe, on which were depicted his war deeds, and a full war bonnet of eagle feathers and buffalo horns. The portrait by Karl Bodmer of Four Bears painted for war, however, also presents a record of the warrior's achievements (Figure 7). Prince Maximilian left a written description to accompany Bodmer's portrait.

Figure 7 (*opposite*).   Four Bears, as Painted by Karl Bodmer in 1834 "Very celebrated and eminent warriors, when most highly decorated, wear in their hair various pieces of wood, as signals of their wounds and heroic deeds. Thus Mato-Topé had fastened transversely in his hair a wooden knife, painted red, and about the length of a hand, because he had killed a Chayenne chief with his knife; then six wooden sticks, painted red, blue, and yellow, with a brass nail at one end, indicating so many musket wounds which he had received. For an arrow wound he fastened in his hair the wing feather of a wild turkey; at the back of his head he wore a large bunch of owl's feathers, dyed yellow, with red tips, as the badge of the Meniss-Ochata (the dog band). The half of his face was painted red, and the other yellow; his body was painted reddish-brown, with narrow stripes, which were produced by taking off the colour with the tip of the finger wetted. On his arms, from the shoulder downwards, he had seventeen yellow stripes, which indicated his warlike deeds, and on his breast the figure of a hand, of a yellow colour, as a sign that he had captured some prisoners." — Prince Maximilian of Wied[5]

FOUR BEARS'S BUFFALO ROBE

Four Bears's buffalo robe attracted the attention of both George Catlin and Karl Bodmer. The Mandans had a long tradition of recording military events on robes; a Mandan buffalo robe painted with scenes of intertribal warfare and collected by Lewis and Clark in 1805 is the earliest documented example of Plains biographical art.[6] Four Bears seems to have carried the tradition to new levels. According to Catlin, he wore "a robe on his back, with the history of all his battles on it, which would fill a book of themselves if they were properly enlarged and translated."[7] Catlin recorded the stories behind these drawings, related by Four Bears as the Indian sat on the robe pointing to the battle scenes and deciphering them one by one. Joseph Kipp, a trader whose wife was a Mandan, translated. Catlin vouched for the truth of Four Bears's achievements: In a country where the warriors were so

> jealous of rank and of standing; and in a community so small also, that every man's deeds of honour and chivalry are familiarly known to all; it would not be reputable, or even safe to life, for a warrior to wear upon his back the representations of battles he never had fought; professing to have done what every child in the village would know he never had done.[8]

Catlin devoted ten pages and four illustrations in his *Letters and Notes* to Four Bears's interpretation of the scenes on the robe (see robe in Figure 8). Beginning at the right-hand side and moving clockwise, the robe depicts

1. Four Bears charging a war party of Assiniboines represented by a mass of heads shown entrenched in a defensive position. Four Bears has black body paint, striped legs, and an eagle feather and wears the sash of his military society over his shoulder.
2. Four Bears, wearing a trailing eagle-feather headdress, wounded and bleeding, stands over the body of a Cheyenne in a frock coat whom he has killed. The tracks leading from the Cheyenne's head indicate the thirty Cheyennes who fought in the battle.
3. Four Bears's most famous deed: killing a Cheyenne chief in hand-to-hand combat. (See the following selection for a more detailed description of this event.)
4. Four Bears, with two eagle feathers in his hair, strikes a Cheyenne with his lance.

Figure 8. Buffalo Robe
Painted by Four Bears.

5. A Cheyenne chief with a long eagle-feather headdress lies on the ground next to his horse and a shield trimmed with eagle feathers. The Cheyenne's wife, who attempted to help her husband in the fight, was also killed.
6. Wearing a headdress and leading a war pony that carries his shield, Four Bears goes alone to an Ojibwa village to avenge the killing of a Mandan. After remaining in hiding for six days, he kills two Ojibwa women, shown on the ground in black dresses.
7. In a huge battle from which the Mandans and Hidatsas retreated before a large Assiniboine war party, Four Bears, holding his lance and shield, is the only man to hold his ground. The tracks before and behind him indicate the attack of the enemy and the retreat of his own people; other marks indicate the bullets flying around him.
8. Four Bears charges the Assiniboines and earns his name: The Assiniboines said he charged them "like four bears" (mato topé).[9]

FOUR BEARS KILLS A CHEYENNE CHIEF

The hand-to-hand combat in which Four Bears killed a Cheyenne chief ranked as his greatest exploit (Figure 9). He gave both George Catlin and Karl Bodmer a blow-by-blow account of the encounter. When Bodmer gave Four Bears a gift of paper, pencils, and watercolors, the Mandan used the new materials and the new techniques he had picked up to execute a colored drawing of the deed. He used fine pencil lines to indicate details like the fringes on his leggings, and he employed the brush and watercolors to display his own body paint and the Cheyenne's leggings in different textures.[10] Prince Maximilian transcribed a record of the fight, as related to him by Four Bears on several occasions.[11]

THE DEATH SPEECH OF FOUR BEARS

When George Catlin and Karl Bodmer met him, Four Bears was at the height of his powers. In his actions and character he exemplified the virtues esteemed in the warrior culture of his time and place: laden with honors, fearless in battle, merciless to his enemies, generous to his people.

Then, in the summer of 1837, Four Bears's world fell to pieces.

Figure 9. Four Bears's Drawing Depicting His Killing of a Cheyenne Chief

"He was, on that occasion, on foot, on a military expedition, with a few Mandans, when they encountered four Chayennes, their most virulent foes, on horseback. The chief of the latter, seeing that their enemies were on foot, and that the combat would thereby be unequal, dismounted, and the two parties attacked each other. The two chiefs fired, missed, threw away their guns, and seized their naked weapons; the Chayenne, a tall, powerful man, drew his knife, while Mato-Topé, who was lighter and more agile, took his battle-axe. The former attempted to stab Mato-Topé, who laid hold of the blade of the knife, by which he, indeed, wounded his hand, but wrested the weapon from his enemy, and stabbed him with it, on which the Chayennes took to flight. Mato-Topé's drawing of the scene in the above-named plate, shows the guns which they had discharged and thrown aside, the blood flowing from the wounded hand of the Mandan chief, the footsteps of the two warriors, and the wolf's tail at their heels — the Chayenne being distinguished by the fillet of otter skin on his forehead." — Prince Maximilian of Wied[12]

Following the smallpox epidemic on the central plains in 1831, the U.S. government began a vaccination program among the Indian tribes of the Missouri River. Some three thousand people were vaccinated on the lower Missouri, but the program did not reach the Mandans, Arikaras, and Hidatsas upriver.[13] On the afternoon of June 19, 1837, an American Fur Company steamboat stopped at the Mandan villages. Some of the passengers had smallpox. Within a month, the first smallpox cases broke out among the Mandans. Confined to their densely populated earthen lodge villages by Sioux enemies out on the plains, the Mandans had no chance. By midsummer, their villages were a nightmare of rotting corpses, mourning relatives, and suicides. People were dying at such a rate that observers were unable to keep a record. Many Indians threatened the whites with death for bringing them the disease. Four Bears caught the disease and "watched every one of his family die about him, his wives and his little children."[14] He "got crazy," disappeared from the village for a time, and starved himself. But on July 30 he made a speech to his people that was recorded by the American trader at Fort Clark, Francis Chardon.

FOUR BEARS

Speech to the Arikaras and Mandans
July 30, 1837

My Friends one and all, Listen to what I have to say — Ever since I can remember, I have loved the Whites, I have lived With them ever since I was a Boy, and to the best of my Knowledge, I have never Wronged a White Man, on the Contrary, I have always Protected them from the insults of Others, Which they cannot deny. The 4 Bears never saw a White Man hungry, but what he gave him to eat, Drink, and a Buffaloe skin to sleep on, in time of Need. I was always ready to die for them, Which they cannot deny. I have done every thing that a red Skin could do for them, and how have they repaid it! With ingratitude! I have Never Called a White

Annie Heloise Abel, ed., *Chardon's Journal at Fort Clark, 1834–1839* (Pierre: State of South Dakota, Dept. of History, 1932; reprinted Freeport, N.Y.: Books for Libraries Press, 1970), 124–25.

Man a Dog, but to day, I do Pronounce them to be a set of Black harted Dogs, they have deceived Me, them that I always considered as Brothers, has turned Out to be My Worst enemies. I have been in Many Battles, and often Wounded, but the Wounds of My enemies I exhalt in, but to day I am Wounded, and by Whom, by those same White Dogs that I have always Considered, and treated as Brothers. I do not fear *Death* my friends. You Know it, but to *die* with my face rotten, that even the Wolves will shrink with horror at seeing Me, and say to themselves, that is the 4 Bears the Friend of the Whites —

Listen well what I have to say, as it will be the last time you will hear Me. think of your Wives, Children, Brothers, Sisters, Friends, and in fact all that you hold dear, are all Dead, or Dying, with their faces all rotten, caused by those dogs the whites, think of all that My friends, and rise all together and Not leave one of them alive. The 4 Bears will act his Part. . . .

Four Bears died the same day. The Mandans, who had numbered between 1,600 and 2,000 in June 1837 were reduced to about 138 by October of the same year. In one of the villages, only fourteen people survived of a population of six hundred. The epidemic cut Arikara and Hidatsa populations in half, killed thousands of Assiniboines, Blackfeet, Sioux, and Crows, and spread as far as Texas and California.[15] Remembering in her old age the horror of the smallpox epidemic she witnessed as a young girl, Buffalo Bird Woman, a Hidatsa, said: "We had corn aplenty and buffalo meat in the Five [Hidatsa] Villages, and there were old people and little children in every lodge. Then smallpox came. More than half of my tribe died in the smallpox winter [1837]. Of the Mandans only a few families were left alive. All the old people and little children died."[16] A handful of Mandan survivors joined other tribes, most of them moving eventually to the Fort Berthold reservation in North Dakota.

NOTES

[1] George Catlin, *Letters and Notes on the Manners, Customs, and Conditions of North American Indians.* 2 vols. (London: Author, 1844), 1:145.
[2] W. Raymond Wood and Thomas D. Thiessen, eds., *Early Fur Trade on the Northern Plains: Canadian Traders among the Mandan and Hidatsa Indians, 1738–1818* (Norman:

University of Oklahoma Press, 1985); James P. Ronda, *Lewis and Clark among the Indians* (Lincoln: University of Nebraska Press, 1984); Reuben G. Thwaites, ed., *Original Journals of the Lewis and Clark Expedition, 1804–1806.* 7 vols. (New York: Dodd, Mead, 1904–05), esp. 6:80–120.

3 John C. Ewers, "Early White Influence upon Plains Indian Painting," in his *Indian Life on the Upper Missouri* (Norman: University of Oklahoma Press, 1968), 98–116.

4 "Prince Maximilian of Wied's Travels in the Interior of North America, 1832–1834," in Reuben G. Thwaites, ed., *Early Western Travels, 1748–1846*, vols. 22–25 (Cleveland: The Arthur H. Clark Co., 1906), 24:58.

5 Ibid., 23:261.

6 The robe is in the Peabody Museum of Archaeology and Ethnology at Harvard University. Evan M. Maurer, et al., *Visions of the People: A Pictorial History of Plains Indian Life* (Minneapolis Institute of Arts, 1992), 188.

7 Catlin, *Letters and Notes,* 1:145.

8 Ibid., 148–54.

9 Maurer, et al., *Visions of the People,* 190–91; cf. Catlin, *Letters and Notes,* 1:148–54.

10 Maurer, et al., *Visions of the People,* 192.

11 George Catlin left a more dramatized and romanticized account of the fight. Catlin, *Letters and Notes,* 1:151–53.

12 "Prince Maximilian's Travels in the Interior of North America," 24:80.

13 Michael K. Trimble, "The 1832 Inoculation Program on the Missouri River," in John W. Verano and Douglas H. Ubelaker, eds., *Disease and Demography in the Americas* (Washington, D.C.: Smithsonian Institution, 1992), 257–65.

14 Catlin, *Letters and Notes,* 2:257–58.

15 Russell Thornton, *American Indian Holocaust and Survival: A Population History since 1492* (Norman: University of Oklahoma Press, 1987), 95–99.

16 *Waheenee: An Indian Girl's Story.* Told by Herself to Gilbert L. Wilson (St. Paul: Webb Publishing Co., 1921; reprinted in *North Dakota History* 38 (Winter-Spring 1971), 9.

5

Counting Coups and Fighting for Survival

Warfare had existed on the Great Plains since prehistoric times,[1] but by 1800 the area had become a vast theater of intertribal conflict. Warriors fought for prestige or revenge and waged ritualized battles in which counting coup carried more honor than inflicting casualties. White observers, especially Army officers accustomed to winning victories by inflicting massive losses, often were bewildered and bemused by Plains Indian warfare, dismissing it as petty skirmishing.

In reality, the *way* Indian warriors fought sometimes obscured the underlying *causes* of war and the severity of the conflicts. As new peoples and new pressures accumulated on the plains, Indians continued to fight for glory and revenge, but they also fought for trade, for hunting territories, and even for survival in a volatile world.[2] The dwindling buffalo herds edged tribes into ever-increasing competition, and "whenever they meet," wrote the Jesuit missionary Pierre-Jean De Smet in 1846, "it is war to the death."[3] Plains Indians launched military expeditions against rival tribes and maintained their societies on a war footing. The documents in this chapter illustrate both aspects of the intertribal warfare waged on the northern plains in the nineteenth century: warriors sought visions and counted coups, but their conflicts were life-and-death struggles, not just dangerous games.

For Plains Indians, war was a sacred activity demanding ritual preparation and supernatural help. Success in war depended as much on spiritual power — war medicine — as on individual courage and prowess. Young men fasted and prayed in the hope of experiencing a vision in which a sacred helper or spiritual guardian appeared to them. Warriors sustained and directed the power that visions conveyed to them through songs and medicine bundles of sacred objects: "Our bundles, the songs belonging to them, and the ceremony for using them were all taught to us in our dreams," explained the Crow warrior Two Leggings. "Together they made our medicine. A man who ordered his life with this help was a good and happy man and lived for a long time." Warriors maintained a respectful relationship with their sacred helpers through prayer and ritual, invoked spiritual protection before going into battle, and listened to their dreams for forecasts of victory or defeat. An impressive war record testified to the strength of an individual's war medicine, and Indians who seemed to court death were demonstrating the power of their spiritual protection; conversely, failure in war stemmed from inadequate spiritual help or improper observance. The warrior cult glorified death in battle, but living to old age proved that one's sacred helper was powerful. "Many men die young on the battlefield," said Two Leggings. "This shows that their sacred helper was not very powerful and lost the game early in the life of his adopted child. Or perhaps the adopted man did not obey his sacred father."[4] As warfare escalated on the Great Plains, and firearms changed the face of battle, Indian warriors did not abandon traditional beliefs and rituals; if anything, they reaffirmed and intensified them because the need for spiritual protection was greater than ever.

Historians have often portrayed intertribal warfare as a conflict between "hereditary" enemies, "as if each group were doled out an allotted number of adversaries at creation with whom they battled mindlessly through eternity."[5] Some tribes developed alliances and identified consistent enemies — for example, the tribes of the Blackfoot Confederacy fought against Crows and Shoshonis, and the Sioux, Cheyennes, and Arapahos combatted Pawnees and Crows — but the situation on the Great Plains was volatile, not static: New pressures and new peoples upset balances of power and produced a world of increasing competition for diminishing resources. As the Sioux moved west onto the Plains, they pushed weaker peoples aside. Struggling to survive against powerful enemies, tribes like the Crows of Montana continued to invoke traditional spiritual assistance but added new terrestrial allies as they enlisted in campaigns with the United States Army.[6]

ACCOUNT OF THREE COYOTES'S EXPEDITION

Like other plains societies, the Hidatsas of North Dakota regarded success in war as the path to status and recognized that such success could not be achieved without spiritual assistance, powerful dreams, and careful preparation. Young men were raised to be warriors. A Hidatsa named Wolf Chief recalled late in life how ancient customs surrounded every aspect of a warrior's life. Training young men for war, he said, was "like driving a wagon along a deeply rutted road. There was no way to get anywhere but by going forward in the same path as others had done before. . . ."[7]

The following account of a conflict between Hidatsas and Sioux illustrates Plains Indian warfare as a contest of war medicines, with certain mutually understood rules governing the counting of coups. Each side believes its war medicine to be strong, and the warriors test their power in the fight. Warriors ritually prepare for battle, take note of omens, and observe key rites even in the midst of battle. Leaders instruct the younger men to make trilling noises whenever an enemy is killed to prove their bravery; Hidatsa warriors sing their war songs so that the enemy's women can hear them, and the Sioux women respond with their own victory songs. The Sioux are unwilling to engage in hand-to-hand combat with enemies who, though inferior in number, appear to have stronger war medicine. The Hidatsas escape, but they have lost two warriors and are unable to count coup on the bodies of their enemies: A successful war party was one that returned with war honors and without casualties.

Born in the mid-nineteenth century, Four Dancers was a member of the Speckled Eagle clan. In the early 1930s he related to ethnologist Alfred Bowers the story of a war party led by the warrior Three Coyotes in which his grandfather, Guts, participated. Guts was notoriously unlucky in war, but he was nonetheless credited with having access to considerable spiritual power because he was keeper of the sacred Earthnaming bundle of his people. Bowers spoke Hidatsa, worked without an interpreter, and recorded everything that Four Dancers said in the Hidatsa text.

FOUR DANCERS

Three Coyotes Leads a Skirmish

When Three Coyotes went out, there were thirty-two men in his party. They did not want Guts along but he went anyway. He was tall and strong; he liked to go on these trips. They traveled to the southwest until they had passed the Black Hills. All the time the scouts were out ahead looking around but the enemy saw them before the scouts did. There was a large camp and soon the enemy drove them into a washout. The enemy came

Alfred W. Bowers, "Hidatsa Social and Ceremonial Organization," *Bureau of American Ethnology, Bulletin* 194 (Washington, D.C.: U.S. Govt. Printing Office, 1965), 238–40.

in great numbers on horseback so that the Hidatsa were unable to run away. When the enemy attacked, one Hidatsa took a red shirt out of a bundle and Guts said to him, "You should not put it on or they will see you. I will put it on. I always seem to bring bad luck. If they kill me they will think that I am a great chief. Then they may stop fighting and let the rest of you go away."

The Sioux did not start the fight right away. First they surrounded the Hidatsa so they could not get away and then the women and children came along bringing their tipis and setting them up nearby where they could watch the fight. They must have sent messages out for soon another large group came up and began setting up their tipis too. While this was going on, the Hidatsa painted up and put on their sacred objects. The Sioux did likewise. The young Sioux boys rode back and forth practicing with their horses, riding so that their bodies did not show, stopping their horses quickly and pretending that they were fighting the enemy. This they did to frighten the Hidatsa boys so that they would not be brave. The Hidatsa all thought that they would surely not be able to save their lives.

When the Sioux were all properly painted to show their honors and medicines, the battle began. Three Coyotes picked out his two best men to be at the corners. One was Black Shield; he was a good shot. His medicine was the gun and whenever he fired it, he was sure to get something. The arrows flew toward the washout in great curves like grasshoppers dropping into the grass.

Before the battle, Black Shield wet some gunpowder and painted his face; he put white cloth on his head and white paint on his lips and eyes just as he had seen these things in his dream. He had a young man beside him who loaded the gun each time. They agreed to make a great noise each time an enemy was killed so that the enemy would be afraid to come into the fort. Each time Black Shield shot, an enemy was killed; then they came closer to get their dead for fear the Hidatsa would go out and scalp them. After a while, one of the Hidatsa would go out of the fort, shoot an enemy, and run back. Just as he went out, a Prairie Dog Owl flew above him and the others knew that he was not shot because this bird was his god.

When the dead were taken back to camp, the Hidatsa could hear the relatives crying. All the while the older Hidatsa would repeat to the young men who had not been out before, "They will cut your scalps off, but be brave and do not cry."

While the Sioux were taking back their dead, the Hidatsa painted themselves anew for they knew that the enemy were not done fighting.

They could not leave the fort or the Sioux would run them down. During the lull in the fighting, Guts said to a friend, "Let's go up on top of the hill and sing our war songs. I think there are some Sioux women who can hear us from there."

So they went up on the hill and sang their war songs and when they had finished, the Sioux howled in recognition of their bravery. Then the Sioux sang their war songs for the Hidatsa who were showing such bravery.

Then the two Sioux bands went together. They knew then that their enemy was brave so the Sioux selected a man who impersonated a bear, and could not be shot through, to lead for he was so brave. He was their greatest medicine man. The Bear man was ahead and Black Shield would shoot at him but he would not fall down. Then Black Shield knew that the Bear man really had great supernatural powers. When Black Shield had dreamed of the gun, his gods had told him if his life was ever in extreme danger he should hold the gun to the north, pour powder from his left ear, shot from the right ear, and put the powder and shot in the gun while he sang the song that should be used only in extremely critical situations.

So Black Shield did. He shot at the Bear medicine man who fell down. Black Shield shouted so the enemy could hear, "You were foolish; you didn't have any power. You should have known that mine was greater."

When the Bear man fell, the Sioux stopped fighting and took his body away, for they did not want to give the Hidatsa the honor of scalping their holiest man. Then the Sioux set the prairie on fire so that the smoke would cover their advance. Some of the enemy went onto the hill where Guts had sung the war songs. They hit the sickly young man who had been filling Black Shield's gun and one other but the Sioux would not attack the fort. Again the fighting stopped. The Sioux dragged their dead away so that they could not be scalped and as word got around in their camp, the women set up a loud howl as they cried for their dead relatives.

The Hidatsa were tired and thought that they would surely lose their lives the next time. There was brush about a mile away. Some thought they could run for it, but others thought that it was too far. Three Coyotes and his coleaders decided to run for the brush, fighting their way through the Sioux lines. He selected Guts, who was a great medicine man, and Black Shield, who was a good shot, to take the two ends while the others sneaked out, following a narrow coulee part of the way. The two went onto the hill to attract the Sioux's attention and when the others were on the flat, they ran too. When all were near the brush, the Sioux rode in front of them but they were not prepared for the attack and were easily driven out of the way. When they got into the brush, the Sioux returned to their camp and did not try to follow them further.

The two on the corners were the ones who saved them, one a great medicine man, the other a good shot. The sickly one had been killed at the fort and one other was lost running towards the brush.

Because they lost two, even though killing many of the enemy that they could not strike, the party came back in mourning. But the Sioux kept Three Coyotes from dancing the victory dances for they kept their dead out of reach of the Hidatsa. It was too bad that he could not possess any of them for the Sioux camp was in mourning when they left from losing so many young men. If Three Coyotes had taken even one scalp, the relatives of the two dead men would have called for the victory dances after a period of mourning.

FIGHTING FOR CROW COUNTRY

[handwritten: Some groups started out together]

The Crow Indians were relatives of the Hidatsas. According to tradition, they separated from them and migrated west following a hunting dispute. The split probably took several generations, but by the early eighteenth century the Crows had emerged as a people with their own identity.[8] The Crows moved into Big Horn and upper Yellowstone country in present-day Montana, edging out Shoshonis, Comanches, and other peoples, and made it their home. Crow country was a hunters' paradise, and the Crows had to fight to keep it. Crow traditions assert that when First Worker created the world he gave the Crows strong hearts, placed them on the best lands, and told them they would always have to fight to hold their country. "Look at our country, and look at our enemies," Crows told their agent in 1870; "they are all around it; the Sioux, Blackfeet, Cheyennes, Arapahoes, and Flatheads, all want our country, and kill us when they can."[9] The following speech by the Crow chief Arapooish, or Rotten Belly, recorded by Captain Bonneville of the United States Army in the early 1830s, indicates why Crow country was so loved by the Crows and so coveted by their neighbors.

ARAPOOISH

Speech on Crow Country

The Crow country . . . is a good country. The Great Spirit has put it exactly in the right place; while you are in it you fare well; whenever you go out of it, whichever way you travel, you fare worse.

If you go to the south, you have to wander over great barren plains; the water is warm and bad, and you meet the fever and ague.

To the north it is cold; the winters are long and bitter, with no grass; you cannot keep horses there, but must travel with dogs. What is a country without horses?

On the Columbia they are poor and dirty, paddle about in canoes, and eat fish. Their teeth are worn out; they are always taking fish-bones out of their mouths. Fish is poor food.

To the east, they dwell in villages; they live well; but they drink the muddy water of the Missouri — that is bad. A Crow's dog would not drink such water.

About the forks of the Missouri is a fine country; good water; good grass; plenty of buffalo. In summer, it is almost as good as the Crow country; but in winter it is cold; the grass is gone; and there is no salt weed for the horses.

The Crow country is exactly in the right place. It has snowy mountains and sunny plains; all kinds of climates and good things for every season. When the summer heats scorch the prairies, you can draw up under the mountains, where the air is sweet and cool, the grass fresh, and the bright streams come tumbling out of the snow-banks. There you can hunt the elk, the deer, and the antelope, when their skins are fit for dressing; there you will find plenty of white bears and mountain sheep.

In the autumn, when your horses are fat and strong from the mountain pastures, you can go down into the plains and hunt the buffalo, or trap beaver on the streams. And when winter comes on, you can take shelter in the woody bottoms along the rivers; there you will find buffalo meat for yourselves, and cotton-wood bark for your horses: or you may winter in the Wind River valley, where there is salt weed in abundance.

The Crow country is exactly in the right place. Everything good is to be found there. There is no country like the Crow country.

Washington Irving, *The Adventures of Captain Bonneville, U.S.A.* (1837; reprint, Norman: University of Oklahoma Press, 1961), 165.

TWO LEGGINGS'S QUEST FOR POWER

For almost a hundred years the Crows lived in a state of virtual siege as they waged guerilla warfare against their many enemies. War became literally a matter of life and death not only for individual warriors but for the people as a whole. Anthropologist Robert H. Lowie, who did extensive fieldwork among the Crows, concluded that war was "not the concern of a class nor even of the male sex, but of the whole population, from cradle to grave."[10]

The autobiography of the Crow warrior Two Leggings, as recorded by William Wildschut in the summer of 1919 and edited by Peter Nabokov almost half a century later, shows a man all of whose aspirations and endeavors are shaped by the warrior culture of his times. In his old age, Two Leggings related more than twenty years' worth of war parties, which, to him, constituted what was important in a life. His assessment of his own life also shows that he sees himself as someone who has not fully achieved his goals and, as a result, has had to settle for second best. Two Leggings seems never to have risen above the rank of pipe holder, "roughly the equivalent of a platoon lieutenant."[11] The central theme of Two Leggings's life is the quest for the religious power that will enable him to win a name for himself on the warpath. Unfortunately, it always eludes him. His earlier raids were not particularly successful and he was, in fact, tempting fate by going out without medicine or power received through a vision. Unable to achieve a powerful vision, he resorted to the second-rate alternative of purchasing medicine property from someone else, but even that never brought him the success he craved. For Two Leggings, war was life. Even though he lived for another forty years, he ended his autobiography at the point when the Crows were confined to their reservation: "Nothing happened after that. We just lived. There were no more war parties, no capturing of horses from the Piegans and the Sioux, no buffalo to hunt. There is nothing more to tell."[12]

The following selection illustrates the impetuosity of a Crow warrior anxious for the chance to win fame; it also shows that not all dreams carried equal power and that those which came true could have a hidden cost. Two Leggings had a dream in which four enemies fell dead and he acquired a beautiful buckskin horse. He built a sweat lodge, gave thanks for his dream, and prayed for success as he prepared to go on a raid. Two Belly and other older Crows advised against it: The camp would be left unprotected, and Crooked Arm had dreamed that if Two Leggings left someone would be killed. Two Leggings promised to reconsider, but he had no intention of giving up his raid. When the village awoke to find that Sioux raiders had stolen horses during the night, Two Leggings seized the opportunity to pursue.

TWO LEGGINGS
The Dream and Reality of a Raid

Outside I joined Young Mountain and we ran for the horses. Camp was wide awake with most men jumping on the first horse they found. The women and children were crying over their stolen horses; the men were singing war songs.

Riding up to my tipi I dashed inside for my gun and medicine and ran out. When I jumped on my horse to catch up with the others, Young Mountain was close behind. Everyone seemed to be spreading out. I noticed someone near the river bank calling to us. It was Black Head, who had discovered where the Sioux had crossed.

He told me to lead since I had been planning a raid and had said my dream was good. But he said that the earth does not move and by traveling steadily we could overtake them. He wanted to be sure our horses would not lose their strength.

After fording the river and picking up their tracks on the other side I made them stop so I could make medicine. Kneeling on the Sioux tracks which headed north over a group of ridges toward the Bull Mountains, I drew a straight line across their trail with my finger. Then I formed a dirt bank along the line's far side and made a smudge of white pine needles. Sitting on the trail I faced where the Sioux had gone and smoked my pipe. I pointed the stem and told the Sioux to smoke this and wait until I caught up with them. Now their trail would be rough and they would grow sleepy.

After I stood up I unwrapped my medicine and prayed to the Great Above Person through whom I had received it, saying that I had acted as he had said and asking him to have pity on the women and children crying over their horses.

As I finished a stolen horse walked out of the brush toward us. Here I said was the sign of my medicine's power. We were eight but Black Head

Peter Nabokov, *Two Leggings: The Making of a Crow Warrior* (New York: Thomas Crowell, 1967), 122–26.

asked me to wait for others. Whenever we were about to leave, men would call to us from the opposite bank.

About the middle of the day we finally left. It grew very hot and I prayed this would make the Sioux sleepy. Their trail led east and north, directly toward the spot where I had seen the four bodies. Now I knew that everything would come true.

Late that afternoon we came to where they had killed a buffalo and made a fire. I would never have stopped for a meal the first day out; already they were growing careless.

Young Mountain, Hawk High Up, and I rode ahead to a nearby hill. If we saw anything we were to ride our horses back and forth. But when we searched through my telescope there was no sign of Sioux, and we signaled for the others to join us. After doing the same thing on the next ridge my men killed a deer and cooked some meat. We rode to a third hill, picketed our horses near the top, and crawled to the cover of some tall bushes. A big basin lay before us and at the far end I could see the Bull Mountains covered with pine trees. By the time the rest had caught up the shadows were long. But we had ridden slowly during the day and our horses were still fresh. I told my friends we would travel the shortest route to the pine-covered ridge in my dream, close to the Musselshell River.

The moon shone brightly enough for us to ride apart from the Sioux tracks. I did not want to come upon them in the night. Soon after the first streaks of dawn showed in the east we reached the ridge. Black Head had noticed a big buffalo herd to the east. The Sioux had not yet passed.

After picketing our horses we took off our saddles and rested. Young Mountain, One Blue Bead, Paints His Body Red, and I kept a careful lookout from behind the trees on top.

Noticing movement on the hills several rifle-shot distances to the south, I picked up my telescope. Horses broke out of some timber with men riding behind, all heading for us. I counted five Sioux and recognized our horses.

I left One Blue Bead and ran down to the others. We painted our faces and unwrapped our medicines, tying them where we had been told in our dreams. Bobtail Wolf painted seven red spots on his face running from one side of his jawbone over his forehead to the other and representing the dipper. He tied his foretop with a piece of otter skin, fastened some feathers to the back of his head, and sang a medicine song: "My son is coming."

Boils His Leggings sang a medicine song for Young Mountain, painted a red bar over his mouth, and fastened a red-painted eagle feather in his hair. Making him face the Sioux, he pointed to the sun and said that he wanted Young Mountain to do some brave thing so the people would know him. He called him his son and told him to look into the sky. Bobtail Wolf sang a medicine song for his brother Goes First. Then he fastened an otter-skin strip to his brother's forehead and gave him a shield painted with the thunderbird. He sang another medicine song, repeating it until Black Head and Few warned him to stop.

Black Head asked me to sing a medicine song for the whole party. Seeing that the Sioux were still far away, I sang one. Bobtail Wolf was singing another medicine song for his brother: "My child, I am coming toward you."

He told his brother that it was strong medicine and would protect him. He sang again: "I am coming toward you today."

Telling my men to stand close together, I rode around them four times, praying for the Great Above Person to help us recover our horses and kill some Sioux. Then I sang my medicine song: "Anywhere I go I will always thank you. Thank long ago. I will be a chief."

Bobtail Wolf was still singing for his brother. When we tried to stop him he said we meant nothing to him. We felt sorry for his brother.

Taking my eagle-tail medicine out of its wrappings, I whistled seven times and looked under the hoop. Four enemies lay on the ground and a number of horses ran toward me. Black Head had watched and asked what would happen. I told him not to be afraid, that I had seen my true dream again.

One Blue Bead ran down to say they were getting close. When he had first looked through my telescope he had recognized a pinto, a roan, a baldface, and a black horse. These were among our fastest horses; it would have been difficult to catch them. A Sioux was leading the pinto as if he meant to ride it and another man was on the black. But just before One Blue Bead had left, this man on the black had changed mounts to chase a small buffalo herd to the north.

I sent Young Mountain up the ridge, telling him to signal when they were within rifle shot. I told my men to shoot straight because One Blue Bead had reported that they all carried good guns and one also had a bow. The younger men were very excited and I had trouble holding them back.

Then Young Mountain made signs and jumped on his horse. Yelling our war cries, we whipped our horses over the ridge. When the Sioux heard us they dropped the stolen horses and raced to a nearby hill, dismounting and shooting from behind rocks.

Some of us rounded up our horses while the rest surrounded the Sioux. When we had driven them a safe distance I left some younger men as guards and rode back. Our men were riding in fast circles around the Sioux, hanging over their horses' sides and shooting from under their necks.

One of their horses broke loose and galloped in front of me. When I caught its reins I saw the beautiful buckskin of my dream. Now I was sure we would kill the four men. We had seen the fifth Sioux return from his hunting and run off when he saw his friends surrounded.

We were not hitting anyone so I told my men to dismount and crawl up. A Sioux called to us, waving his knife over his head. Loud Hawk said that he was calling us women and asking us to come near so he could stab us. I told my men to close in and not let the yelling make them nervous.

Big Lake was lying in front behind a boulder. As he lifted his rifle he fell back. We thought he was dead but his forehead had only been grazed. We dragged him out of the shooting. After a quick council we decided to charge. The first time we were thrown back but then we drove them out of the rocks and into a coulee. The one who had called us women had run first. Big Lake recovered and now crawled to the coulee's edge and shot into it. A Sioux stumbled out with blood pouring from his forehead, threw out his arms, and fell on his back.

As Goes First ran to join Big Lake, singing his medicine song, he was shot through the heart. This was because his brother had sung too many songs over him.

We were all angry and charged the three remaining men. One was killed immediately but we did not know who did it, he was hit so many times. Young Mountain was in front of me running down the coulee with his head bent forward. A bullet struck him in the neck, coming out his spine. Another bullet cut a hole in my shirt but I kept running and shot into the head of the man who had killed Young Mountain. Pulling out my knife, I slashed at his scalp. Then I began crying and shot him again and again. I forgot everything until I heard sounds like animals growling and turned to see Old Tobacco holding the last Sioux's rifle barrel. We could not aim because they were jumping around so much. Old Tobacco gave a wrench and the Sioux slipped on a stone. As he fell he pulled the trigger and the bullet hit Old Tobacco in the forearm, coming out the middle of his upper arm. Before the Sioux could get to his feet two bullets knocked him on his back. He was still trying to stand when Bobtail Wolf ran up and stabbed him twice in the neck. Blood poured out and he fell dead.

We scalped only three because the last man's hair was short and dirty. We let that fifth man get away. After carrying my partner and Goes First to the top of a high bluff we covered their bodies with rocks.

Figure 10. Crow Indians Pursue Sioux in a Running Battle
This war record was drawn by New Bear in 1884.

My dream had come true, but our homecoming was sad. Crooked Arm's dream had also come true. Young Mountain's death was a great sorrow for me. I could not be content with our success and made up my mind to take revenge.

When we returned Two Belly called me to his tipi and reminded me that he had wanted to go to the Arrowhead Mountains. Now I had lost my best friend and another man also. He said that my dream might have been true but that if I had listened to the older men's advice I could have found another opportunity. Their dreams, he said, had more truth than those of young men.

He was right and I kept silent. Immediately we broke camp and moved to Arrow Creek, traveling through Hits With The Arrows towards the Buffalo Heart Mountain. As our camp moved from place to place, following the buffalo, I would often walk into the hills to weep over Young Mountain.

A WOMAN'S VIEW OF WAR

Plains Indian women participated in the warrior cultures of their societies. They raised their sons to be warriors, celebrated their husbands' achievements in war, and took part in victory dances. On occasion, they also fought: At the Battle of the Rosebud in June 1876 a Cheyenne woman called Buffalo Calf Road displayed great courage in rescuing her brother, Comes In Sight; in the same battle, The Other Magpie, a Crow woman, rode to war to exact revenge on the Sioux for killing her brother. As Pretty Shield points out in this passage, however, escalating intertribal warfare also caused wives and mothers their own kind of hell.

PRETTY SHIELD

"Like Talking to Winter-Winds"

Of course the Lacota, Striped-feathered-arrows [Cheyenne], Arapahoes, Pecunnies [Piegans], and other tribes never let us rest, so that there was always war. When our enemies were not bothering *us,* our warriors were bothering *them,* so there was always fighting going on somewhere. We women sometimes tried to keep our men from going to war, but this was like talking to winter-winds; and of course there was always some woman, sometimes many women, mourning for men who had been killed in war. These women had to be taken care of. Somebody had to kill meat for them. Their fathers or uncles or brothers did this until the women married again, which they did not always do, so that war made more work for everybody. There were few lazy ones among us in those days. . . .

Even in my days young men were always going to war, or to steal horses, leaving the village short of warriors, because they could not marry until they had counted coup, or had reached the age of twenty-five years. Young men do not like to wait so long. . . .

My man, Goes-ahead, was a Fox [member of that secret society] and although we women had no secret societies we sided with our men, so that my heart was always strong for the Foxes. The Foxes were warlike. We women did not like war, and yet we could not help it, because our men loved war. Always there was some man missing, and always some woman was having to go and live with her relatives, because women are not hunters. And then there were the orphans that war made. They had to be cared for by somebody. You see that when we women lost our men we lost our own, and our children's, living. I am glad that war has gone forever. It was no good — *no good!*

"THE ONLY WAY OPEN TO US"

Pretty Shield's husband, Goes Ahead, served as a scout for George Custer in 1876. Crow scouts wept openly when they heard of Custer's defeat at the Little Big Horn; they had good reason to lament the outcome of a battle that was fought on their reservation.[13]

Frank B. Linderman, *Pretty-shield, Medicine Woman of the Crows* (Lincoln: University of Nebraska Press, 1972), 167–69.

As the Teton Sioux pushed westward in the nineteenth century, they encroached on the rich Crow hunting grounds; buffalo herds in other areas of the country were diminishing, and the Sioux needed to feed their large population. In 1842, American explorer John C. Fremont reported that the Sioux intended to wage a war of extermination against the Crows "in order to take from them their country, which is now the best buffalo country in the west."[14] By midcentury, the Lakotas posed the major threat to Crow survival. In their embattled situation, alliance with the new and growing power on the plains was a logical strategy for the Crows. They signed their first treaty with the United States in 1825. In 1876, a chief named Old Crow explained why Crow warriors enlisted as scouts and allies with the United States Army in a speech recorded by newspaper correspondent John Finerty. The Sioux had stolen Crow lands, hunted on Crow mountains, murdered Crow women and children. "The Sioux have trampled upon our hearts," he said. "We shall spit upon their scalps."[15] In his old age, the Crow chief Plenty Coups offered a more moderate explanation of the same strategy: Alliance with the United States constituted the Crows' last and best hope of preserving their homelands from old enemies. The strategy worked. The Crows employed the Americans as allies in *their* wars and survived with much of their land and culture intact. Despite repeated encroachments by whites, the Crow reservation today stands in the heart of the territory Crow warriors battled to defend in the nineteenth century.[16]

PLENTY COUPS

On Alliance with the United States

The Absarokees are red men, . . . and so are their enemies, the Sioux, Cheyenne, and Arapahoe, three tribes of people, speaking three different languages, who always combined against us and who greatly outnumbered the Crows. When I was young they had better weapons too. But in spite of all this we have held our beautiful country to this day. War was always with us until the white man came; then because we were not

Frank B. Linderman, *Plenty Coups, Chief of the Crows* (Lincoln: University of Nebraska Press, 1962), 153–54.

against him he became our friend. Our lands are ours by treaty and not by chance gift. I have been told that I am the only living chief who signed a treaty with the United States.

I was a chief when I was twenty-eight [1875], and well remember that when white men found gold in the Black Hills the Sioux and Cheyenne made war on them. The Crows were wiser. We knew the white men were strong, without number in their own country, and that there was no good in fighting them; so that when other tribes wished us to fight them we refused. Our leading chiefs saw that to help the white men fight their enemies and ours would make them our friends. We had always fought the three tribes, Sioux, Cheyenne, and Arapahoe, anyway, and might as well do so now. The complete destruction of our old enemies would please us. Our decision was reached, not because we loved the white man who was already crowding other tribes into our country, or because we hated the Sioux, Cheyenne, and Arapahoe, but because we plainly saw that this course was the only one which might save our beautiful country for us. When I think back my heart sings because we acted as we did. It was the only way open to us.

NOTES

[1] John C. Ewers, "Intertribal Warfare as the Precursor of Indian-White Warfare on the Northern Great Plains," *Western Historical Quarterly* 6 (1975), 398–99.

[2] W. W. Newcomb, Jr., "A Re-examination of the Causes of Plains Warfare," *American Anthropologist* 52 (1950), 317–30.

[3] Hiram M. Chittenden and Alfred T. Richardson, eds., *Life, Letters, and Travels of Father Pierre-Jean De Smet, S.J., 1801–1873*. 4 vols. (New York: Francis P. Harper, 1905), 3:948.

[4] Peter Nabokov, *Two Leggings: The Making of a Crow Warrior* (New York: Thomas Y. Crowell, 1967), 26–28.

[5] Richard White, "The Winning of the West: The Expansion of the Western Sioux in the Eighteenth and Nineteenth Centuries," *Journal of American History* 65 (1978), 342.

[6] Colin G. Calloway, "'The Only Way Open to Us': The Crow Struggle for Survival in the Nineteenth Century," *North Dakota History* 53 (Summer 1986), 24–34.

[7] Alfred W. Bowers, "Hidatsa Social and Ceremonial Organization," *Bureau of American Ethnology, Bulletin 194* (Washington, D.C.: U.S. Govt. Printing Office, 1965), 220.

[8] For a convenient overview of Crow history see Frederick E. Hoxie, *The Crow* (New York: Chelsea House, 1989). The same author's *Parading through History: The Making of the Crow Nation in America, 1805–1935* (New York: Cambridge University Press, 1995) offers the best study of Crow history.

[9] *Annual Report of the Commissioner of Indian Affairs for 1870* (Washington, D.C.: U.S. Govt. Printing Office, 1871), 663.

[10] Robert H. Lowie, *The Crow Indians* (New York: Holt, Rinehart and Winston, 1965 reissue), 215; see also Fred W. Voget, "Warfare and the Integration of Crow Culture," in

Ward H. Goodenough, ed., *Explorations in Cultural Anthropology* (New York: McGraw Hill, 1964), 483–509.

[11] Nabokov, *Two Leggings,* xii.

[12] Ibid., 197.

[13] Colin G. Calloway, "Army Allies or Tribal Survival: The 'Other Indians' in the 1876 Campaign," in Charles E. Rankin, ed., *Legacy: New Perspectives on the Battle of Little Bighorn* (Helena: Montana Historical Society, 1996).

[14] Donald Jackson and Mary Lee Spence, eds., *The Expeditions of John Charles Fremont.* 2 vols. (Urbana: University of Illinois Press, 1970), 1:493.

[15] Milo M. Quaife, ed., *War Path and Bivouac: The Big Horn and Yellowstone Expedition. By John F. Finerty* (Chicago: R. R. Donnelley, 1955), 104.

[16] Calloway, "'The Only Way Open to Us': The Crow Struggle for Survival in the Nineteenth Century," 24–34.

6

The Agony and Anger
of the Eastern Sioux

By the middle of the nineteenth century, the Sioux nation stretched from Minnesota to the Dakotas and Wyoming. The eastern Sioux tribes, known as the Santee, or in their own language the Dakotas, occupied western Minnesota and the upper Mississippi valley. Between the Mississippi and the Missouri lived the Yanktons and Yanktonais, or Nakotas. West of the Missouri ranged the Teton, or Lakotas, who constituted about half of the entire Sioux population and were themselves divided into seven bands, or subtribes. The Santee Sioux — the Mdewakantons, the Wahpetons, the Wahpekutes, and the Sissetons — were the first to come into sustained contact with Americans and the first to endure dispossession and defeat at the hands of the United States. Their experiences in the early 1860s presaged what their western relatives would have to deal with in subsequent decades.

In August 1862, while the United States was divided and distracted by civil war, the Santees rose up in furious revolt against white settlers in southern Minnesota. The Great Sioux Uprising, one of the bloodiest conflicts in frontier history, is often portrayed as a classic racial conflict: Pressures from whites produced deep resentments among the Indians that finally led to a bloodbath that cost the lives of hundreds of settlers before the Army defeated the Indians and exacted grim retribution. Though accurate in its broad outlines, however, such a portrayal obscures the complexities of a conflict that was also a civil war within Dakota society.

In the eyes of Americans at the time, and many historians since, the Mdewakanton chief, Little Crow, or Taoyateduta, was the villain of the piece, masterminding a bloody uprising against unprotected settlers while American forces were busy in the East. In fact, Little Crow had been a strong advocate of peace. He had led his people in a policy of accommodation, accepting some aspects of American culture while trying to preserve crucial elements of traditional life. At the Treaties of Traverse des Sioux in 1851, and again in 1858, the Sioux gave up large areas of their homeland in return for the promise of annuities in cash and food and assistance in education and agriculture to help them follow "the white man's road." By 1862, Little Crow had been to Washington and seen American power firsthand, and he wore his hair cut short, lived in a frame house, and attended church.[1]

But the United States failed to honor its promises. Corrupt agents and bureaucratic indifference deprived the Sioux of food and clothing and produced suffering and anger in Sioux villages. There were few schools or teachers, and the Indians received inadequate training for the difficult transition from hunting to farming. Having obtained title to Sioux lands, white settlers no longer felt the need to treat Sioux people with respect. The winter of 1861–62 was severe. Tensions escalated and young warriors clamored for war. Bowing to the inevitable, Little Crow was forced to abandon his accommodationist policies and lead his warriors in a war he did not want and knew he could not win. Other Sioux people faced equally difficult choices: Generations of intermarriage with whites had produced a complex web of kinship networks and family ties. How were mixed-bloods and full-bloods with white relatives to act? Many Indians went to war reluctantly; others tried to protect friends and relatives in the communities that were attacked.

Defeated and hunted down by American troops, Sioux warriors were tried for their "war crimes": Thirty-eight died in the largest mass execution in American history; 326 more were imprisoned for three years in Davenport, Iowa, where more than one-third of them died, while their families were confined near Fort Snelling. Little Crow died ignominiously. He was shot down while picking raspberries, his body dismembered. The war left a bitter legacy of interracial conflict in Minnesota, but it also tore apart Dakota society and shattered bonds of kinship and coexistence that had been forged over generations.[2] It was also the first major conflict in a series of wars between the Sioux and the United States that would last almost thirty years.

The selections in this chapter provide a view of the war through the eyes of one Sioux participant and testimony from Sioux people that the root causes of the war remained unresolved three years after the conflict.

BIG EAGLE'S ACCOUNT OF THE GREAT SIOUX UPRISING

Born in 1827, Jerome Big Eagle was a prominent Mdewakanton chief who tried to pursue a new life as a farmer, as agreed in a treaty with the United States. Like Little Crow, he joined the warriors reluctantly, but he led them in battles at New Ulm, Fort Ridgley, Birch Coulee, and Wood Lake. After he surrendered, a military commission sentenced Big Eagle to death, but he was granted a reprieve, and after serving time at the prison camp at Davenport was pardoned by President Lincoln in 1864. Thirty years later, a newspaper reporter interviewed Big Eagle regarding his role in the war. Now sixty-seven years old, Big Eagle recalled the frustrations that produced the war, some of the divisions and disagreements among the Sioux, and his experiences after the surrender. With memories of the war still fresh in the minds of many Minnesotans, Indians who ventured to speak of their participation in the conflict often were anxious to disassociate themselves from those guilty of committing atrocities.

JEROME BIG EAGLE
A Sioux Story of the War
ca. 1894

Of the causes that led to the outbreak of August, 1862, much has been said. Of course it [going to war] was wrong, as we all know now, but there were not many Christians among the Indians then, and they did not understand things as they should. There was great dissatisfaction among the Indians over many things the whites did. The whites would not let them go to war against their enemies. This was right, but the Indians did not then know it. Then the whites were always trying to make the Indians give up their life and live like white men — go to farming, work hard and do as they did — and the Indians did not know how to do that, and did not want to anyway. It seemed too sudden to make such a change. If the Indians had tried to make the whites live like them, the whites would have resisted, and it was the same way with many Indians. The Indians wanted to live as they did before the treaty of Traverse des Sioux [1851] — go where they pleased and when they pleased; hunt game wherever they could find it, sell their furs to the traders, and live as they could.

Jerome Big Eagle, "A Sioux Story of the War," *Collections of the Minnesota Historical Society* 6 (1894), 382–400. Reprinted and edited in Gary Clayton Anderson and Alan L. Woolworth, eds., *Through Dakota Eyes: Narrative Accounts of the Minnesota Indian War of 1862* (St. Paul: Minnesota Historical Society Press, 1988), 23–27, 55–56, 237.

Then the Indians did not think the traders had done right. The Indians bought goods off them on credit, and when the government payments came the traders were on hand with their books, which showed that the Indians owed so much and so much, and as the Indians kept no books they could not deny their accounts, but had to pay them, and sometimes the traders got all their money. I do not say that the traders always cheated and lied about these accounts. I know many of them were honest men and kind and accommodating, but since I have been a citizen I know that many white men, when they go to pay their accounts, often think them too large and refuse to pay them, and they go to law about them and there is much bad feeling. The Indians could not go to law, but there was always trouble over their credits. Under the treaty of Traverse des Sioux the Indians had to pay a very large sum of money to the traders for old debts, some of which ran back fifteen years, and many of those who had got the goods were dead and others were not present, and the traders' books had to be received as to the amounts, and the money was taken from the tribe to pay them. Of course the traders often were of great service to the Indians in letting them have goods on credit, but the Indians seemed to think the traders ought not to be too hard on them about the payments, but do as the Indians did among one another, and put off the payment until they were better able to make it.

Then many of the white men often abused the Indians and treated them unkindly. Perhaps they had excuse, but the Indians did not think so. Many of the whites always seemed to say by their manner when they saw an Indian, "I am much better than you," and the Indians did not like this. There was excuse for this, but the Dakotas did not believe there were better men in the world than they. Then some of the white men abused the Indian women in a certain way and disgraced them, and surely there was no excuse for that.

All these things made many Indians dislike the whites. Then a little while before the outbreak there was trouble among the Indians themselves. Some of the Indians took a sensible course and began to live like white men. The government built them houses, furnished them tools, seed, etc., and taught them to farm. At the two agencies, Yellow Medicine and Redwood, there were several hundred acres of land in cultivation that summer. Others stayed in their tepees. There was a white man's party and an Indian party. We had politics among us and there was much feeling. A new chief speaker for the tribe was to be elected. There were three candidates — Little Crow, myself, and Wa-sui-hi-ya-ye-dan ("Traveling Hail"). After an exciting contest Traveling Hail was elected. Little Crow felt sore over his defeat. Many of our tribe believed him responsible for the sale of the north ten-mile strip, and I think this was why he was defeated. I did not care much about it. Many whites think that Little Crow was the principal chief of the Dakotas at this time, but he was not. Wabasha was the principal chief, and he was of the white man's party; so was I; so was old Shakopee, whose band was very large. Many think if old Shakopee had lived there would have been no war, for he was for the white men and had great influence. But he died that summer, and was succeeded by his son, whose real name was Ea-to-ka ("Another Language"), but when he became chief he took his father's name, and was afterwards called "Little Shakopee," or "Little Six," for in the Sioux language "Shakopee" means six. This Shakopee was against the white men. He took part in the outbreak, murdering women and children, but I never saw him in a battle, and he was caught in Manitoba and hanged in 1864. My brother, Medicine Bottle, was hanged with him.

As the summer advanced, there was great trouble among the Sioux — troubles among themselves, troubles with the whites, and one thing and another. The war with the South was going on then, and a great many men had left the state and gone down there to fight. A few weeks before the outbreak the president [Abraham Lincoln] called for many more men, and a great many of the white men of Minnesota and some half-breeds enlisted and went to Fort Snelling to be sent South. We understood that the South was getting the best of the fight, and it was said that the North would be whipped. . . .

It began to be whispered about that now would be a good time to go to war with the whites and get back the lands. It was believed that the men who had enlisted last had all left the state, and that before help could be sent the Indians could clean out the country, and that the Winnebagoes, and even the Chippewas, would assist the Sioux. It was also thought that a war with the whites would cause the Sioux to forget the troubles among themselves and enable many of them to pay off some old scores. Though I took part in the war, I was against it. I knew there was no good cause for it, and I had been to Washington and knew the power of the whites and that they would finally conquer us. We might succeed for a time, but we would be overpowered and defeated at last. I said all this and many more things to my people, but many of my own bands were against me, and some of the other chiefs put words in their mouths to say to me. When the outbreak came Little Crow told some of my band that if I refused to lead them to shoot me as a traitor who would not stand up for his nation, and then select another leader in my place.

But after the first talk of war the counsels of the peace Indians prevailed, and many of us thought the danger had all blown over. The time of the government payment was near at hand, and this may have had something to do with it. There was another thing that helped to stop the war talk. The crops that had been put in by the "farmer" Indians were looking well, and there seemed to be a good prospect for a plentiful supply of provisions for them the coming winter without having to depend on the game of the country or without going far out to the west on the plains for buffalo. It seemed as if the white men's way was certainly the best. Many of the Indians had been short of provisions that summer and had exhausted their credits and were in bad condition. "Now," said the farmer Indians, "if you had worked last season you would not be starving now and begging for food." The "farmers" were favored by the government in every way. They had houses built for them, some of them even had brick houses, and they were not allowed to suffer. The other Indians did not like this. They were envious of them and jealous, and disliked them because they were favored. They called them "farmers," as if it was disgraceful to be a farmer. They called them "cut-hairs," because they had given up the Indian fashion of wearing the hair, and "breeches men," because they wore pantaloons, and "Dutchmen," because so many of the settlers on the north side of the river and elsewhere in the country were Germans. I have heard that there was a secret organization of the Indians called the "Soldiers' Lodge," whose object was to declare war against the whites, but I knew nothing of it.

At last the time for the payment came and the Indians came in to the agencies to get their money. But the paymaster did not come, and week after week went by and still he did not come. The payment was to be in gold. Somebody told the Indians that the payment would never be made. The government was in a great war, and gold was scarce, and paper money had taken its place, and it was said the gold could not be had to pay us. Then the trouble began again and the war talk started up. Many of the Indians who had gathered about the agencies were out of provisions and were easily made angry. Still, most of us thought the trouble would pass, and we said nothing about it. I thought there might be trouble, but I had no idea there would be such a war. Little Crow and other chiefs did not think so. But it seems some of the tribe were getting ready for it. . . .

At this time my village was up on Crow creek, near Little Crow's. I did not have a very large band — not more than thirty or forty fighting men. Most of them were not for the war at first, but nearly all got into it at last. A great many members of the other bands were like my men; they took no part in the first movements, but afterward did. The next morning, when the force started down to attack the agency, I went along. I did not lead my band, and I took no part in the killing. I went to save the lives of two particular friends if I could. I think others went for the same reason, for nearly every Indian had a friend that he did not want killed; of course he did not care about anybody's else [sic] friend. The killing was nearly all done when I got there. Little Crow was on the ground directing operations. The day before, he had attended church there [the Episcopal mission] and listened closely to the sermon and had shaken hands with everybody. So many Indians have lied about their saving the lives of white people that I dislike to speak of what I did. But I did save the life of George H. Spencer at the time of the massacre. I know that his friend, Chaska, has always had the credit of that, but Spencer would have been a dead man in spite of Chaska if it had not been for me. I asked Spencer about this once, but he said he was wounded at the time and so excited that he could not remember what I did. Once after that I kept a half-breed family from being murdered; these are all the people whose lives I claim to have saved. I was never present when the white people were willfully murdered. I saw all the dead bodies at the agency. Mr. Andrew Myrick, a trader, with an Indian wife, had refused some hungry Indians credit a short time before when they asked him for some provisions. He said to them: "Go and eat grass." Now he was lying on the ground dead, with his mouth stuffed full of grass, and the Indians were saying tauntingly: "Myrick is eating grass himself."

When I returned to my village that day I found that many of my band had changed their minds about the war, and wanted to go into it. All the other villages were the same way. I was still of the belief that it was not best, but I thought I must go with my band and my nation, and I said to my men that I would lead them into the war, and we would all act like brave Dakotas and do the best we could. All my men were with me; none had gone off on raids, but we did not have guns for all at first. . . .

Soon after the battle [of Wood Lake] I, with many others who had taken part in the war, surrendered to Gen. Sibley. Robinson [Robertson] and the other half-breeds assured us that if we would do this we would only be held as prisoners of war a short time, but as soon as I surrendered I was thrown into prison. Afterward I was tried and served three years in the prison at Davenport and the penitentiary at Rock Island for taking part in the war. On my trial a great number of the white prisoners, women and others, were called up, but not one of them could testify that I had murdered any one or had done anything to deserve death, or else I would have been hanged. If I had known that I would be sent to the penitentiary I would not have surrendered, but when I had been in the penitentiary three years and they were about to turn me out, I told them they might keep me another year if they wished, and I meant what I said. I did not like the way I had been treated. I surrendered in good faith, knowing that many of the whites were acquainted with me and that I had not been a murderer, or present when a murder had been committed, and if I had killed or wounded a man it had been in fair, open fight. But all feeling on my part about this has long since passed away. For years I have been a Christian and I hope to die one. My white neighbors and friends know my character as a citizen and a man. I am at peace with every one, whites and Indians. I am getting to be an old man, but I am still able to work. I am poor, but I manage to get along.

THE COMPLAINTS OF STRIKE THE REE, MEDICINE COW, AND PASSING HAIL

The Sand Creek Massacre in 1864 outraged many Americans in the East and led to demands for investigations of the massacre itself and the overall handling of Indian affairs. In 1865, Wisconsin Republican senator James R. Doolittle headed a special committee to investigate "the condition of the Indian tribes and their treatment by the civil and military authorities of the United States." The work, said Doolittle, "was immense, covering a continent." Three commissioners visited Indian groups on the southern plains and the Southwest; two traveled to the Pacific coast; and two more investigated conditions in Minnesota and the northern plains. Doolittle submitted his report in 1867. In it the commission admitted that "many agents, teachers, and employees of the government are inefficient, faithless, and even guilty of peculations and fraudulent practices upon the government and upon the Indians." Doolittle himself pointed out the reasons for the situation. "Many, perhaps a majority in Congress, would prefer honesty and good faith in an Indian administration," he wrote, "but I have little hope in your action. There are too many hungry politicians to feed, there is too profound an ignorance in your body, and there is too great an indifference among the people."[3]

The testimonies of Strike the Ree and Medicine Cow of the Yanktons and Passing Hail of the Santees reveal the impact on the Sioux of the system of official indifference and ingrained corruption described by Senator Doolittle. The commissioners described the chiefs as "wise and good men" who recognized that their people's survival depended on becoming "civilized" and had worked steadily toward that end. (Medicine Cow told the commissioners, "Since I made the treaty I am an American.")

But they had been betrayed. Strike the Ree was now "bowed to the ea___, as well with age as sorrow for his people," and every speech he made revealed his great disappointment.[4] On one occasion, reminded by the Americans of his duty to remain peaceful and not act like his friends in Minnesota, the old man burst out:

> You blame the Minnesota Indians. They did wrong, but you do not know the cause. We know it! We know it! You do not. For long winters and summers they had been cheated and robbed by the agents and traders. They complained, but the Great Father would not make it right. Their hearts became bad; they thirsted for blood; they got plenty. We have the same cause to kill as our friends in Minnesota. But this (pointing to a cross suspended from his neck) keeps my heart right. I would not let my young men fight. The Yanktons have never killed a white man.[5]

The conditions that had sparked open war in 1862 continued to plague the Sioux in 1865.

STRIKE THE REE, MEDICINE COW, AND PASSING HAIL

Speeches to the Special Joint Committee on the Condition of the Indian Tribes

1865

[Strike the Ree spoke as follows:]

My grandfather, Mr. Redfield, the first agent, did not tell me the same things that my grandfather told me, neither did Agent Burleigh, but both of them told me lies; they filled my belly with lies. Everybody has got a copy of the treaty I made with my grandfather, I suppose. I suppose you are sent by my grandfather to represent the great council. I am here to represent my great council. The money my grandfather sent me has been thrown away. You know who threw it away. The guns, ammunition, wagons, horses, and everything have been thrown away. I can tell who threw them away. The reason the whites have trouble with the Indians is

Report of the Special Joint Committee on the Condition of the Indian Tribes, 39th Congress, 2nd Session (1866–67), Senate Report No. 156, Serial 1279: 368–70; 406–07

on account of the agents. When the goods come they are not according to the treaty; they never fulfil the treaty. When the agent goes away he says he is going to leave these things to be done by his successor. When Agent Burleigh came he made fine promises of what he would do. I asked for my invoice, but he would not let me have it; and I told him what my grandfather told me. I think the agents are all alike. The agent puts his foot on me as though I were a skunk. And the agents are all getting rich and we are getting poor.

My friend, what I am telling you is the truth, and what I have seen. What the agents have done in the night, I cannot tell. That is the reason I am telling you this; I want you to report it to my grandfather. I want to go to Washington; and I wish you to do all you can with my grandfather to induce him to let me come there next winter. I want to see my grandfather to ascertain how much money and goods have been sent me, and that I may know how much has been stolen and who stole it. I would like to have the agents there with my grandfather when I talk to him, that they may hear what I have to say. If there was a bible there for them to swear upon, they could not swear that they had not stolen the goods. . . .

Friends, my people are friendly to the white man. Our grandfather promised us (referring to the treaty of 1858) money, a school-house, and blacksmith shop. I have seen neither, but I believe that it is no fault of our grandfather; he has done all in his power to keep his promise. I believe our money is being kept for us, and when it is paid we shall receive the interest with it; you should pay it. My young men, squaws, and children are starving; the black spots you see on the hills before you are the graves of many of my people. When we receive anything from the white man it is given as you would throw it to a hog. The Indian stands as upon a snow-bank; the sun of prosperity shines brightly for others, but it is gradually melting away his support, and by and by all will be gone. Our grandfather at Washington promised that we should be raised up, but his young men put their feet on us and keep us down; that is the way the white man treats us.

Medicine Cow spoke as follows: . . .

I am glad you are here. You know the cause of the murders in Minnesota; if you do not, I do; the agents were the cause. Our agents never give us what our grandfather sends us. I think when the whites make an agreement with each other they do as they agree with each other. If the whites did as they agree with the Indians, there would not be so much difficulty. The agents bring goods, but do not give them to us. When the agent brought us money we asked him to let us see it; but more than half was carried back to the house and we never received it. One time he got and told us that he would keep it until winter, but he never let us have it. The blacksmith won't work for the common Indians, but works for the chiefs and all white men. If the common Indians go to him he will tell them to go away.

I think all the work Doctor Burleigh had done was done for himself. He purchased lots of cattle and things. When he came there he only had a trunk, but now he is high up — rich. Once in a while I went and asked Doctor Burleigh about the money, and he said he saved it for all the Indians, and we did not get it.

When Agent Conger came there he and Doctor Burleigh were together, and we felt bad to see him with the new agent. We went and told Doctor Burleigh that we wanted him to give us the money which he had taken from us; but he would not. I told him if he did not I would tell my grandfather when I went to see him.

I think a great many of our tribe have frozen to death, and a great many have died of starvation. When I was talking that way to Doctor Burleigh he said he did not care what I said to him; that all up and down the Missouri river all the big men and generals were on his side. The reason I talk this way, the governor said I must not talk so hard against a young man. The doctor told me I was against him. I answered, "Yes; you are always against the Indians; you never try to do anything for us."

Another time Doctor Burleigh came and brought us money, and gave us two dollars in paper money and some three and some one dollar, and we don't know what he did with the gold money, but we want to know, and we want to know if that is the way our grandfather does with us. I think if they had asked the young men to learn at school they would have done so; they would willingly attend the school and learn, but they have never had an opportunity. For my part I think the agents have been an injury to us. When we moved here we had to dig the ground with our fingers. We have done as the whites told us. When Burleigh told us to be soldiers we became soldiers; we burnt the dirt lodges, as he told us; but we were not paid for being soldiers. We tried hard to please the whites. We have often told the same things to the big men before, but it made no difference; but we are glad to see you and hope you will do us some good. One time the doctor (Burleigh) came up and said he had got plenty of goods to keep us all winter; that he had 4,000 sacks of flour, and plenty of blankets; but we found out that he was not telling the truth; he put it into the store and we had to buy it. One time he told us he was going to keep seven large boxes of goods (one containing traps) for another time, to be distributed to us; but we never received any of these goods, excepting three of our young men got three guns and three suits of clothes as a reward for killing a Santee, and that was all we got. I asked Burleigh to do right; but Burleigh's interpreter would not tell him right. I told him to get another interpreter. Things are no better now. The new agent has come, but he is like a man in the middle of the prairie. Burleigh cleaned the agency of everything, and the new agent has nothing to go on with; no cattle, no wagons, no ploughs, in fact nothing; everything has melted away like a snow bank in the summer's sun. I think our grandfather don't know what is done with the money, from what you say to us to-day. I think everything on the agency is gone, and one saw mill does us no good; there is no one to attend to it. It is the business of the agent to attend to it. It would take a month to start it. We have no lumber. There is no one to attend to our blacksmith shop, nor the carpenter shop; all the tools are gone. Sometimes the blacksmith does some things for the Indians, but works mostly for whites. Since the new agent came there is a good blacksmith. When Burleigh came to the agency there were two mules there, and they are there now; and there were also two horses, but Burleigh went away and swapped them away for two bob-tailed horses, and the Indians have never since seen their horses or the bob-tails.

Chief Passing Hail — Wasuhiya-ye-dom — says:
It has been a long time since I have heard such talk, and I am very glad. Myself and three of these chiefs with him here were at Washington, and heard what the grandfather told them, and we know we live by what the government gives them, and we abide by what the government does for us. At Redwood they took all the young and smart men and put them in prison, and they took all the chiefs and women and children and put them in Fort Snelling. They done with us as they would grain, shaking it to get out the best, and then brought our bodies over here; that is, took everything from us and brought us over here with nothing. . . . When the provisions were brought here the agent told us the food was to be divided between us and the Winnebagoes, and only five sacks of flour were given us per week through the winter; they were issued to us each Saturday. They brought beef and piled it up here; they built a box and put the beef in it and steamed it and made soup; they put salt and pepper in it, and that is the reason these hills about here are filled with children's graves; it seemed as though they wanted to kill us. We have grown up among white folks, and we know the ways of white folks. White folks do not eat animals that die themselves; but the animals that died here were piled up with the beef here and were fed out to us; and when the women and children, on account of their great hunger, tried to get the heads, blood, and entrails,

when the butchering was being done, they were whipped and put in the guard-house. It is not right for me to omit anything. The heads, entrails, and liver were piled about here in the stockade, and the agent would keep watch of them, and when he wanted some work done he would pay for the work with the most rotten part of it. He employed the Indians to work, and paid them with the most rotten part, as above stated. Last fall the agent told us to go out on a hunt, and while they were out on the hunt the goods came, and we suppose the reason he wanted us to go on the hunt was, that he did not want us to see what was done with the goods. Last fall the agent called the chiefs and said he would give us the goods. The next day we came up, and the agent, from the top window of the warehouse, threw out the goods; he threw out a dress for each woman and a blanket for each family. I think there were over one hundred blankets given out at that time. They brought us here to a windy country, and we supposed the wind had blown the goods away; but we heard afterwards that there were some round in the houses in the stockade. We heard that the agent traded some of our goods away, and we suppose he traded them for robes and furs. We think if he had not traded them away there would have been plenty to go round, and the women would not have been crying with cold. You told me that you wanted me to tell all that the agent did. . . .

The President gave us some laws, and we have changed ourselves to white men, put on white man's clothes and adopted the white man's ways, and we supposed we would have a piece of ground somewhere where we could live; but no one can live here and live like a white man. I have changed my body to a white man's body. I have not told any lie. You told me to tell the truth, and I have done so. . . .

NOTES

[1] Gary Clayton Anderson, *Little Crow: Spokesman for the Sioux* (St. Paul: Minnesota Historical Society, 1986).

[2] Gary Clayton Anderson, *Kinsmen of Another Kind: Dakota-White Relations in the Upper Mississippi Valley, 1650–1862* (Lincoln: University of Nebraska Press, 1984); Gary Clayton Anderson and Alan R. Woolworth, eds., *Through Dakota Eyes: Narrative Accounts of the Minnesota Indian War of 1862* (St. Paul: Minnesota Historical Society Press, 1988).

[3] *Report of the Joint Special Committee on the Condition of the Indian Tribes*, 39th Congress, 2d session (1866–67), Senate Report No. 156, Serial 1279 (quotations at 3, 7, and 387).

[4] Ibid., 372, 286.

[5] Ibid., 384.

7

Massacres North and South

From almost the first conflicts in North America, colonists resorted to destroying Indian crops and villages as the surest way to defeat Indians. Hundreds of Pequots died when the Puritans burned their village on the Mystic River in Connecticut in 1637; French expeditions into Mohawk country in the 1660s targeted Mohawk villages for destruction, and British troops carried fire and sword to Cherokee towns in 1760. During the American Revolution, patriot troops launched recurrent assaults on Cherokee and Shawnee villages, and General John Sullivan's expedition in 1779 rampaged through Iroquois country burning crops, cutting down orchards, and burning forty towns.

Americans on the plains continued the strategy of waging war against Indian food supplies and Indian villages. Where colonists had destroyed cornfields in previous centuries, Americans slaughtered buffalo herds in the nineteenth century. In addition, American forces regularly endeavored to catch otherwise elusive Plains Indians when they were gathered in winter encampments. As in colonial times, and as the two accounts reproduced here demonstrate, it was not unusual for Indian people living peacefully in their villages to be attacked by soldiers who made no distinction between hostile and friendly bands.

ACCOUNT OF SAND CREEK

The Sioux war in Minnesota in 1862 sent a wave of terror through frontier communities who felt vulnerable owing to the diversion of able-bodied men to the Civil War. Many settlers feared the Indians would seize the opportunity to attack, and rumors that Confederate agents were at work among southern Plains tribes added to the tension. Fears in Colorado reached fever pitch late in 1863 when the military transferred troops from the territory to Missouri despite objections that the inhabitants would be left defenseless. Many historians believe that the authorities in Colorado deliberately set in motion an Indian war as the best way to prevent further troop withdrawals, and that the territorial governor, John Evans, regarded defeating the Indians as the best way of clearing the territory for development and securing statehood with himself as senator. Testifying before a congressional investigating committee, frontiersman Kit Carson said that "the authorities in Colorado, expecting that their troops would be sent to the Potomac, determined to get up an Indian war."[1]

In this tense atmosphere, any thefts or raids committed by Indians were apt to be interpreted as evidence of a major uprising. Tensions with Indians increased in the spring and summer of 1864, and in June four Arapahos killed a family named Hungate near Denver. The mutilated bodies were put on display in Denver, and settlers in Colorado were outraged. Governor Evans issued a proclamation advising "friendly Indians" who wished to avoid being mistaken for hostiles to place themselves under the protection of the military at Fort Lyon. Black Kettle and White Antelope of the Southern Cheyennes and Left Hand of the Southern Arapahos did so and, believing themselves safe, their people set up camp. On November 29, in the face of a snowstorm and anxious to score a victory before their enlistment term expired, the militia of the Third Colorado Cavalry under Colonel John Chivington attacked the village. George Bent, a mixed-blood Cheyenne who was in the village, said, "I looked toward the chief's lodge and saw that Black Kettle had a large American flag tied to the end of a long lodgepole and was standing in front of his lodge, holding the pole, with the flag fluttering in the grey light of the winter dawn. I heard him call to the people not to be afraid, that the soldiers would not hurt them; then the troops opened fire from two sides of the camps."[2] The soldiers killed and mutilated men, women, and children. White Antelope died singing his death song; Black Kettle survived, only to be killed in Custer's attack on his village on the Washita River four years later. Congress demanded an investigation but the massacre sparked the general Indian war that Coloradans had feared and predicted. The following account of the massacre was related by Little Bear to his friend George Bent.

LITTLE BEAR

The Sand Creek Massacre
1864

I got up before daylight to go out to where my brother-in-law Tomahawk had left our pony herd the evening before. He told me where he had left the ponies and said he did not think they would stray far from that place. As soon as I was dressed I went out of the lodge and crossed the creek; but as I was going up on the hill I saw Kingfisher running back toward the camp. He shouted to me that white men were driving off the herds. I looked toward the Fort Lyon Trail and saw a long line of little black objects to the south, moving toward the camp across the bare brown plain. There was some snow on the ground, but only in the hollows. I ran back to the camp as fast as I could, but soldiers had already come up on the other side of the creek and were firing in among the lodges. As I came into camp the people were running up the creek. As I passed Black Kettle's lodge I saw that he had a flag tied to the end of the pole and was standing there holding the pole. I ran to our lodge to get my bow, quiver, shield, and war bonnet. My father, Bear Tongue, had just recently given me these things. I was very young then and had just become a warrior.

By this time the soldiers were shooting into the camp from two sides, and as I put on my war bonnet and took up my shield and weapons, the bullets were hitting the lodge cover with heavy thumps like big hailstones. When I went out again I ran behind the lodges, so that the troops could not get good shots at me. I jumped over the bank into the creek bed and found Big Head, Crow Neck, Cut-Lip-Bear, and Smoke standing there under the high bank. I joined these young men. The people were all running up the creek; the soldiers sat on their horses, lined up on both banks and firing into the camps, but they soon saw that the lodges were now nearly empty, so they began to advance up the creek, firing on the fleeing people. Our party was at the west end of the camps, not one hundred yards from the lodges. At this point the creek made a bend, coming from the north and turning toward the southeast just at the upper end of the village. As the soldiers began to advance, we ran across to the west side of the creek to get under another high bank over there, but just as we reached this bank another body of cavalry came up and opened fire

Savoie Lottinville, ed., *Life of George Bent, Written from His Letters by George E. Hyde* (Norman: University of Oklahoma Press, 1968), 153–54.

on us. We hardly knew what way to turn, but Big Head and the rest soon decided to go on. They ran on toward the west, but passing over a hill they ran into another body of troops just beyond and were surrounded and all killed.

After leaving the others, I started to run up the creek bed in the direction taken by most of the fleeing people, but I had not gone far when a party of about twenty cavalrymen got into the dry bed of the stream behind me. They chased me up the creek for about two miles, very close behind me and firing on me all the time. Nearly all the feathers were shot out of my war bonnet, and some balls passed through my shield; but I was not touched. I passed many women and children, dead and dying, lying in the creek bed. The soldiers had not scalped them yet, as they were busy chasing those that were yet alive. After the fight I came back down the creek and saw these dead bodies all cut up, and even the wounded scalped and slashed. I saw one old woman wandering about; her whole scalp had been taken off and the blood was running down into her eyes so that she could not see where to go.

I ran up the creek about two miles and came to the place where a large party of the people had taken refuge in holes dug in the sand up against the sides of the high banks. I stayed here until the soldiers withdrew. They were on both banks, firing down on us, but not many of us were killed. All who failed to reach these pits in the sand were shot down.

THE MASSACRE ON THE MARIAS (1870)

The Blackfeet Indians — the Siksika, Blood, and Piegan tribes — were the dominant power on the northwestern plains in the late eighteenth and early nineteenth century. Endeavoring to protect their monopoly of the gun trade to the north, the Blackfeet, and particularly the southernmost Piegans, resisted American intrusions, clashing with the Lewis and Clark expedition in 1806 and earning a reputation as ferocious enemies of American trappers during the era of the Rocky Mountain fur trade.[3] But recurrent epidemics of smallpox — in 1781, 1837, and 1869 — broke Blackfoot power before the American Army had to deal with them as a military force.

Nevertheless, tensions and conflicts continued to mark Blackfeet-American relations through the 1860s, as American settlers and miners encroached on Piegan lands in Montana. Piegan warriors killed isolated settlers, and Indians who went to Many-Houses (Fort Benton) to trade were beaten and even killed. Things came to head when Owl Child and a Piegan war party killed a rancher named Malcolm Clark (known to the Piegans as Four Bears), a man of violent temper who had beaten Owl Child and seduced his wife.[4]

Bombarded with requests for protection, the Army took action. General Philip Sheridan thought the best way to deal with the "marauders" was to apply the same tactics he had used with grim effect among the southern Plains tribes a couple of years earlier: "Let me find out exactly where these Indians are going to spend the winter," he said, "and about the time of a good heavy snow I will send out a party and try and strike them." General Alfred Sully first called a conference with the Piegan chiefs and demanded that Clark's murderers be handed over. The chiefs — Heavy Runner, Little Wolf, Big Lake, and Gray Eyes of the Bloods — promised to do what they could, but Owl Child was a member of Mountain Chief's band, and Mountain Chief did not attend the meeting. With little expectation of seeing their demands met, the Army prepared for war. "If the lives and property of the citizens of Montana can best be protected by striking Mountain Chief's band," telegraphed Sheridan, "I want them struck." He ordered Colonel Eugene M. Baker to lead the campaign and "to strike them hard."[5]

In January 1870, in subzero temperatures and howling winds, Baker led his troops in search of Mountain Chief's village. At daybreak on January 23, the seizers (as the Blackfeet called the soldiers) attacked a village of some thirty-seven lodges on the Marias River. The Blackfeet, huddling in the cold and reeling from a recent smallpox epidemic, were caught totally off guard. The soldiers killed 173 people, mostly women, children, and old men, and slaughtered 300 horses (Figure 11). One soldier died; another hurt his leg falling from his horse. But this was not Mountain Chief's village; the victims were members of Heavy Runner's band, one of the "friendly" Piegan chiefs who had been working for peace. Owl Child lay dying of smallpox in Mountain Chief's village seventeen miles away.

Baker claimed he did not know he was attacking the wrong village; Piegans said that Heavy Runner was shot down as he walked toward the attacking soldiers holding up his hands and waving his identification paper. White settlers in Montana approved of the massacre and the Army defended its actions, but a storm of protest brewed in the East and killed a move to relocate the Indian Bureau to the War Department. Congressman John A. Logan of Illinois, a Civil War veteran and former supporter of transferring the Indian Bureau, now voted against it: The reports of the Piegan massacre, he said, "made my blood run cold in my veins."[6]

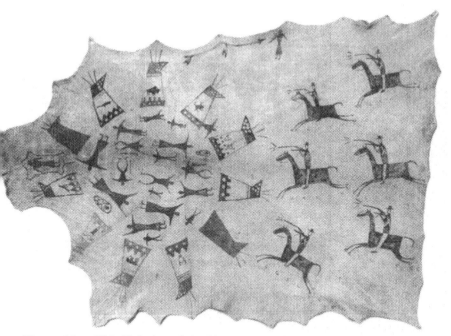

Figure 11.   Hide Painting of the Massacre on the Marias (ca. 1930)
In this painting, Piegan artist George Bull Child (b. 1891) depicts the bodies of men, women, children, and infants in cradles lying dead on the ground. Nine of the eleven tepees are painted with dream visions and images.

The Blackfeet never again faced the United States Army in battle. Even when the government's failure to deliver promised provisions produced starvation in 1883–84, the Blackfeet remained at peace. But bitter memories of Baker's massacre of Heavy Runner's band persisted. James Willard Schultz, a white American who married a Blackfoot woman and took the name Apikuni, lived with the Blackfeet from 1877 until his wife's death in 1903. He then moved to Los Angeles, became literary critic for the *Los Angeles Times,* and made a career as a writer. He returned often to Montana and wrote several books about his life and experiences with the Blackfeet. Schultz first met Bear Head in 1879, when he was a young Piegan warrior. Not until he was an old man, sixty-five years after the Massacre on the Marias, however, did Bear Head relate the story of that event to Schultz. "I want you to write it for the whites to read," he said, "for the whites of this time to learn what their fathers did to us."[7]

BEAR HEAD

Account of the Massacre on the Marias

In Falling-Leaves Moon (September) we moved back across Big River, and were camped on Two Medicine Lodges River when winter came. All the other bands of our tribe were east of us, here and there along Bear (Marias) River. A white man called "Big Nose" (Hiram Baker), who had come with a wagonload of cartridges and other things to trade for our buffalo robes and furs, told that the whites were more and more angry about the killing of Four Bears, and were trying to get their seizers (soldiers) to make a big killing of our tribe and so avenge his death. However, the seizer chiefs (army officers) seemed not to listen to their demand. Our chiefs talked over that news and thought little of it. As Heavy Runner said, the killing of Four Bears did not concern us. If the whites wanted to get revenge for it, they should kill Owl Child.

As the winter wore on the buffalo herds drifted farther and farther away from the mountains, and we had to follow them or starve. We moved down to the mouth of Two Medicine Lodges River; then in Middle-Winter Moon (January), moved down on Bear River and camped in a bottom that Mountain Chief's band had just left, they going a little way farther down the river. It was an unhappy time: the whites had given us of their terrible white-scabs disease (smallpox), and some of our band were dying. And the buffalo herds remained so far out from the river that we had to go for a two or three days' hunt in order to get meat for our helpless ones. One evening I arranged to go on a hunt with a number of our band. We were to travel light, take only two lodges to accommodate us all; my mother and one of my sisters were to go with me to help with my kills. Came morning and I set out for my horses; could not find them on the plain. Sought them in the timbered bottoms of the valley; did not come upon them until late in the day. The hunting party had long since gone. I told my mother that we would join the next party of hunters to go out. We still had dried meat to last us for some days.

On the following morning I found my horses in the timber well above camp and was nearing it with them when, suddenly, I ran into a multitude of white men: seizers. I was so astonished, so frightened, that I could not move. One of the seizers came and grasped my arm; spoke; tapped his

James Willard Schultz (Apikuni), *Blackfeet and Buffalo: Memories of Life among the Indians* (Norman: University of Oklahoma Press, 1962), 300–02.

lips with his fingers: I was not to speak, shout. He was a chief, this seizer, had strips of yellow metal on his shoulders, had a big knife, a five-shots pistol. He made me advance with him; all of the seizers were advancing. We came to the edge of the camp; close before us were the lodges. Off to our right were many more seizers looking down upon them. It was a cold day. The people were all in their lodges, many still in their beds. None knew that the seizers had come.

A seizer chief up on the bank shouted something, and at once all of the seizers began shooting into the lodges. Chief Heavy Runner ran from his lodge toward the seizers on the bank. He was shouting to them and waving a paper writing that our agent had given him, a writing saying that he was a good and peaceful man, a friend of the whites. He had run but a few steps when he fell, his body pierced with bullets. Inside the lodges men were yelling; terribly frightened women and children, screaming — screaming from wounds, from pain as they died. I saw a few men and women, escaping from their lodges, shot down as they ran. Most terrible to hear of all was the crying of little babies at their mothers' breasts. The seizers all advanced upon the lodges, my seizer still firmly holding my arm. They shot at the tops of the lodges; cut the bindings of the poles so the whole lodge would collapse upon the fire and begin to burn — burn and smother those within. I saw my lodge so go down and burn. Within it my mother, my almost-mothers, my almost-sisters. Oh, how pitiful were their screamings as they died, and I there, powerless to help them!

Soon all was silent in the camp, and the seizers advanced, began tearing down the lodges that still stood, shooting those within them who were still alive, and then trying to burn all that they tore down, burn the dead under the heaps of poles, lodge-skins, and lodge furnishings; but they did not burn well.

At last my seizer released my arm and went about with his men looking at the smoking piles, talking, pointing, laughing, all of them. And finally the seizers rounded up all of our horses, drove them up the valley a little way, and made camp.

I sat before the ruin of my lodge and felt sick. I wished that the seizers had killed me, too. In the center of the fallen lodge, where the poles had fallen upon the fire, it had burned a little, then died out. I could not pull up the lodge-skin and look under it. I could not bear to see my mother, my almost-mothers, my almost-sisters lying there, shot or smothered to death. When I went for my horses, I had not carried my many-shots gun. It was there in the ruin of the lodge. Well, there it would remain.

From the timber, from the brush around about, a few old men, a few women and children came stealing out and joined me. Sadly we stared at our ruined camp; spoke but little; wept. Wailed wrinkled old Black Antelope: "Why, oh, why had it to be that all of our warriors, our hunters, had to go out for buffalo at this time. But for that, some of the white seizers would also be lying here in death."

"One was killed. I saw him fall," I said.

"*Ah.* Only one seizer. And how many of us. Mostly women and children; newborn babies. Oh, how cruel, how terribly cruel are the white men," old Curlew Woman wailed.

"Killed us off without reason for it; we who have done nothing against the whites," said old Three Bears, and again we wept.

As we sat there, three men arrived from Mountain Chief's camp below. They stared and stared at our fallen, half-burned lodges, at our dead, lying here and there, and could hardly believe what they saw. They rode over to us, asked what had happened, and when we had told them of the white seizers' sudden attack upon us, it was long before they could speak. And then they said that we were to live with them; they would take good care of us poor, bereaved ones.

NOTES

[1] Stan Hoig, *The Sand Creek Massacre* (Norman: University of Oklahoma Press, 1961), includes a discussion of the escalating hostilities. See also Donald J. Berthrong, *The Southern Cheyennes* (Norman: University of Oklahoma Press, 1963), chaps. 7–9. Carson's testimony is in "The Chivington Massacre," 39th Congress, 2d Session, Senate Report No. 156, appendix, 96–98.

[2] Savoie Lottinville, ed., *Life of George Bent, Written from His Letters by George E. Hyde* (Norman: University of Oklahoma Press, 1968), 152.

[3] James P. Ronda, *Lewis and Clark among the Indians* (Lincoln: University of Nebraska Press, 1984), 241-44.

[4] For more information see John C. Ewers, *The Blackfeet: Raiders on the Northwestern Plains* (Norman: University of Oklahoma Press, 1958), chap. 14; James Willard Schultz, *Blackfeet and Buffalo: Memories of Life among the Indians* (Norman: University of Oklahoma Press, 1962), 298–99. These events also feature prominently in James Welch's novel *Fools Crow* (New York: Penguin, 1987).

[5] Ewers, *The Blackfeet,* 247–49.

[6] Ibid., 250–52; *Second Annual Report of the Board of Indian Commissioners for 1870* (Washington, D.C.: U.S. Govt. Printing Office, 1871), 89–93.

[7] Schultz, *Blackfeet and Buffalo,* 282.

8

Talking to the Peace Commissioners: The Treaty of Medicine Lodge, 1867

With the Civil War won, the United States turned to rebuilding the defeated states in the South and to resolving the Indian question in the West. The government aimed ultimately to concentrate the Indians of the plains on two large reservations: one south of Kansas and the other north of Nebraska. Not only would this clear a corridor for American expansion across the central plains, but it would also begin the process of eradicating the Plains Indians' way of life, something the government regarded as essential to lasting peace. The United States intended to achieve these ends by peaceful negotiation if possible, and by force if necessary. As a result, federal Indian policy toward Plains Indians vacillated between peace and war, even though the ultimate objective — the dispossession and acculturation of the Indians — was basically the same. Plains Indians fought to defend both their lands and their way of life.

In 1867, President Andrew Johnson appointed a peace commission to meet with the various tribes on the plains, induce them to accept life on reservations, and encourage farming and stock-raising. The commission was to include Nathaniel G. Taylor, Commissioner of Indian Affairs, Senator John B. Henderson, Chairman of the Senate Committee on Indian Affairs, Samuel F. Tappan, John B. Sanborn, and three Army officers "not below the rank of brigadier general": William S. Harney, Alfred H. Terry, and Christopher C. Augur.[1] Meetings with Brulé, Oglala, and Cheyenne delegates at North Platte, Nebraska, in September proved unproductive, and Red Cloud refused even to come in and talk, so the commissioners headed south and convened a meeting with the tribes of the southern plains at Medicine Lodge Creek, Kansas, in late October. More than five thousand Kiowas, Comanches, Plains Apaches, Kiowa Apaches, Southern Arapahos, and Southern Cheyennes gathered at the treaty grounds to hear the commissioners outline their vision of the future. Thirty wagon loads of provisions and presents lumbered to the site, accompanied by three companies of cavalry and a battery of gatling guns. Newspaper reporters also were there in force, preserving detailed accounts of the treaty and of the speeches made by Indian leaders, several of whom impressed them as colorful personalities.[2]

The American commissioners spelled out what they regarded as the limited choices facing Plains Indians: Only by adopting the white man's ways and agreeing to the reservation system could they hope to survive. "What we say to you may at first be unpleasant," Senator Henderson told the assembled tribes, "but if you follow our advice it will bring you good, and you will soon be happy." The whites were settling the country and resistance was futile, asserted the senator. Now was the time for the Indians to set aside some lands for their exclusive use before it was too late. "We say to you that the buffalo will not last for ever. They are now becoming few, and you must know it. When that day comes, the Indian must change the road his father trod, or he must suffer, and probably die. We tell you that to change will make you better. We wish you to live, and we will now offer you the way."[3]

"The way" involved giving up the life of nomadic warrior-hunters and settling down on reservations to begin a new life as farmers with government assistance. The United States would provide food and supplies, seeds and farming equipment, schools and churches ("medicine lodges"), and peace. The Kiowas and the Comanches signed the treaty on October 21, the Apaches on October 25, and the Arapahos and some Cheyennes on October 28 (Figure 12). The Indians pledged to live in peace with the United States and reserved the right to continue hunting in certain areas, but also agreed to live on reservation lands set aside for them below Kansas.[4]

As the following speeches by Kiowa and Comanche chiefs indicate, however, some of the Indians who signed the treaty agreed to things they clearly stated they did not want and voiced opposition to the new way of life being offered them. Tooshaway, or Silver Brooch, a chief of the Penateka band of Comanches, said, "I have tried the life the Great Father told me to follow. . . . I am tired of it." He went on to say that the government had not kept its promises in the past, and if it failed to do so this time, "I and my young men will return to our wild brothers to live on the prairie."[5] Various newspaper reporters recorded different versions of the Indians' speeches, but the sentiments they expressed were consistent. Although aware that it was no longer possible to live their traditional way of life, the Indian chiefs who negotiated with the American representatives were determined to make clear that theirs was not a surrender at any cost.

Figure 12.   Council with Army Officers
Painted by Soaring Eagle, a Southern Cheyenne.

"WHEN WE SETTLE DOWN WE GROW PALE AND DIE."

The Kiowa chief Satanta, or White Bear, initially impressed the newspaper reporters at the treaty as the Orator of the Plains. He was a physically impressive man, a noted warrior, and a capable speaker. Henry Morton Stanley, who recorded the following speech (and who later gained fame for his "Dr. Livingstone, I presume" greeting in Africa), said, "Satanta has a knack of saying boldly what he needs, regardless of what anybody thinks." As the meeting wore on, however, Satanta wore thin. The reporters began to view him as a self-important, hard-drinking, strutting individual who loved to hear himself speak and whose professions of peace and friendship meant little. The following speech was met by shouts of approval from the Kiowas but, said Stanley, "produced a rather blank look upon the faces of the Peace Commissioners."[6]

SATANTA

Speech at the Treaty of Medicine Lodge

The Commissioners have come from afar to listen to our grievances. My heart is glad, and I shall hide nothing from you. I understood that you were coming down here to see us. I moved away from those disposed to war, and I also came from afar to see you. The Kiowas and Comanches have not been fighting. We were away down south when we heard that you were coming to see us.

The Cheyennes are those who have been fighting with you. They did it in broad daylight, so that all could see them. If I had been fighting I would have done so also. Two years ago I made peace with General Harney, Sanborn, and Colonel Leavenworth at the mouth of the Little Arkansas. That peace I have never broken. When the grass was growing this spring, a large body of soldiers came along on the Santa Fe road. I had not done anything, and therefore was not afraid.

All the chiefs of the Kiowas, Comanches, and Arapahoes are here to-day. They have come to listen to the good word. We have been waiting here a long time to see you, and we are getting tired. All the land south of the Arkansas belongs to the Kiowas and Comanches, and I don't want to give away any of it. I love the land and the buffalo, and will not part with any. I want you to understand also that the Kiowas don't want to fight, and have not been fighting since we made the treaty. I hear a good deal of fine talk from these gentlemen, but they never do what they say. I don't want any of these medicine homes built in the country; I want the papooses brought up just exactly as I am. When I make peace it is a long and lasting one; there is no end to it. We thank you for your presents.

Henry M. Stanley, *My Early Travels and Adventures in America and Asia* (London: Sampson, Low, Marston and Co., 1895), 1:247–49.

All these chiefs and head men feel happy. They will do what you want. They know that you are doing the best you can. I and they will do so also. There is one big chief lately died — Jim Pockmark, of the Caddoes — he was a great peacemaker, and we are sorry he is dead.

When I look upon you I know you are all big chiefs. While you are in the country we go to sleep happy, and are not afraid. I have heard that you intend to settle us on a reservation near the mountains. I don't want to settle there. I love to roam over the wide prairie, and when I do it I feel free and happy, but when we settle down, we grow pale and die.

Hearken well to what I say. I have laid aside my lance, my bow, and my shield, and yet I feel safe in your presence. I have told you the truth. I have no little lies hid about me, but I don't know how it is with the Commissioners; are they as clear as I am? A long time ago this land belonged to our fathers, but when I go up to the river I see a camp of soldiers, and they are cutting my wood down, or killing my buffalo. I don't like that, and when I see it my heart feels like bursting with sorrow. I have spoken.

"I WANT TO LIVE AND DIE AS I WAS BROUGHT UP."

Ten Bears, the gray-haired old head chief of the Yamparika Comanches, was one of the most influential men on the southern plains. He told the commissioners at Medicine Lodge, "What I say is law for the Comanches, but it takes half-a-dozen to speak for the Kiowas." After a heated argument with Satanta, the old Comanche succeeded even in silencing the loquacious Kiowa.[7] Ten Bears had visited President Lincoln in Washington in 1863 and had become a consistent advocate of peace. He wore gold-rimmed spectacles as he addressed the commissioners. Some versions of Ten Bears's speech are more embellished than the one reprinted here as recorded by Henry Stanley.

TEN BEARS

Speech at the Treaty of Medicine Lodge

My people do not trouble the white man at all; but two years ago, on this road, your soldiers commenced killing my young men, and on the Canadian also. My young men returned the fire, and fought your soldiers. Your men then attacked our villages; we retorted as well as we could, but we finally made peace, and there was an end of it. We have been at peace since.

There is one thing which is not good in your speeches; that is, building us medicine houses. We don't want any. I want to live and die as I was brought up. I love the open prairie, and I wish you would not insist on putting us on a reservation. We prefer to roam over the prairie when we want to do so. If the Texans were kept from our country, then we might live upon a reserve, but this country is so small we cannot live upon it. The best of my lands the Texans have taken, and I am left to shift as I can best do. If you have any good words from the Great Father I shall be happy to hear them. I love to get presents, for it reminds me that the Great Father has not forgotten his friends the Comanches. I want my country to be pure and clean.

"TEACH US THE ROAD TO TRAVEL."

Satank, or Sitting Bear, was a prominent Kiowa chief and medicine man, a warrior and a peacemaker. He had played a major role in bringing about the great peace between the Kiowas and the Cheyennes in 1840. Unlike Satanta, Satank kept his own counsel through most of the proceedings at Medicine Lodge. When he did speak, however, bidding the Americans farewell, he moved treaty commissioners and newspaper correspondents alike with the power of his words. One reporter, no friend of Indians, said he had sat through stirring speeches in Congress and fiery sermons from pulpits, but "never have I known true eloquence before this day."[8] The speech was reprinted in full in the *New York Tribune* on November 30, 1867.

Henry M. Stanley, *My Early Travels and Adventures in America and Asia* (London: Sampson, Low, Marston and Co., 1895), 1:252–53.

SATANK

Speech at the Treaty of Medicine Lodge

It has made me glad to meet you, who are the commissioners of the Great Father. You no doubt are tired of the much talk of our people. Many of them have put themselves forward and filled you with their sayings. I have kept back and said nothing, not that I did not consider myself still the principal chief of the Kiowa nation, but others, younger than I, desired to talk, and I left it to them. Before leaving, however, as I now intend to go, I come to say that the Kiowas and Comanches have made with you a peace, and they intend to keep it. If it brings prosperity to us, we, of course, will like it better. If it brings poverty and adversity we will not abandon it. It is our contract and it shall stand.

Our people once carried on war against Texas. We thought the Great Father would not be offended, for the Texans had gone out from among his people and become his enemies. You now tell us they have made peace and returned to the great family. The Kiowa and Comanche will now make no bloody trail in their land. They have pledged their word, and that word shall last unless the whites shall break their contract and invite the horrors of war.

We do not break treaties. We make but few contracts, and them we remember well. The whites make so many they are liable to forget them. The white chief seems not to be able to govern his braves. The Great Father seems powerless in the face of his children. He sometimes becomes angry when he sees the wrongs of his people committed on the red man, and his voice becomes loud as the roaring winds. But, like the wind, it soon dies away, and leaves the sullen calm of unheeded oppression. We hope now that a better time has come.

If all would talk and then do as you have done, the sun of peace would shine forever. We have warred against the white man, but never because it gave us pleasure. Before the day of oppression came, no white man came to our villages and went away hungry. It gave us more joy to share with him than it gave him to partake of our hospitality. In the far-distant past there was no suspicion among us. The world seemed large enough for both the red man and the white man. Its broad plains seem now to

New York Tribune, Nov. 30, 1867; reprinted in W. C. Wanderwerth, comp., *Indian Oratory: Famous Speeches by Noted Indian Chieftains* (Norman: University of Oklahoma Press, 1971), 135–37.

contract, and the white man grows jealous of his red brother. He once came to trade; he comes now to fight. He once came as a citizen; he now comes as a soldier. He once put his trust in our friendship, and wanted no shield but our fidelity, but now he builds forts and plants big guns on their walls. He once gave us arms and powder, and bade us hunt the game. We then loved him for his confidence. He now suspects our plighted faith, and drives us to be his enemies. He now covers his face with a cloud of jealousy and anger, and tells us to be gone, as the offended master speaks to his dog.

We thank the Great Spirit that all these wrongs are now to cease, and the old day of peace and friendship to come again. You came as friends. You talked as friends. You have patiently heard our many complaints. To you they have seemed trifling; to us they are everything.

You have not tried, as many do, to get from us our lands for nothing. You have not tried to make a new bargain merely to get the advantage. You have not asked to make our annuities smaller; but, unasked, you have made them larger. You have not withdrawn a single gift, but voluntarily you have provided new guarantees for our education and comfort.

When we saw these things we then said, "These are the men of the past." We at once gave you our hearts. You now have them. You know what is best for us. Do for us what is best. Teach us the road to travel, and we will not depart from it forever. For your sakes the green grass shall not be stained with the blood of the whites. Your people shall again be our people, and peace shall be our mutual heritage. If wrong comes, we shall look to you for the right. We know you will not forsake us, and tell your people to be as you have been. I am old and will soon join my father, but those who come after me will remember this day. It is now treasured up by the old, and will be carried by them to the grave, and then handed down to be kept as a sacred tradition by their children and their children's children.

There is not a drop of my blood in the veins of any creature living, and when I am gone to the happy land, who will mourn for Satank? And now the time has come that I must go. Good by! You may never see me more, but remember Satank as the white man's friend!

When he had finished speaking, Satank shook hands with the commissioners, mounted his pony, and rode off into the plains. A future of peace did not await him or his people. Leaving Medicine Lodge, the American commissioners traveled north and the next spring made peace with the

Sioux at the Treaty of Fort Laramie. The United States agreed to abandon its forts along the Bozeman Trail and guaranteed Sioux hunting rights in unceded territory, but the treaty also established the boundaries of the "Great Sioux Reserve" and contained provisions for acculturation similar to those in the Treaty of Medicine Lodge.[9] The Fort Laramie treaty maintained a fragile peace on the northern plains until the Americans discovered gold in the Black Hills six years later.

The peace established at Medicine Lodge proved short-lived indeed. Congress failed to appropriate funds for the provisions the peace commissioners had promised the southern tribes and, after a hungry winter, young warriors headed for restricted hunting grounds in Kansas. Hostilities soon broke out, and General Sherman moved quickly to punish the "hostile tribes" in 1868. Satank's eldest son was killed during a raid in Texas in 1870; the old man recovered his son's bones, wrapped them in a blanket, and carried them on a pony wherever he went. In May 1871, both Satanta and Satank were arrested for the massacre of a party of Texas teamsters. As he was being taken to jail in an army wagon, Satank sang his death song, tore the manacles from his hands, and seized a soldier's rifle. He was shot to death in a hail of bullets.[10] Satanta was imprisoned in Huntsville, Texas, released for a time, then sent back to jail. In 1878, having been told he would never be released, Satanta committed suicide by jumping from a window of the prison hospital.[11] Ten Bears died in 1872, exhausted after another trip to Washington for talks with the Great Father. The destruction of the buffalo herds on the southern plains and defeat in the Red River War of 1874–75 left southern plains tribes little choice but to accept the way of life that was held out to them at Medicine Lodge.

NOTES

[1] Francis Paul Prucha, ed., *Documents of United States Indian Policy* (Lincoln: University of Nebraska Press, 1975), 105.

[2] Douglas C. Jones, *The Treaty of Medicine Lodge: The Story of the Great Treaty Council as Told by Eyewitnesses* (Norman: University of Oklahoma Press, 1966).

[3] Henry M. Stanley, *My Early Travels and Adventures in America and Asia.* 2 vols. (London: Sampson, Low, Marston and Co., 1895), 1:254–55.

[4] Charles J. Kappler, ed., *Indian Affairs: Laws and Treaties.* 2 vols.(Washington, D.C.: U.S. Govt. Printing Office, 1904), 2:977–84.

[5] Stanley, *My Early Travels and Adventures*, 1:249.

[6] Jones, *Treaty of Medicine Lodge,* 115–16, 135.

[7] Stanley, *My Early Travels and Adventures*, 1:233; Jones, *Treaty of Medicine Lodge*, 205.

[8] Jones, *Treaty of Medicine Lodge*, 157.

[9] Kappler, ed., *Indian Affairs*, 2:998–1003.

[10] Jones, *Treaty of Medicine Lodge*, 158.

[11] Donald Worcester, "Satanta," in R. David Edmunds, ed., *American Indian Leaders: Studies in Diversity* (Lincoln: University of Nebraska Press, 1980), 128–29.

9

The Slaughter of the Buffalo

In the Treaty of Medicine Lodge with the southern plains tribes in 1867 and the Treaty of Fort Laramie with the Sioux in 1868, the United States government guaranteed to the Indians the right to continue hunting on certain lands "so long as the buffalo may range thereon in such numbers as to justify the chase."[1] But even as the American peace commissioners offered the Indians assurances that they would be allowed to continue their buffalo-hunting way of life, the United States was poised to destroy that way of life by systematically slaughtering the buffalo herds.

A variety of species of buffalo once inhabited virtually all of North America. Estimates of buffalo populations in precontact times are usually exaggerated, suggesting as many as sixty million, but to Indians and early whites on the plains the buffalo seemed without number.[2] Indians hunted buffalo on foot for thousands of years before the arrival of the horse, when mounted hunters were able to harvest the vast buffalo herds with unprecedented efficiency. Buffalo provided the Plains Indians with virtually everything they needed: food; tepee skins, robes, and clothing; weapons, tools, utensils, and glue made from horns, bones, and hooves; bags and buckets made from beef paunches or the membranes around the heart; bowstrings made from buffalo gut. Buffalo became the economic foundation of Plains Indian life, figured prominently in religious ceremonies, and were ingrained in the culture. The buffalo herds were the source of Plains Indians' independence and prosperity: Recalling the buffalo-hunting years of his youth, Wooden Leg said, "As I now think back upon those days, it seems that no people in the world ever were any richer than we were."[3]

Unfortunately, the buffalo herds also constituted the Plains Indians' Achilles heel. Unable to defeat elusive equestrian Indian enemies in pitched battle, the United States Army waged war on the animals on which the Indians depended.

Euro-Americans tried to induce Plains Indians to give up buffalo hunting and become farmers almost from the moment they met them.

After defeating the Comanche war leader Cuerno Verde in 1779 and negotiating peace between New Mexico and the Comanches in 1786, Governor Juan Bautista de Anza tried to persuade the Comanches to settle in permanent villages and turn to farming. He had few takers.[4] Confronted with the arguments of Europeans or Americans who sought to save them from their way of life, Plains Indians usually shared the sentiments expressed by the Pawnee chief Sharitarish in Washington in 1822, and by most of the speakers at Medicine Lodge in 1867: They preferred to hunt buffalo so long as there were buffalo to hunt. "The time has not come for us yet to go a-farming," said one Sioux speaker at a council on the North Platte in 1867. "When the game is all gone, I will let [you] know that we are willing." Another said he had eaten wild meat all his life. "My father and grandfather ate wild meat before me. *We cannot give up quickly the customs of our fathers.*" The Crow chief Bear's Tooth said simply to the American commissioners: "Father, you talk about farming, and about raising cattle. I don't want to hear it; I was raised on buffalo, and I love it."[5]

But the way of life Bear's Tooth loved and hoped to preserve, already slipping away, was about to be demolished completely. In fact, recent research has indicated that buffalo populations on the plains were in decline and under serious pressures even before white hunters began to eradicate them. As Indian peoples moved onto the plains in greater numbers, developed new and more efficient buffalo-hunting techniques, and began to hunt for European markets as well as to feed their own people, they seem to have initiated a decline in the herds. At the same time, drought reduced the carrying capacity of the plains and new bovine diseases, such as anthrax, tuberculosis, and brucellosis also thinned the herds. "We have long since noticed the decrease of the buffalo, and we are well aware it cannot last much longer," said the Southern Cheyenne chief Yellow Wolf in 1846. There were reports of Indian people starving by 1850.[6]

After the end of the American Civil War in 1865, the pressures on those Indians who wished to maintain their traditional way of life increased tremendously. Whereas missionaries and others formerly had urged the Indians to give up buffalo-hunting in order to become "civilized," after the war the buffalo herds were targeted for destruction to make room for railroads, ranchers, and settlers and to end Indian resistance by creating starvation and dependency. As industrializing America expanded westward, Indians and buffalo had to make way. Reflecting on the slaughter of the buffalo after the fact, General Nelson Miles justified the carnage:

The buffalo, like the Indian, stood in the way of civilization and in the path of progress, and the decree had gone forth that they must both give way. . . . The same territory which a quarter of a century ago was supporting those vast herds of wild game, is now covered with domestic animals which afford the food supply for hundreds of millions of people in civilized countries.[7]

Generals like William Tecumseh Sherman and Philip Sheridan, who had defeated the Confederacy by waging total war, applied the same strategy in their assaults on Plains Indians and their way of life. Professional hide hunters, sportsmen from the United States and Europe, and the United States Army collaborated to bring the buffalo herds of the Great Plains to the brink of extinction. Sometimes they shot buffalo for sport and left the carcasses to rot on the plains, a practice that enraged Indian people: "Have the white men become children," the Kiowa chief Satanta asked the American commissioners at Medicine Lodge in 1867, "that they should kill meat and not eat?"[8] "You can see that the men who did this were crazy," declared the Oglala holy man Black Elk in his old age according to John G. Neihardt, "they just killed and killed because they liked to do that."[9]

The first transcontinental railroad, completed in 1869, split the great buffalo herds of the plains in two. The southern herd was destroyed in the early 1870s, the northern herd between 1876 and 1883. The Kiowa Apaches had hunted buffalo for countless generations on the southern plains (Figure 13) but when Jim Whitewolf, born about 1878, was a small boy, "there were only antelopes, deer, and wild turkeys. I don't remember any buffalo."[10] As a military measure, killing buffalo was easier than killing Indians and a more effective means of defeating them: Warriors whose families were starving came in to the reservations and accepted government rations. By 1883 the buffalo were almost gone from Blackfoot country, and more than a quarter of the Blackfeet died of starvation the following winter. In 1884 a party of Piegans found and killed four lone buffalo near the Sweetgrass Hills in southwest Saskatchewan. It was the end of an era and the end of a way of life for the Blackfeet: They turned to a life of dependence on the government.[11] By 1895, fewer than one thousand buffalo survived in the United States.[12] The impact on Indian people was devastating. "A cold wind blew across the prairie when the last buffalo fell — a death wind for my people," said Sitting Bull.[13] The Crow chief Plenty Coups recalled that "when the buffalo went away the hearts of my people fell to the ground, and they could not lift them up again. After this nothing happened. There was little singing anymore."[14]

Figure 13. Buffalo Hunting in the Old Days by Howling Wolf

"When I hunted the Buffalo I was not poor . . . but here I am poor. I would like to go out on the planes a gain whare I could rome at will and not come back a gain." — Howling Wolf, back on the reservation after three years of captivity at Fort Marion[15]

FIRST HIDE HUNTERS

Born in the 1860s, Luther Standing Bear grew up as a way of life was falling apart. Known as Plenty Kill when he was a boy, he was raised in the traditional Lakota way but lived through the painful era of transition to a modern world imposed by outsiders. After he graduated from Carlisle Indian School, he published several books on Indian culture and history in the early twentieth century. He recalled how, soon after his first buffalo hunt, his band had to move south from the Dakotas into Nebraska in search of buffalo and there saw at first hand the work of white hide hunters.

LUTHER STANDING BEAR

"The Plains Were Covered with Dead Bison."

Our scouts, who had gone out to locate the buffalo, came back and reported that the plains were covered with dead bison. These had been shot by the white people. The Indians never were such wasteful, wanton killers of this noble game animal. We kept moving, fully expecting soon to run across plenty of live buffalo; but we were disappointed. I saw the bodies of hundreds of dead buffalo lying about, just wasting, and the odor was terrible.

Now we began to see white people living in dugouts, just like wild bears, but without the long snout. These people were dirty. They had hair all over their faces, heads, arms, and hands. This was the first time many of us had ever seen white people, and they were very repulsive to us. None of us had ever seen a gorilla, else we might have thought that Darwin was right concerning these people.

Outside these dugouts we saw bale after bale of buffalo skins, all packed, ready for market. These people were taking away the source of the clothing and lodges that had been provided for us by our Creator, and they were letting our food lie on the plains to rot. They were to receive money for all this, while the Indians were to receive only abuse. We

Luther Standing Bear, *My People the Sioux* (Boston: Houghton Mifflin, 1928), 67–68.

thought these people must be devils, for they had no sympathy. Do you think such treatment was fair to the Indian?

But some of you may say, "Oh, the plains had to be cleared of the buffalo, and that was the only way." That may all be very true; but did you ever stop to think of the thousands of Indians who had to go hungry in consequence of this wholesale slaughter? Why not look at it this way: Suppose a man had a farm with lots of cattle, and it was thought a good idea to build a town on his farm. Should you consider it right if other people had gone in and shot and killed all the farmer's cattle without paying him for the slaughter? No, you would not consider such a proposition fair or just. They would first have to pay the farmer for destroying his herds, so he could buy clothing and food for his family.

When we camped at this place where the dugouts were built, I remember that our mothers told us to hurry and go to sleep, or the hairy men would "get us." We knew they carried long sticks which made a great noise, with which they killed our buffalo. These "sticks" we called "mazawaken," or "holy iron." These people cared nothing for us, and it meant nothing to them to take our lives, even through starvation and cold. This was the beginning of our hatred for the white people. But still we did not kill them.

THE END OF THE BUFFALO ROAD

Born in 1891, Arapaho artist Carl Sweezy learned most of what he knew about buffalo-hunting from stories he heard as a boy. Once independent hunters, the Arapahos were living on government rations and adjusting to a new life as farmers by the time Sweezy was born. Sweezy's life linked the old and new ways of his people: He attended government schools and learned modern techniques in art studios, but he also drew on the traditions of the hide-painters of prereservation days. His paintings often portrayed vivid scenes from the way of life his people once lived. Sweezy's life story reflected the Arapahos' transition from traditional to modern, and their detour from the "buffalo road" they had traveled for generations.

CARL SWEEZY

On Taking "the New Road"

We never killed more buffalo than we could use, to eat and to bring back in the form of hides and robes, dried meat and pemmican and tallow. So, we believed, the Indians and the buffalo would hold out together as long as grass grew. It was white men who slaughtered buffalo without limit, and brought our long-traveled buffalo road to an end. Some of them killed whole herds, for no reason except that they wanted to be rid of them. Men who built railroads and those who wanted to establish farms and towns had no use for them. A good many of these men had no use for Indians either, and the Indians and the buffalo were disappearing together.

The last of our hunts, before Reservation days began, were fights with white men as well. We hated the white men who slaughtered bulls and cows and calves alike and left them to rot on the prairies, and whenever we found them at it we attacked them. They had wagons and mules and camp gear to set up as barricades, and more ammunition than we had. But our horses were better trained than theirs, and we were better riders and sometimes better marksmen. Still, there were too many white men crossing the country to get to California, settling on the land to farm it, and building railroads and bridges. Each year the herds grew fewer and smaller, and our scouts went farther in search of them. By the time of the Medicine Lodge treaty, we had seen signs that the day had come when there would be no more buffalo. We wanted to believe what we had always believed, that the buffalo came up out of a hole in the ground somewhere out on the western Plains and that if we held our dances and used the buffalo as we had been taught to do, there would always be more. But our medicine was gradually losing its power.

After we came to the Reservation, we could not hunt beyond its boundaries. For a few years we still had good hunts, and came in with plenty of meat and robes and hides. The white people at the Agency thought we were irresponsible and lazy, when we left our gardens and field crops to go on the summer hunt, or when we took our children from school to go in winter time. But buffalo came first, in our minds, as long as any were left; we "went to buffalo" when buffalo were plenty, not when crops were laid by or schools dismissed. And since the promised Govern-

Althea Bass, *The Arapaho Way: A Memoir of an Indian Boyhood* (New York: Clarkson N. Potter, 1966), 41–44.

ment issues of food and calico and lodge cloth were often delayed, so that we went cold and hungry while we waited, it is small wonder that, among the older people especially, the buffalo road seemed the one to follow. When I was growing up, old people on the Reservation still remembered those last buffalo hunts as the best thing they had ever known. Sometimes the Indians found white people within the Reservation boundaries, illegally shooting deer and antelope and turkey and prairie chickens, cutting our timber, stealing our horses and cattle. Even then we could not make war on the trespassers because we had pledged ourselves to peace, and the Agents reported that, considering the situation, the crimes we committed were very few. The last good buffalo hunt on the Reservation was in 1874. The next winter was very cold; the hunt was a failure; our lodge skins were worn out and our ponies thin for want of grazing; our annuity goods were long delayed; there was much sickness and hunger and death. Even the Cheyenne, most of whom had refused to send their children to school until then, began to see that they must take the new road. The old one had come to an end.

"WAR BETWEEN THE BUFFALO AND THE WHITE MEN"

According to Kiowa tradition, the buffalo originally lived in a cave underground, from which they had been released by the Kiowas' great hero Sinti and scattered over the plains for the benefit of his Indian children. The destruction of the buffalo herds reduced the Kiowas to eating their horses to prevent starvation. For many Indian people the mass slaughter of the buffalo was a calamity too terrible to comprehend, and instead they explained it in traditional terms: The white man had shut the buffalo underground once more so as to be able to subjugate the Indians; but they could be released again by prayer and sacred ceremony. A Kiowa calendar shows that in the summer of 1882 a young medicine man endeavored to make the buffalo return.[16] As this Kiowa woman's account of the passing of the buffalo indicates, such measures were in vain.

OLD LADY HORSE

The Last Buffalo Herd

Everything the Kiowas had came from the buffalo. Their tipis were made of buffalo hides, so were their clothes and moccasins. They ate buffalo meat. Their containers were made of hide, or of bladders or stomachs. The buffalo were the life of the Kiowas.

Most of all, the buffalo was part of the Kiowa religion. A white buffalo calf must be sacrificed in the Sun Dance. The priests used parts of the buffalo to make their prayers when they healed people or when they sang to the powers above.

So, when the white men wanted to build railroads, or when they wanted to farm or raise cattle, the buffalo still protected the Kiowas. They tore up the railroad tracks and the gardens. They chased the cattle off the ranges. The buffalo loved their people as much as the Kiowas loved them.

There was war between the buffalo and the white men. The white men built forts in the Kiowa country, and the woolly-headed buffalo soldiers [the Tenth Cavalry, made up of Negro troops] shot the buffalo as fast as they could, but the buffalo kept coming on, coming on, even into the post cemetery at Fort Sill. Soldiers were not enough to hold them back.

Then the white men hired hunters to do nothing but kill the buffalo. Up and down the plains those men ranged, shooting sometimes as many as a hundred buffalo a day. Behind them came the skinners with their wagons. They piled the hides and bones into the wagons until they were full, and then took their loads to the new railroad stations that were being built, to be shipped east to the market. Sometimes there would be a pile of bones as high as a man, stretching a mile along the railroad track.

The buffalo saw that their day was over. They could protect their people no longer. Sadly, the last remnant of the great herd gathered in council, and decided what they would do.

The Kiowas were camped on the north side of Mount Scott, those of them who were still free to camp. One young woman got up very early in the morning. The dawn mist was still rising from Medicine Creek, and as she looked across the water, peering through the haze, she saw the last buffalo herd appear like a spirit dream.

Alice Marriott and Carol K. Rachlin, *American Indian Mythology* (New York: Thomas Y. Crowell, 1968), 169–70.

Straight to Mount Scott the leader of the herd walked. Behind him came the cows and their calves, and the few young males who had survived. As the woman watched, the face of the mountain opened.

Inside Mount Scott the world was green and fresh, as it had been when she was a small girl. The rivers ran clear, not red. The wild plums were in blossom, chasing the red buds up the inside slopes. Into this world of beauty the buffalo walked, never to be seen again.

"THEY STARED AT THE PLAINS, AS THOUGH DREAMING."

Like the Crow warrior Two Leggings, who refused to talk about life after the days of intertribal warfare, the Crow woman Pretty Shield had little to say about her life after the buffalo disappeared except that once mobile and active people became sedentary and idle. However, toward the end of her life story as related to Frank Linderman, the old woman did respond to the question of how old she was when the buffalo had gone.

PRETTY SHIELD

When the Buffalo Went Away

"Tst, tst, tst! I haven't seen a buffalo in more than forty years," she said slowly, as though she believed herself to be dreaming.

"The happiest days of my life were spent following the buffalo herds over our beautiful country. My mother and father and Goes-ahead, my man, were all kind, and we were so happy. Then, when my children came I believed I had everything that was good on this world. There were always so many, many buffalo, plenty of good fat meat for everybody.

"Since my man, Goes-ahead, went away twelve snows ago my heart has been falling down. I am old now, and alone, with so many grandchildren to watch," . . .

"Tell me what happened when the buffalo went away," I urged.

Frank B. Linderman, *Pretty-shield, Medicine Woman of the Crows* (Lincoln: University of Nebraska Press, 1972), 248–51.

"Sickness came, strange sickness that nobody knew about, when there was no meat," she said, covering her face with both hands as though to shut out the sight of suffering. "My daughter stepped into a horse's track that was deep in the dried clay, and hurt her ankle. I could not heal her; nobody could. The white doctor told me that the same sickness that makes people cough themselves to death was in my daughter's ankle. I did not believe it, and yet she died, leaving six little children. Then my other daughter died, and left hers. These things would not have happened if we Crows had been living as we were intended to live. But how could we live in the old way when everything was gone?

"Ahh, my heart fell down when I began to see dead buffalo scattered all over our beautiful country, killed and skinned, and left to rot by white men, many, many hundreds of buffalo. The first I saw of this was in the Judith basin. The whole country there smelled of rotting meat. Even the flowers could not put down the bad smell. Our hearts were like stones. And yet nobody believed, even then, that the white man could kill *all* the buffalo. Since the beginning of things there had always been so many! Even the Lacota, bad as their hearts were for us, would not do such a thing as this; nor the Cheyenne, nor the Arapahoe, nor the Pecunnie; and yet the white man did this, even when he did not want the meat.

"We believed for a long time that the buffalo would again come to us; but they did not. We grew hungry and sick and afraid, all in one. Not believing their own eyes our hunters rode very far looking for buffalo, so far away that even if they had found a herd we could not have reached it in half a moon. 'Nothing; we found nothing,' they told us; and then, hungry, they stared at the empty plains, as though dreaming. After this their hearts were no good any more. If the Great White Chief in Washington had not given us food we should have been wiped out without even a chance to fight for ourselves.

"And then white men began to fence the plains so that we could not travel; and anyhow there was now little good in traveling, nothing to travel for. We began to stay in one place, and to grow lazy and sicker all the time. Our men had fought hard against our enemies, holding them back from our beautiful country by their bravery; but now, with everything else going wrong, we began to be whipped by weak foolishness. Our men, our leaders, began to drink the white man's whisky, letting it do their thinking. Because we were used to listening to our chiefs in the buffalo days, the days of war and excitement, we listened to them now; and we got whipped. Our wise-ones became fools, and drank the white man's whisky. But what else was there for us to do? We knew no other way than to listen to our chiefs and head men. Our old men used to be different; even our children were different when the buffalo were here."

NOTES

[1] Charles J. Kappler, ed., *Indian Affairs: Laws and Treaties*. 2 vols. (Washington, D.C.: U.S. Govt. Printing Office, 1904), 2:1002.

[2] The standard work on the buffalo, its place in Indian life, and its destruction is Frank Gilbert Roe, *The North American Buffalo: A Critical Study of the Species in Its Wild State* (Toronto: University of Toronto Press, 1970).

[3] Thomas B. Marquis, interpreter, *Wooden Leg, A Warrior Who Fought Custer* (Minneapolis: The Midwest Co., 1931), 35.

[4] Dan Flores, "Bison Ecology and Bison Diplomacy: The Southern Plains, 1800–1850," *Journal of American History* 78 (1991), 465.

[5] Henry M. Stanley, *My Early Travels and Adventures in America and Asia*. 2 vols. (London: Sampson, Low, Marston and Co., 1895), 1:203, 204, 270.

[6] Flores, "Bison Ecology and Bison Diplomacy," 465–85. Yellow Wolf's speech is in Appendix to Report of the Commissioner of Indian Affairs, 1847, Senate Executive Document, No. 1, 30th Congress, 1st session, p. 242, and quoted in Stan Hoig, *The Peace Chiefs of the Cheyennes* (Norman: University of Oklahoma Press, 1980), 32–33.

[7] David D. Smits, "The Frontier Army and the Destruction of the Buffalo: 1865–1883," *Western Historical Quarterly* 25 (1994), 313–38; quote at 333. William A. Dobak questions Smits's evidence of Army involvement in the destruction in *Western Historical Quarterly* 26 (1995), 197–202.

[8] Stanley, *My Early Travels and Adventures,* 1:228–29.

[9] John G. Neihardt, *Black Elk Speaks: Being the Life Story of a Holy Man of the Oglala Sioux* (Lincoln: University of Nebraska Press, 1988 ed.), 213.

[10] Charles S. Brant, ed. *The Autobiography of a Kiowa Apache* (New York: Dover Publications, 1991 ed.), 52.

[11] John C. Ewers, *Indian Life on the Upper Missouri* (Norman: University of Oklahoma Press, 1968), 173.

[12] Russell Thornton, *American Indian Holocaust and Survival* (Norman: University of Oklahoma Press, 1987), 52.

[13] Smits, "The Frontier Army and the Destruction of the Buffalo," 338.

[14] Frank B. Linderman, *Plenty Coups, Chief of the Crows* (Lincoln: University of Nebraska Press, 1962), 311.

[15] Karen Daniels Peterson, *Howling Wolf: A Cheyenne Warrior's Graphic Interpretation of His People* (Palo Alto, Cal.: American West Publishing Co., 1968), 21.

[16] James Mooney, "Calendar History of the Kiowa Indians," *17th Annual Report of the Bureau of American Ethnology,* 1895–96, part 1 (Washington, D.C.: U.S. Govt. Printing Office, 1898), 349.

10

The Battle on
the Greasy Grass, 1876

Few conflicts in American history are more famous than the Battle of the Little Big Horn, or the Greasy Grass as the Sioux called it. Few moments in American history are as clearly etched in the popular imagination as the last stand of Lieutenant Colonel George Armstrong Custer and his Seventh Cavalry. The image of Custer and his gallant band surrounded by hordes of Indian warriors has served as a symbol of Indian-white conflict, of "civilization" battling "savagery," of America's frontier identity. Yet the enduring image of the last stand — promoted and perpetuated by generations of writers, artists, and movie makers — is one created by people who were not there. This chapter reproduces several views of the battle by people who lived through it and told their stories in later life: an Arikara scout for the Seventh Cavalry; a Cheyenne warrior; a Sioux council chief; a Sioux who was fourteen years old at the time; and a Sioux woman who recalled the battle from the viewpoint of the village the soldiers attacked.

In the winter of 1875–76, in violation of the 1868 Treaty of Fort Laramie, the government pressured the Sioux to sell the sacred Black Hills and to leave the Powder River country and go to the reservation. Sitting Bull, Crazy Horse, and their followers resisted. In the spring of 1876, the United States Army launched a campaign to drive the "hostile" bands of Sioux and Cheyennes off the plains and onto the reservation. Some 2,500 men advanced in three columns, to catch the Indians in their pincers. The Oglala Sioux chief Red Cloud warned General George Crook what to expect: The Sioux had many warriors, guns, and ponies, he said. "They are brave and ready to fight for their country. They are not afraid of the soldiers nor of their chief. Many braves are ready to meet them. Every lodge will send its young men, and they will all say of the Great Father's dogs, 'Let them come.' "[1] Crazy Horse fought Crook to a standstill at the Battle of the Rosebud in June. Meanwhile, Custer and about five hundred troops headed for the Little Big Horn River in southeastern Montana and the Indian village that was reported to be in the area. Disregarding the warnings of his Crow and Arikara scouts about the immense size of the village, Custer divided his command and ordered an attack on the morning of June 25. Captain Frederick Benteen led three companies — about 125 men — to scout the hills overlooking the Indian village. Major Marcus Reno attacked the southern end of the village. Custer and five companies — about 210 men — swung north to attack the village from the opposite end.

Things quickly went wrong. The soldiers were attacking one of the largest encampments ever encountered on the plains, and soon were fighting for their lives against as many as 2,500 warriors. Recovering from their initial surprise, the Indians quickly routed Reno's command and pinned the survivors down in a defensive position above the river. When Benteen came up he could do no more than dig in alongside Reno's beleaguered troops. Then most of the Indians swung away to meet Custer's threat at the other end of the village. In less than an hour they overwhelmed and annihilated Custer's entire command. "It took about as long as a hungry man to eat his dinner," recalled Cheyenne chief Two Moons in later life.[2] "I feel sorry that too many were killed on each side," said Sitting Bull, "but when Indians must fight, they must."[3] The United States had suffered a humiliating defeat in the year of its centennial celebrations, and the Army's grand campaign lay in shambles.

In the years after the battle, Indian participants were reluctant to talk openly about their experiences, fearing retribution. Those who were interviewed often were evasive and only gave answers about troop movements and specific incidents. The narratives and pictures reprinted in this chapter are not intended to give a complete account of the battle, nor do they offer the full story from the Indians' perspective. All of the participants had only a partial view of what was going on. Some of the accounts show evidence of hindsight; some no doubt were recounted with a white audience very much in mind. But they do present views of the battle by some of the Indian people involved, and they offer more realistic images of the conflict than that which has dominated the national mythology for so long.[4]

The United States Army held investigations and courts of inquiry to establish responsibility for the disaster. Military historians have long debated the reasons for Custer's defeat, sometimes going into minute detail and timing movements with impressive precision.[5] For many Indian people, however, the reasons for their victory were quite simple. During a sun dance in which he sacrificed one hundred pieces of his own flesh, Sitting Bull had a vision in which he saw soldiers falling into camp without ears. For the Sioux, the victory on the Greasy Grass was religiously sanctioned and divinely ordained.[6] Pretty Shield, whose husband, Goes Ahead, was one of Custer's Crow scouts, hinted at something similar: Custer, she said, "was like a feather blown by the wind, and *had* to go. . . . He *had* to fight, because he *had* to die."[7]

SIOUX SIGNS AND ARIKARA PREMONITIONS

The Battle of the Little Big Horn stands as the classic Indian-white conflict. It is easy to forget that it was also an Indian-Indian conflict, in which Crows and Arikaras served as scouts and allies for U.S. forces against Sioux and Cheyenne enemies.[8] Like the Crows, the Arikaras had good reason to serve with the Americans. Even after the Arikaras, Mandans, and Hidatsas congregated in Like-a-Fishook village on the Fort Berthold reservation in the wake of the 1837 smallpox epidemic, the Sioux continued to raid them. About forty Arikaras enlisted as scouts for the 1876 campaign. The Army also hired two interpreters: Frederick Gerard, an Indian trader who was post interpreter at Fort Lincoln, and Isaiah Dorman, an African American married to a Sioux woman. When the scouts first cut the Sioux trail, Gerard told them to sing their death songs.

The narratives of the surviving Arikara scouts, collected and recorded in 1912, offer an additional dimension to the view of the Little Big Horn as simply a clash between the Sioux and the Seventh Cavalry. The following selection from the narrative of Red Star (known at the time of the battle as Strikes the Bear) shows Indian scouts reading "Indian signs" as the cavalry approached their objective. The Arikaras sensed that the Sioux had powerful medicine and realized that Custer was heading into combat with an enemy that was both powerful and confident of a victory. Many of the Arikara scouts were young and inexperienced. They spat on clay they had brought from their homeland and rubbed it on their chests as good medicine. But the thin line of Arikaras fighting on the left of Reno's men was overwhelmed by the Sioux. Bloody Knife, known as Custer's favorite scout, had his brains blown out. Bob-tailed Bull died surrounded by circling Sioux warriors.[9] The Arikaras' premonitions had been well founded.

RED STAR

Reading the Sioux Signs

Next morning . . . the bugle sounded and we saddled up, Custer ahead, the scouts following and flanking the army that marched behind. Bob-tailed Bull was in charge, with Strikes Two and others on one side. About nightfall they came to an abandoned Dakota camp where there were signs of a sun dance circle. Here there was evidence of the Dakotas having made medicine, the sand had been arranged and smoothed, and pictures had been drawn. The Dakota scouts in Custer's army said that this meant the enemy knew the army was coming. In one of the sweat lodges was a long heap or ridge of sand. On this one Red Bear, Red Star, and Soldier saw figures drawn indicating by hoof prints Custer's men on one side and the Dakota on the other. Between them dead men were drawn lying with their heads toward the Dakotas. The Arikara scouts understood this to mean that the Dakota medicine was too strong for them and that they would be defeated by the Dakotas. Here they camped, the scouts at the left on the right bank under Bob-tailed Bull. They brought in two Dakota horses which had been discovered by Strikes Two. Bob-tailed Bull brought in one of them, a bald-faced bay, and Little Brave brought in the other, a black with white on the forehead (this indicated that the Dakotas had hurried away from the camp in great haste). On the right bank of the Rosebud as they marched they saw Dakota inscriptions on the sandstone of the hills at their left. One of these inscriptions showed two buffalo fighting, and various interpretations were given by the Arikara as to the meaning of these figures. Young Hawk saw in one of the sweat lodges, where they had camped, opposite the entrance, three stones near the middle, all in a row and painted red. This meant in Dakota sign language that the Great Spirit had given them victory, and that if the whites did not come they would seek them. Soldier saw offerings, four sticks standing upright with a buffalo calfskin tied on with cloth and other articles of value, which was evidence of a great religious service. This was also seen by Strikes Two, Little Sioux, and Boy Chief. All the Arikara knew what this meant, namely, that the Dakotas were sure of winning. Soldier said he heard later that Sitting Bull had performed the ceremonies here in this camp. After they passed this inscription of

O. G. Libby, ed., "The Arikara Narrative of the Campaign Against the Hostile Dakotas, June 1876," *North Dakota State Historical Society Collections* 6 (1920): 75–80.

the two buffaloes charging, they came to the fork of the Rosebud River (about where the Cheyennes are now located). Six of the Crow scouts with their interpreter had been out scouting and they returned at this camp. They reported many abandoned Dakota camps along the Rosebud. The whole army stopped here and ate dinner on a hill.

REPELLING RENO

The Northern Cheyenne warrior Wooden Leg provided one of the fullest accounts of the Battle of the Little Big Horn. Cheyenne tribal historian John Stands in Timber said that Wooden Leg erred in some of his statements and that he later retracted his claim that many of the soldiers were drunk and committed suicide.[10] Nevertheless, Wooden Leg's narrative is extremely valuable for the picture it affords of Indian warriors fighting out of their village to defend homes and families against enemy assault. It also conveys some of the confusion of the conflict as the Indians recovered from their surprise and rushed to repulse Reno's thrust.

WOODEN LEG

A Cheyenne Account of the Battle

In my sleep I dreamed that a great crowd of people were making lots of noise. Something in the noise startled me. I found myself wide awake, sitting up and listening. My brother too awakened, and we both jumped to our feet. A great commotion was going on among the camps. We heard shooting. We hurried out from the trees so we might see as well as hear. The shooting was somewhere at the upper part of the camp circles. It looked as if all of the Indians there were running away toward the hills to the westward or down toward our end of the village. Women were screaming and men were letting out war cries. Through it all we could hear old men calling:

"Soldiers are here! Young men, go out and fight them."

We ran to our camp and to our home lodge. Everybody there was

Thomas B. Marquis, *Wooden Leg: A Warrior Who Fought Custer* (Minneapolis: The Midwest Co., 1931), 217–21.

excited. Women were hurriedly making up little packs for flight. Some were going off northward or across the river without any packs. Children were hunting for their mothers. Mothers were anxiously trying to find their children. I got my lariat and my six shooter. I hastened on down toward where had been our horse herd. I came across three of our herder boys. One of them was catching grasshoppers. The other two were cooking fish in the blaze of a little fire. I told them what was going on and asked them where were the horses. They jumped on their picketed ponies and dashed for the camp, without answering me. Just then I heard Bald Eagle calling out to hurry with the horses. Two other boys were driving them toward the camp circle. I was utterly winded from the running. I never was much for running. I could walk all day, but I could not run fast nor far. I walked on back to the home lodge.

My father had caught my favorite horse from the herd brought in by the boys and Bald Eagle. I quickly emptied out my war bag and set myself at getting ready to go into battle. I jerked off my ordinary clothing. I jerked on a pair of new breeches that had been given to me by an Uncpapa Sioux. I had a good cloth shirt, and I put it on. My old moccasins were kicked off and a pair of beaded moccasins substituted for them. My father strapped a blanket upon my horse and arranged the rawhide lariat into a bridle. He stood holding my mount.

"Hurry," he urged me.

I was hurrying, but I was not yet ready. I got my paints and my little mirror. The blue-black circle soon appeared around my face. The red and yellow colorings were applied on all of the skin inside the circle. I combed my hair. It properly should have been oiled and braided neatly, but my father again was saying, "Hurry," so I just looped a buckskin thong about it and tied it close up against the back of my head, to float loose from there. My bullets, caps, and powder horn put me into full readiness. In a moment afterward I was on my horse and was going as fast as it could run toward where all of the rest of the young men were going. My brother already had gone. He got his horse before I got mine, and his dressing was only a long buckskin shirt fringed with Crow Indian hair. The hair had been taken from a Crow at a past battle with them.

The air was so full of dust I could not see where to go. But it was not needful that I see that far. I kept my horse headed in the direction of movement by the crowd of Indians on horseback. I was led out around and far beyond the Uncpapa camp circle. Many hundreds of Indians on horseback were dashing to and fro in front of a body of soldiers. The soldiers were on the level valley ground and were shooting with rifles. Not many bullets were being sent back at them, but thousands of arrows

Figure 14. Seizing a Soldier's Gun at the Battle of the Little Big Horn
Drawn by Wooden Leg.

were falling among them. I went on with a throng of Sioux until we got
beyond and behind the white men. By this time, though, they had
mounted their horses and were hiding themselves in the timber. A band
of Indians were with the soldiers. It appeared they were Crows or
Shoshones. Most of these Indians had fled back up the valley. Some were
across east of the river and were riding away over the hills beyond.
Our Indians crowded down toward the timber where were the soldiers. More and more of our people kept coming. Almost all of them
were Sioux. There were only a few Cheyennes. Arrows were showered
into the timber. Bullets whistled out toward the Sioux and Cheyennes.
But we stayed far back while we extended our curved line farther and
farther around the big grove of trees. Some dead soldiers had been left
among the grass and sagebrush where first they had fought us. It
seemed to me the remainder of them would not live many hours longer.
Sioux were creeping forward to set fire to the timber.
Suddenly the hidden soldiers came tearing out on horseback, from the
woods. I was around on that side where they came out. I whirled my horse
and lashed it into a dash to escape from them. All others of my companions did the same. But soon we discovered they were not following us.

They were running away from us. They were going as fast as their tired horses could carry them across an open valley space and toward the river. We stopped, looked a moment, and then we whipped our ponies into swift pursuit. A great throng of Sioux also were coming after them. My distant position put me among the leaders in the chase. The soldier horses moved slowly, as if they were very tired. Ours were lively. We gained rapidly on them.

I fired four shots with my six shooter. I do not know whether or not any of my bullets did harm. I saw a Sioux put an arrow into the back of a soldier's head. Another arrow went into his shoulder. He tumbled from his horse to the ground. Others fell dead either from arrows or from stabbings or jabbings or from blows by the stone war clubs of the Sioux. Horses limped or staggered or sprawled out dead or dying. Our war cries and war songs were mingled with many jeering calls, such as:

"You are only boys. You ought not to be fighting. We whipped you on the Rosebud. You should have brought more Crows or Shoshones with you to do your fighting."

Little Bird and I were after one certain soldier. Little Bird was wearing a trailing warbonnet. He was at the right and I was at the left of the fleeing man. We were lashing him and his horse with our pony whips. It seemed not brave to shoot him. Besides, I did not want to waste my bullets. He pointed back his revolver, though, and sent a bullet into Little Bird's thigh. Immediately I whacked the white man fighter on his head with the heavy elk-horn handle of my pony whip. The blow dazed him. I seized the rifle strapped on his back [Figure 14]. I wrenched it and dragged the looping strap over his head. As I was getting possession of this weapon he fell to the ground. I did not harm him further. I do not know what became of him. The jam of oncoming Indians swept me on. But I had now a good soldier rifle.

RED HORSE:
PICTORIAL RECORD OF THE BATTLE

In 1881, just five years after the event, Dr. Charles E. McChesney, Acting Assistant Surgeon, United States Army, at the Cheyenne River reservation in South Dakota, persuaded a Miniconjou warrior named Red Horse to produce a set of drawings of the battle. Red Horse, who described himself as a "chief in the council lodge" at the time of the fight, made forty-two drawings, the largest pictorial record of the conflict. McChesney sent the drawings to Garrick Mallery, who published some

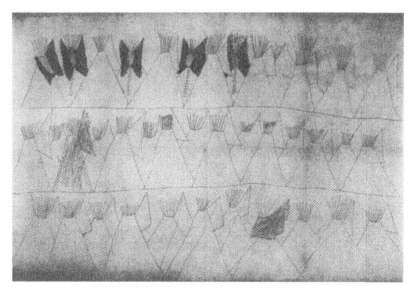

Figure 15.   The Indian Village in the Valley of the Little Big Horn

Figure 16.   Soldiers Charging the Indian Village

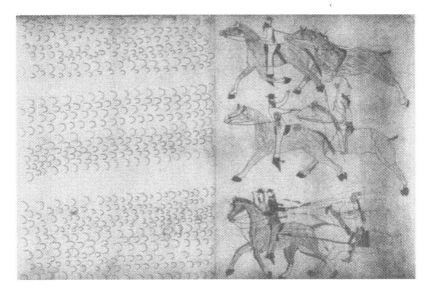

Figure 17.   Repulsing the Attack, as Indicated by the Cavalry Being Forced Back over Their Own Hoofprints

"All the Sioux now charged the soldiers and drove them in confusion across the river," said Red Horse.[11]

Figure 18.   The Sioux Fighting Custer's Command

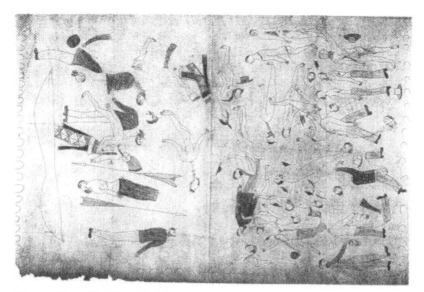

Figure 19.   The Dead Soldiers and Indians

Figure 20.   The Indians Leaving the Battlefield as They Hear that Relief Columns of Infantry Are Approaching

of them in his study of Indian picture writing, along with Red Horse's own account of the battle.[12] Many of the drawings depict similar episodes (there are five pages of soldiers approaching the village, for example), or generic fighting rather than specific actions. The six drawings reproduced here (Figures 15–20), convey the flow of events and suggest the battle had elements of a rout rather than of a heroic last stand. Like Wooden Leg, Red Horse suggested that many of the soldiers "became foolish" and, throwing away their guns, begged the Sioux for mercy.[13]

"THE SOLDIERS WERE ALL RUBBED OUT."

The cavalry's attack on their village brought youths as well as seasoned warriors into the fight. Iron Hawk, a Hunkpapa Sioux, was fourteen years old in June 1876. Many years later, in 1931, as John G. Neihardt interviewed Black Elk, Iron Hawk and other veterans of the battle listened and offered their own comments. Iron Hawk gave this account of his participation in the final stages of the fight on "Custer Hill."

IRON HAWK

Killing Custer's Men

By now a big cry was going up all around the soldiers up there and the warriors were coming from everywhere and it was getting dark with dust and smoke.

We saw soldiers start running down hill right towards us. Nearly all of them were afoot, and I think they were so scared that they didn't know what they were doing. They were making their arms go as though they were running very fast, but they were only walking. Some of them shot their guns in the air. We all yelled "Hoka hey!" and charged toward them, riding all around them in the twilight that had fallen on us.

I met a soldier on horseback, and I let him have it. The arrow went through from side to side under his ribs and it stuck out on both sides.

John G. Neihardt, *Black Elk Speaks: Being the Life Story of a Holy Man of the Oglala Sioux* (Lincoln: University of Nebraska Press, 1988 ed.), 119–25.

He screamed and took hold of his saddle horn and hung on, wobbling, with his head hanging down. I kept along beside him, and I took my heavy bow and struck him across the back of the neck. He fell from his saddle, and I got off and beat him to death with my bow. I kept on beating him awhile after he was dead, and every time I hit him I said "Hownh!" I was mad, because I was thinking of the women and little children running down there, all scared and out of breath. These Wasichus wanted it, and they came to get it, and we gave it to them. I did not see much more. I saw Brings Plenty kill a soldier with a war club. I saw Red Horn Buffalo fall. There was a Lakota riding along the edge of the gulch, and he was yelling to look out, that there was a soldier hiding in there. I saw him charge in and kill the soldier and begin slashing him with a knife.

Then we began to go towards the river, and the dust was lifting so that we could see the women and children coming over to us from across the river. The soldiers were all rubbed out there and scattered around.

The women swarmed up the hill and began stripping the soldiers. They were yelling and laughing and singing now. I saw something funny. Two fat old women were stripping a soldier, who was wounded and playing dead. When they had him naked, they began to cut something off that he had, and he jumped up and began fighting with the two fat women. He was swinging one of them around, while the other was trying to stab him with her knife. After awhile, another woman rushed up and shoved her knife into him and he died really dead. It was funny to see the naked Wasichu fighting with the fat women.

By now we saw that our warriors were all charging on some soldiers that had come from the hill up river to help the second band that we had rubbed out. They ran back and we followed, chasing them up on their hill again where they had their pack mules. We could not hurt them much there, because they had been digging to hide themselves and they were lying behind saddles and other things. I was down by the river and I saw some soldiers come down there with buckets. They had no guns, just buckets. Some boys were down there, and they came out of the brush and threw mud and rocks in the soldiers' faces and chased them into the river. I guess they got enough to drink, for they are drinking yet. We killed them in the water.

Afterwhile it was nearly sundown, and I went home with many others to eat, while some others stayed to watch the soldiers on the hill. I hadn't eaten all day, because the trouble started just when I was beginning to eat my first meal.

"THE WOMEN AND CHILDREN CRIED."

Most accounts of the Battle of the Little Big Horn are written — and most movies filmed — from the perspective of the attackers as they advance toward and then recoil from their objective. Rarely do we get a view of the battle from the village in the valley. The wife of the Hunkpapa warrior Spotted Horn Bull related her story of the fight to the St. Paul *Pioneer Press* in 1883 and again, when she was in her sixties, to Major James McLaughlin, formerly Indian agent at Standing Rock reservation, who knew her well.[14] McLaughlin reprinted her account in his book, *My Friend the Indian,* published in 1910. When Walter Campbell (pen name Stanley Vestal) was doing field work among the Sioux, some of the Hunkpapa men complained that McLaughlin had taken his account of the battle from a woman, rather than from a warrior who was in the fight: "In their opinion war is the business of a man and not a thing which women should be quoted on."[15] As McLaughlin pointed out, however, Mrs. Spotted Horn Bull was there, she had a remarkable memory, and she was eloquent. The male veterans of the battle may have had a clearer grasp of the fighting outside the village, but they could not share her memories of what it meant to be a noncombatant in the village while the battle raged.

MRS. SPOTTED HORN BULL

A View from the Village

Like that the soldiers were upon us. Through the tepee poles their bullets rattled. The sun was several hours high and the tepees were empty. Bullets coming from a strip of timber on the west bank of the Greasy Grass passed through the tepees of the Blackfeet and Hunkpapa. The broken character of the country across the river, together with the fringe of trees on the west side, where our camp was situated, had hidden the advance of a great number of soldiers, which we had not seen until they were close upon us and shooting into our end of the village, where, from seeing the direction taken by the soldiers we were watching, we felt comparatively secure.

The women and children cried, fearing they would be killed, but the men, the Hunkpapa and Blackfeet, the Oglala and Minniconjou, mounted

James McLaughlin, *My Friend the Indian* (Boston: Houghton Mifflin, 1910), 167–72.

their horses and raced to the Blackfeet tepees. We could still see the soldiers of Long Hair marching along in the distance, and our men, taken by surprise, and from a point whence they had not expected to be attacked, went singing the song of battle into the fight behind the Blackfeet village. And we women wailed over the children, for we believed that the Great Father had sent all his men for the destruction of the Sioux. Some of the women put loads on the travois and would have left, but that their husbands and sons were in the fight. Others tore their hair and wept for the fate that they thought was to be the portion of the Sioux, through the anger of the Great Father, but the men were not afraid, and they had many guns and cartridges. Like the fire that, driven by a great wind, sweeps through the heavy grass-land where the buffalo range, the men of the Hunkpapa, the Blackfeet, the Oglala, and the Minniconjou rushed through the village and into the trees, where the soldiers of the white chief had stopped to fire. The soldiers [Reno's] had been sent by Long Hair to surprise the village of my people. Silently had they moved off around the hills, and keeping out of sight of the young men of our people, had crept in, south of what men now call Reno Hill; they had crossed the Greasy Grass and climbed the bench from the bank. The way from the river to the plateau upon which our tepees stood was level, but the soldiers were on foot when they came in sight of the Blackfeet. Then it was that they fired and warned us of their approach. . . .

The shadow of the sun had not moved the width of a tepee pole's length from the beginning to the ending of the first fight; . . . Even the women, who knew nothing of warfare, saw that Reno had struck too early, and the warriors who were generals in planning, even as Long Hair was, knew that the white chief would attempt to carry out his plan of the attack, believing that Reno had beaten our young men. There was wild disorder in our camp, the old women and children shrieked and got in the way of the warriors, and the women were ordered back out of the village, so that they might not be in the way of our soldiers. And our men went singing down the river, confident that the enemy would be defeated, even as we believed that all of Reno's men had been killed. And I wept with the women for the brave dead and exulted that our braves should gain a great victory over the whites led by Long Hair, who was the greatest of their chiefs, and whose soldiers could then be plainly seen across the river. From a hill behind the camp, at first, and then from the bank of the river, I watched the men of our people plan to overthrow the soldiers of the Great Father; and before a shot was fired, I knew that no man who rode with Long Hair would go back to tell the tale of the fight that would begin when the soldiers approached the river at the lower end of the village. . . .

From across the river I could hear the music of the bugle and could see the column of soldiers turn to the left, to march down to the river to where the attack was to be made. All I could see was the warriors of my people. They rushed like the wind through the village, going down the ravine as the women went out to the grazing-ground to round up the ponies. It was done very quickly. There had been no council the night before — there was no need for one; nor had there been a scalp-dance: nothing but the merry-making of the young men and the maidens. When we did not know there was to be a fight, we could not be prepared for it. And our camp was not pitched anticipating a battle. The warriors would not have picked out such a place for a fight with white men, open to attack from both ends and from the west side. No; what was done that day was done while the sun stood still and the white men were delivered into the hands of the Sioux. . . .

I cannot remember the time. When men fight and the air is filled with bullets, when the screaming of horses that are shot drowns the war-whoop of the warriors, a woman whose husband and brothers are in the battle does not think of the time. But the sun was no longer overhead when the war-whoop of the Sioux sounded from the river-bottom and the ravine surrounding the hill at the end of the ridge where Long Hair had taken his last stand. The river was in sight from the butte, and while the whoop still rung in our ears and the women were shrieking, two Cheyennes tried to cross the river and one of them was shot and killed by Long Hair's men. Then the men of the Sioux nation, led by Crow King, Hump, Crazy Horse, and many great chiefs, rose up on all sides of the hill, and the last we could see from our side of the river was a great number of gray horses. The smoke of the shooting and the dust of the horses shut out the hill, and the soldiers fired many shots, but the Sioux shot straight and the soldiers fell dead. The women crossed the river after the men of our village, and when we came to the hill there were no soldiers living and Long Hair lay dead among the rest. There were more than two hundred dead soldiers on the hill, and the boys of the village shot many who were already dead, for the blood of the people was hot and their hearts bad, and they took no prisoners that day.

NOTES

1 James C. Olson, *Red Cloud and the Sioux Problem* (Lincoln: University of Nebraska Press, 1965), 218.

2 James Welch, *Killing Custer: The Battle of the Little Big Horn and the Fate of the Plains Indians* (New York: Penguin, 1995), 175, 294.

[3] Robert M. Utley, *The Lance and the Shield: The Life and Times of Sitting Bull* (New York: Henry Holt and Co., 1993), 161.

[4] In recent years, scholars have paid increasing attention to Indian accounts of the battle. See, for example, Jerome A. Greene, ed., *Lakota and Cheyenne: Indian Views of the Great Sioux War, 1876–1877* (Norman: University of Oklahoma Press, 1994).

[5] For example, John S. Gray, *Custer's Last Campaign: Mitch Boyer and the Little Big Horn Reconstructed* (Lincoln: University of Nebraska Press, 1991).

[6] Raymond J. DeMallie, "'These Have No Ears': Narrative and the Ethnohistorical Method," *Ethnohistory* 40 (1993), 515–38. The fact that the soldiers in the vision lacked ears refers to their unwillingness to heed Sioux warnings, rather than to mutilation of their bodies.

[7] Frank B. Linderman, *Pretty-shield: Medicine Woman of the Crows* (Lincoln: University of Nebraska Press, 1972), 235.

[8] Colin G. Calloway, "Army Allies or Tribal Survival?: The 'Other' Indians in the 1876 Campaign," in Charles E. Rankin, ed. *Legacy: New Perspectives on the Little Battle of Bighorn* (Helena: Montana Historical Society, 1996).

[9] O. G. Libby, ed., "The Arikara Narrative of the Campaign Against the Hostile Dakotas, June 1876," *Collections of the North Dakota State Historical Society* 6 (1920), 11–12, 84. The names of the Arikara scouts are given on 49–51; biographies of some of the scouts are on 177–209. See also David Humphreys Miller, *Custer's Fall: The Indian Side of the Story* (London: Corgi Books, 1953), 27–28.

[10] John Stands in Timber and Margot Liberty, *Cheyenne Memories* (Lincoln: University of Nebraska Press, 1972), 205. Wooden Leg's statements relating to whiskey and suicide are in Thomas B. Marquis, *Wooden Leg: A Warrior Who Fought Custer* (Minneapolis: The Midwest Co., 1931), 231–32, 246. Another Northern Cheyenne, Soldier Wolf, also said the soldiers acted drunk or panic-stricken. Greene, ed., *Lakota and Cheyenne*, 51.

[11] Garrick Mallory, "Picture-Writing of the American Indians," *10th Annual Report of the Bureau of Ethnology, 1888–89* (Washington, D.C.: U.S. Govt. Printing Office, 1893), 565.

[12] Evan M. Maurer, et al. *Visions of the People: A Pictorial History of Plains Indian Life* (Minneapolis: Minneapolis Institute of Arts, 1992), 200–01; Mallery, "Picture-Writing of the American Indians," 563–66.

[13] Mallery, "Picture-Writing of the American Indians," 565.

[14] Colonel W. A. Graham, *The Custer Myth: A Source Book of Custeriana* (New York: Bonanza Books, 1953), 81–87.

[15] Stanley Vestal, *New Sources of Indian History* (Norman: University of Oklahoma Press, 1934), 181.

11

The End of Freedom

As the United States Army defeated the Plains Indians in battle, the United States government endeavored to eradicate their way of life. Plains Indian people were confined to reservations where they were subjected to policies of acculturation by coercion and where their lives were controlled by government laws and agents (Figure 21). Divisions grew between traditionalists and those people who accepted many of the new ways. Indian people experienced poverty, powerlessness, dependency, and despair. "You see this barren waste," Red Cloud told a white visitor to Pine Ridge. "Think of it! I, who used to own rich soil in a well-watered country so extensive that I could not ride through it in a week on my fastest pony, am put down here. . . . Now I, who used to control five thousand warriors, must tell Washington when I am hungry. I must beg for that which I own. If I beg hard, they put me in the guardhouse. We have trouble. Our girls are getting bad. Coughing sickness every winter carries away our best people. My heart is heavy. . . ."[1]

Time and again, Indians complained about the corruption of their agents, the failure of the government to keep its promises, the aridness of the lands assigned to them, and the starvation and disease that thinned their numbers. According to John G. Neihardt, Black Elk recalled the end of the days of freedom with bitterness:

> All our people now were settling down in square gray houses, scattered here and there across this hungry land, and around them the Wasichus [whites] had drawn a line to keep them in. The nation's hoop was broken, and there was no center any longer for the flowering tree. The people were in despair. They seemed heavy to me, heavy and dark; so heavy that it seemed they could not be lifted; so dark that they could not be made to see any more. Hunger was

Figure 21 (*opposite*).   Plains Indian Reservations, ca. 1889

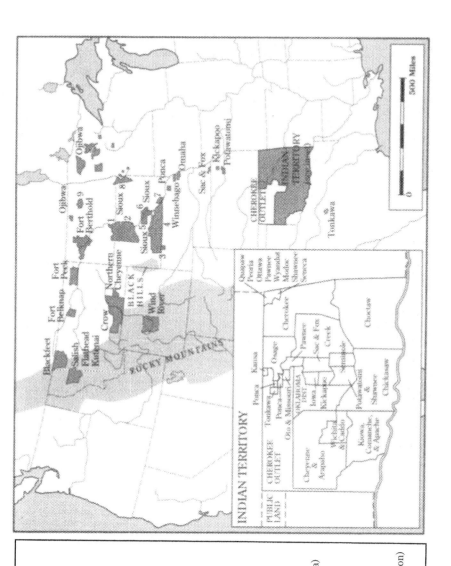

Fort Belknap
Assiniboine
Gros Ventre

Fort Peck
Assiniboine
Sioux

Fort Berthold
Mandan
Hidatsa
Arikara

Wind River
Eastern Shoshoni
Northern Arapaho

Sioux Reservations
1. Standing Rock (Hunkpapa)
2. Cheyenne River (Miniconjou and others)
3. Pine Ridge (Oglala)
4. Rosebud (Brulé)
5. Lower Brulé
6. Crow Creek
7. Yankton
8. Sisseton
9. Devil's Lake (Sisseton/Wahpeton)

Figure 22.   Kiowa Husbands and Wives Going to a Dance
In this ledger drawing (ca. 1880) an anonymous Kiowa artist uses new materials and depicts a new subject while employing many of the conventions used in the stylized pictographic war records of old. The two couples are dressed in their finest, wear decorative face paint and silver jewelry, and carry eagle fan feathers and a colorful umbrella. They, and the artist, find occasion for festivity and celebration amid a life of poverty and demoralization.

among us often now, for much of what the Great Father in Washington sent us must have been stolen by Wasichus who were crazy to get money. There were many lies, but we could not eat them. The forked tongue made promises.[2]

Other people, asked to recall the end of the old ways and the transition to a new way of life, could or would say nothing. Crow chief Plenty Coups refused to speak of it;[3] Two Leggings said nothing happened: "We just lived."[4] Yet Two Leggings was wrong. The reservation era, often depicted as the end of Indian history, in fact saw Indian people confront new threats, adjust to new conditions, and create new ways of life on the ruins of the old. Charles Eastman spoke of his people's being entrenched "in the warfare of civilized life."[5] In this struggle, human capacities for survival surfaced and people found meaning and moments of humor in the midst of alcoholism, hunger, and misery (Figure 22). "I like to laugh," said Pretty Shield. "I always did. Our hearts stay young if we let them." In her old age, she worried how her grandchildren would fare: Would they receive the lease money that the government owed them for allowing white ranchers to graze cattle on their land? "Or will they have to wear out their moccasins going to the Agency office to ask for it, as I do?" she wondered. "But then," she added quickly, the light of fun leaping to her eyes, "I suppose they will be wearing the white man's shoes, because shoes last longer than moccasins."[6]

The documents in this chapter illustrate several aspects of the reservation experience: lamentation for a way of life that has gone forever, adjustments made to meet the acculturative demands of the government, and resilience of the human spirit.

"WE ARE MELTING LIKE SNOW ON THE HILLSIDE."

After his victory in the so-called Red Cloud War of 1866–67, the Oglala chief never again took up arms against the United States. He became a "reservation chief" and was denounced by some of the resistant Sioux as the leader of the "hang-around-the-fort Indians." But Red Cloud had not given up the fight just because he had given up fighting. He continued to champion his people's interests in dealing with the government, proved a thorn in the side of Indian agents, and constantly reminded Americans of their broken promises. The government aimed to transform the Indians on the reservations into hard-working farmers, but Red Cloud had other ideas: "The white man can work if he wants to," he said, "but the Great Spirit did not make us to work. The white man owes us a living for the lands he has taken from us."[7]

In 1870, Red Cloud, Spotted Tail, and other Sioux chiefs traveled to Washington to visit the Great White Father. They met President and Mrs. Grant, ate strawberries and ice cream at the White House, and traveled on to New York, where Red Cloud spoke to a packed house at the Cooper Union and received a standing ovation. He made the following speech to Secretary of the Interior Jacob Cox the day after he met with the president. The attention lavished on him and the impressive display of power and wealth to which he was treated did not divert the Oglala chief from the main purpose of his visit.

RED CLOUD

Speech to the Secretary of the Interior
1870

The Great Spirit has seen me naked; and my Great Father, I have fought against him. I offered my prayers to the Great Spirit so I could come here safe. Look at me. I was raised on this land where the sun rises — now I come from where the sun sets. Whose voice was first sounded on this land? The voice of the red people, who had but bows and arrows. The Great Father says he is good and kind to us. I don't think so. I am good to his white people. From the word sent me I have come all the way to his home. My face is red; yours is white. The Great Spirit has made you to read and write, but not me. I have not learned. I come here to tell my Great Father what I do not like in my country. You are all close to my Great Father, and are a great many chiefs. The men the Great Father sends to us have no sense — no heart. What has been done in my country I did not want, did not ask for it; white people going through my country. Father, have you, or any of your friends here, got children? Do you want to raise them? Look at me; I come here with all these young men. All of them have children and want to raise them. The white children have surrounded me and have left me nothing but an island. When we first had this land we were strong, now are melting like snow on the hillside, while you are grown like spring grass. Now I have come a long distance to my Great Father's house — see if I have left any blood in his land when I go. When the white man comes in my country he leaves a trail of blood behind him. Tell the Great Father to move Fort Fetterman away and we will have no more trouble. I have two mountains in that country — the Black Hills and the Big Horn Mountain. I want the Great Father to make no roads through them. I have told these things three times; now I have come here to tell them the fourth time.

I do not want my reservation on the Missouri; this is the fourth time I have said so. Here are some people from there now. Our children are dying off like sheep; the country does not suit them. I was born at the forks of the Platte, and I was told that the land belonged to me from north, south, east, and west. The red man has come to the Great Father's house. The Ogallallas are the last who have come here; but I come to hear and

First Annual Report of the Board of Indian Commissioners for 1870 (Washington, D.C.: U.S. Govt. Printing Office, 1871), 41.

listen to the words of the Great Father. They have promised me traders, but we have none. At the mouth of Horse Creek they had made a treaty in 1862,[8] and the man who made the treaty is the only one who has told me truths. When you send goods to me, they are stolen all along the road, so when they reached me they were only a handful. They held a paper for me to sign, and that is all I got for my lands. I know the people you send out there are liars. Look at me. I am poor and naked. I do not want war with my Government. The railroad is passing through my country now; I have received no pay for the land — not even a brass ring. I want you to tell all this to my Great Father.

AN OLD WOMAN'S DREAM

Buffalo Bird Woman was born around 1839 in a Hidatsa earthen lodge. She grew up learning the ways and skills that gave women status in the traditional Hidatsa world, but in her life she saw that world replaced by a new and often bewildering one. She remained a dignified and conservative woman, using some of the new material culture but regretting the passing of a way of life that she deemed superior.

Wolf Chief, her brother, also received a traditional upbringing, but he more readily adjusted to the new ways and achieved a measure of success in education and business. Buffalo Bird Woman's son, Goodbird, grew up in an earthen lodge but went to school in a frame house; he learned to hunt buffalo and to raise cattle; he became a Christian but also went on vision quests. Buffalo Bird Woman's memory in old age of the ways of life she knew and loved as a girl convey the sadness induced by massive and uncontrollable change. To many white Americans, her words also reinforced the image of the unchanging Indian, unable to adjust and survive in a new world. But the life stories of her family clearly reveal how individuals coped with radical change without surrendering to it.

BUFFALO BIRD WOMAN
Recalling the Old Days

I am an old woman now. The buffaloes and black-tail deer are gone, and our Indian ways are almost gone. Sometimes I find it hard to believe that I ever lived them.

My little son grew up in the white man's school. He can read books, and he owns cattle and has a farm. He is a leader among our Hidatsa people, helping teach them to follow the white man's road.

He is kind to me. We no longer live in an earth lodge, but in a house with chimneys; and my son's wife cooks by a stove.

But for me, I cannot forget our old ways.

Often in summer I rise at daybreak and steal out to the cornfields; and as I hoe the corn I sing to it, as we did when I was young. No one cares for our corn songs now.

Sometimes at evening I sit, looking out on the big Missouri. The sun sets, and dusk steals over the water. In the shadows I seem again to see our Indian village, with smoke curling upward from the earth lodges; and in the river's roar I hear the yells of the warriors, the laughter of little children as of old. It is but an old woman's dream. Again I see but shadows and hear only the roar of the river; and tears come into my eyes. Our Indian life, I know, is gone forever.

"I JUST LISTENED, SAID NOTHING, AND DID NOTHING."

Many Indian people accepted roles in the reservation system, notably as police officers and judges. While their apparent compliance played into the government's hands and allowed it to divide and rule, they chose to participate for their own reasons and not necessarily because they had sold out. For young men, serving as a policeman helped fill the void created by the suppression of their warrior culture; for older men, serving as judges and "government chiefs" allowed them to exert an influence in the implementation of government policies on the reservation, to work within the system, and to bend rather than to break under the onslaught

Gilbert Wilson, *Waheenee: An Indian Girl's Story, Told by Herself* (St. Paul: Webb Publishing Co., 1921; reprinted in *North Dakota History* 38 (Winter-Spring 1971), 175–76.

of new ways and new values. Wooden Leg had fought against Custer at the Little Big Horn, but later on the Northern Cheyenne reservation he served as a tribal judge. As such, he was responsible for implementing such policies as the prohibition of polygamy as the government attempted to produce what amounted to a social revolution in Indian communities. Such policies caused heartbreak and split families. Charles Eastman recalled the reaction of a Sioux named Old White Bull on being told he must give up one of his two wives:

> What! . . . these two women are sisters, both of whom have been my wives for over half a century. I know the ways of the white man; he takes women unknown to each other and to his law. These two have been faithful to me and I have been faithful to them. Their children are my children and their grandchildren are mine. We are now living together as brother and sisters. All the people know that we are happy together, and nothing but death can separate us.[9]

Wooden Leg described himself as "a tamed old man" during this period of his life, but, as the following excerpt from his autobiography suggests, he found subtle ways to resist and subvert the process of acculturation, buying time to allow people to change at their own pace.

WOODEN LEG

Serving as Judge

A policeman came to my place, one time, and told me that [Agent] Eddy wanted to see me at the agency office. He did not say what was wanted. I thought: "What have I done?" I went right away. I never had been much about the agency, and I did not know Eddy very well. But the people all the time were saying he was a good man, so I was not afraid. When I got there, a strange white man was at the office. The interpreter told me this man was from Washington. Eddy and the other man talked to me a little while, about nothing of importance. Then Eddy said:

"We want you to be judge."

The Indian court was held at the agency. My home place was where it now is, over a divide from the agency and on the Tongue river side of

Thomas B. Marquis, *Wooden Leg, A Warrior Who Fought Custer* (Minneapolis: The Midwest Co., 1931), 366–69.

the reservation. I accepted the appointment. I was paid ten dollars each month for going to the agency and attending to the court business one or two times each month. Not long after I had been serving as judge, Eddy called me into his office. He said:

"A letter from Washington tells me that Indians having two or more wives must send away all but one. You, as judge, must do your part toward seeing that the Cheyennes do this."

My heart jumped around in my breast when he told me this. He went on talking further about the matter, but I could not pay close attention to him. My thoughts were racing and whirling. When I could get them steady enough for speech, I said to him:

"I have two wives. You must get some other man to serve as judge."

He sat there and looked straight at me, saying nothing for a little while. Then he began talking again:

"Somebody else as judge would make you send away one of your wives. It would be better if you yourself managed it. All of the Indians in the United States are going to be compelled to put aside their extra wives. Washington has sent the order."

I decided to keep the office of judge. It appeared there was no getting around the order, so I made up my mind to be the first one to send away my extra wife, then I should talk to the other Cheyennes about the matter. I took plenty of time to think about how I should let my wives know about what was coming. Then I allowed the released one some further time to make arrangements as to where she should go. The first wife, the older one, had two daughters. The younger wife had no children. It seemed this younger one ought to leave me. I was in very low spirits. When a wagon came to get her and her personal packs I went out and sat on a knoll about a hundred yards away. I could not speak to her. It seemed I could not move. All I could do was just sit there and look down at the ground. She went back to her own people, on another reservation. A few years later I heard that she was married to a good husband. Oh, how glad it made my heart to hear that!

I sent a policeman to tell all Cheyennes having more than one wife to come and see me. One of them came that same afternoon. After we had smoked together, I said:

"The agent tells me that I as the judge must order all Cheyennes to have only one wife. You must send away one of yours."

"I shall not obey that order," he answered me.

"Yes, it will have to be that way," I insisted.

"But who will be the father to the children?" he asked.

"I do not know, but I suppose that will be arranged."

"Wooden Leg, you are crazy. Eddy is crazy."
"No. If anybody is crazy, it is somebody in Washington. All of the Indians in the United States have this order. If we resist it, our policemen will put us into jail. If much trouble is made about it, soldiers may come to fight us. Whatever man does not put aside his extra wife may be the cause of the whole tribe being killed."
Many of our men were angered by the order. My heart sympathized with them, so I never became offended at the strong words they sometimes used. Finally, though, all of them sent away their extra wives. Afterward, from time to time, somebody would tell me about some man living a part of the time at one place with one wife and a part of the time at another place with another wife. I just listened, said nothing, and did nothing. These were old men, and I considered it enough of change for them that they be prevented from having two wives at the same place.

On the southern plains, Quanah Parker also successfully evaded this aspect of the government's assault on his way of life. Formerly a prominent warrior, Quanah Parker emerged as the tribal leader on the Comanche reservation in Oklahoma. He assured the government he intended to follow the white man's path "so far as I was able." He visited Washington, D.C., was a judge on the Court of Indian Offenses, became a supporter of the government's program of education for his children, accumulated considerable wealth, usually wore the white man's clothes, and lived in an impressive ranch house. But he kept his hair long and, in defiance of government policy, he practiced polygamy and the peyote religion. When the government learned he had five or six wives it applied pressure to make him give them up. In 1894 Quanah swore "to give up and relinquish all claims to To-pay, as my wife," but To-pay stayed with him and bore him two children. Quanah's "much married condition" eventually cost him his judgeship, but he refused to give in on this issue, "stating that he had children by all of his wives, he loved them equally and loved his children and cared for them equally." He still had two wives when he died in 1911.[10]

LEARNING TO LIKE *WOHAW*

Unlike many people, Arapaho artist Carl Sweezy was able to look back on the painful period of transition from "the buffalo road" to "the corn road" without bitterness. He remembered competent, honest, and humane agents like Brinton Darlington and John Miles, and he recalled how his people found humor and pleasure even as they had to learn to live in a difficult new world and had to develop a taste for *wohaw* (beef) rather than buffalo meat.

CARL SWEEZY
Learning the White Man's Ways

We had everything to learn about the white man's road. We had come to a country that was new to us, where wind and rain and rivers and heat and cold and even some of the plants and animals were different from what we had always known. We had to learn to live by farming instead of by hunting and trading; we had to learn from people who did not speak our language or try to learn it, except for a few words, though they expected us to learn theirs. We had to learn to cut our hair short, and to wear close-fitting clothes made of dull-colored cloth, and to live in houses, though we knew that our long braids of hair and embroidered robes and moccasins and tall, round lodges were more beautiful. . . .

We had never made brick or sawed lumber or had a wooden door to open and shut. Although some of us had visited the forts and the trading posts before we came to the Reservation, and a few of us had seen the white man's towns and cities, hardly any of us had ever been in houses where families lived. We thought windows were put in the walls so that we might look in to see how white people did their work and ate their meals and visited with each other. We pulled up some of the first little trees that were planted at Darlington, to see why the white people had put sticks in the ground in rows. There is a story that one of our men, given a little pig to raise so that when it grew up he could have pork and bacon, returned it to the Agency to be kept for him until it grew too big to get through the holes in his fence. He did not realize that he could repair the fence to suit the size of his pig.

We knew nothing about how to harness a work horse or turn a furrow

Althea Bass, *The Arapaho Way: A Memoir of an Indian Boyhood* (New York: Clarkson N. Potter, 1966), 45–55.

in a field or cut and store hay; and today I suppose there are men living in cities who know no more about these things than we did. Our women did not know how to build a fire in a cook-stove or wash clothes in a tub of water. It was a long time before we knew what the figures on the face of a clock meant, or why people looked at them before they ate their meals or started off to church. We had to learn that clocks had something to do with the hours and minutes that the white people mentioned so often. Hours, minutes, and seconds were such small divisions of time that we had never thought of them. When the sun rose, when it was high in the sky, and when it set were all the divisions of the day that we had ever found necessary when we followed the old Arapaho road. When we went on a hunting trip or to a sun dance, we counted time by sleeps.

My people had everything to learn about the white man's road, but they had a good time learning it. How they laughed when a war pony, not understanding what it was supposed to do when it was hitched to a plough or a wagon, lunged and jumped away and threw them flat on the ground, with the plough or the wagon riding high in the air.

How puzzled they were when they found that old men and women, among the white people, had teeth they could take out of their mouths and put back in again. They gave Brinton Darlington the name "Tosimeea," "He Who Takes Out His Teeth," when he showed them that he could do this, and they wondered how he had come by that strange power. But when Mr. Miles came, he could do the same thing. It must be, they thought, something all Agents had the power to do; so the movement of taking out and putting back a set of teeth became the word for Agent in our sign language. . . .

We Arapaho had always been a sociable people. In our old way of life it had been necessary for us to live in bands, or villages of tipis, and to carry on all our important undertakings together; so we found it hard, in the early days on the Reservation, to learn to work and plan as individuals. Every occasion that brought us together gave us pleasure. We gathered for it early and wore the best we had and made the most of the chance to visit and feast and celebrate. So grass payments and annuity issues meant big times in our lives.

The grass money was rental for lands on our Reservation that we leased to white men for cattle grazing. Since nobody owned the land individually and there was far more of it than we could cultivate and farm, it was leased in large tracts in the name of the Cheyenne and the Arapaho tribes, through the Agent, and the money for the leases was paid to us once a year. Every man, woman, and child received an equal share. Often many of us had spent most of our money in advance, before it was paid to us, but all of us went to the Agency anyhow at the time of the grass payments. Sometimes we had spent our money wisely, for farm implements or household goods; sometimes we hardly knew where it had gone, for one thing or another at the commissary or at the store, where we had been given credit. But we made a good thing of the gathering. Even though the Agents tried to persuade us to come to the pay table wearing no paint and dressed in what they called civilized clothing, and even though many of us had little or no cash to take home with us when the traders had deducted what we owed them, we were all there and in a good mood. There was trading at the stores and feasting in the tipis and visiting everywhere, and everybody went away happy.

By the terms of the treaty at Medicine Lodge, the United States Government was to furnish us what we needed to live on, after we sat down on the Reservation, until we had time to learn to provide for ourselves. It was also to give us schools and teachers, and farm implements and blacksmiths and Agency farmers, to start us on the corn road. All this was paid for out of the fund credited to us for our claim to lands that we surrendered when we moved to the Reservation. Each winter, under this plan, we received an issue of what was called annuity goods. What we were given varied from year to year, but usually there were blankets, strouding for lodge covers, calico and denim for the women to use in making clothing, coats and trousers and shoes and stockings, axes and knives, and needles and thread and kettles and frying pans. Often the goods, which were supposed to reach us at the beginning of winter for use during the cold months ahead, were delayed a long time in the shipping; often, too, they had been carelessly packed and handled, so that the cloth was stained and mildewed and the knives and pans were rusty. And although the Agent and his men were good at figures, there was always some mistake in the count and not enough of any one thing for everyone. Sometimes there was a new lodge covering for only one family in three, or one pair of shoes for every two men. We laughed at some of these shortages and made the best of them. If a man's share of shoes was only one instead of a pair, that was reason enough for the men to sell their shoes and wear moccasins. And if only part of the men got trousers, that was a good excuse to cut them up and wear them as leggings, as the older men usually wore them anyhow.

Each Agent distributed the goods according to his own system, but usually he portioned out whatever we were to get among the village chiefs, to be divided as they thought best. They were responsible men and knew the needs of each family, and they almost never failed to make a fair distribution as far as the goods went. Often we were disappointed over what Washington sent us, but I never heard of any quarrels between Indians over the issue, even when there was far too little to go around and the need was great.

Sometimes the Agents threatened to withhold the annuity goods, to compel us to send our children to school or to give up our medicine dances or to break sod and plant crops. They even threatened to withhold the goods from families of men who refused to cut their hair and to wear trousers. But there was nothing in the terms of the Medicine Lodge treaty to permit this kind of withholding, and the Agents learned not to try it. It made us sullen and uncooperative, and turned us back toward the old road rather than forward to the new.

Wherever we lived on the Reservation — and as the years went on, some of our villages were as much as sixty-five miles away — everyone that could make the trip was on hand at the Agency for the annuity issue. Many of the people, coming from a distance, brought their tipis and camping equipment with them and settled down at Darlington to visit and enjoy life together until the distribution was over. They walked or rode on ponies with a travois dragging behind or came in wagons, and a few of them rode in carriages. The Agents and the teachers argued against an Indian's buying a carriage when he needed, they said, to buy a stove and beds and chairs and farm equipment, but the Indian who managed to get together enough money to buy a carriage argued that he had been told to try to do as the white people did, and white people rode in carriages. We couldn't do everything at once; so we did first what pleased us most.

All of us wore our best to the Agency for the annuity issue. The women came dressed in their buckskin jackets and leggings, or in calico dresses with bright shawls or blankets over them; they carried their babies on cradle boards and led along small children wearing beaded buckskin or calico or denim, with small shawls and blankets of their own. The men with long hair oiled their braids and bound them with otter skin or with colored string, and wore hats on top of these, if they had hats. There was every color and every kind of clothing to be seen, and everyone was in good spirits. Annuity meant a happy, sociable time for everyone. The children played such Indian games as the hoop-and-stick and the mud-ball game, or prisoner's base and drop-the-handkerchief that they had learned from white children; the young men raced their ponies up and down the Agency streets, showing off; the older people, who hadn't seen one another in a long time, sat together for hours in the lodges, visiting and telling stories of the old days. Hunting stories, war stories, stories of brave marches and hard winters and perfect summers when the buffalo grew fat and the bushes were loaded with wild fruit, were told over by those who remembered them. All around the Agency, for two or three miles up and down the river, the tipis glowed at night from the center fires inside.

When the goods were distributed, everyone put on something new — a blanket or a hat or a coat or a shirt or a shawl. If a man got a pair of shoes or trousers that he did not want, he sold them or traded them off for something he fancied for himself or his family. There was trading going on everywhere, and those who came out of a deal with something to sell or with some money to spend now went to the traders' stores to see what they could get. We were always glad to have coffee and sugar and flour, and maybe some canned goods, to take home with us. By the time the gathering broke up, everyone had something new and everyone was happy.

Food was issued on a different plan. At first when we raised no crops and had no knowledge of how to do any kind of work that would give us employment at the Agency, nearly all of our food had to be issued to us. Beef was issued only after we no longer had buffalo meat or when smaller game was not to be had. Every two weeks other items of food that white people considered necessary to live on were distributed to us: bacon and salt pork, flour, sugar, salt, coffee, and lard. Some of these things, especially the bacon and the salt pork, we had to learn to eat, because they were too salty for our taste. Later, when the buffalo were all gone and even small game was less plentiful, but when many of us began to have foodstuffs from our farms and some money to buy part of our supplies, only beef and flour were issued. These rations were supposed to be enough to last each family for two weeks, but it was hard for any Indian to learn to divide what he had on hand and make it last fourteen days. It had always been our custom to feast when food was plenty and to share all we had when there were visitors. We had our own laws of hospitality and our own faith that the powers we prayed to would provide for us. The advice our Agents gave us to cut wood in summer when it was hot to use in winter when it would be cold, to stack hay before frost, to dry corn and beans and save sugar and flour for the future was hard for us to follow. The Agents thought we were wasteful and blind to every-thing but the present, but they had never grown up in a village that used and enjoyed whatever food and fuel and pasture was at hand and then moved on to where there was sure to be more.

Among the Arapaho, and many other Indians, the word for beef was "wohaw." This was not an Indian word, in the old sense. We had never seen cattle until we saw white men driving their ox teams across the country. The driver had a good deal of whacking and yelling to do to keep them going, and "Wo!" and "Haw!" were what he yelled at them. So, having no word for the oxen in our language, we called them wohaw. When we slaughtered a beef and ate it, we called that wohaw too.

Our older people had to learn to like wohaw. Meat had always been their principal food, and whatever else they had they were always hungry without it. But beef had a different smell and a different taste from buffalo; it was stronger and not so sweet. And since the contractors who supplied the beef bought range cattle, often thin and of poor grade, for the commissary, the meat was likely to be tough. It took long cooking to make a range steer tender, and we had always eaten our buffalo meat rare. But we children who had been born on the Reservation liked the white man's meats, beef and bacon and salt pork, from the beginning.

Mondays were beef-issue days, wohaw days. At first the beeves were all issued by the Government clerk from one station, the big corral across the river from the Agency, southeast of Fort Reno. This meant that every two weeks some member of a family had to be on hand to get his beef, and for those families living at a distance from the Agency this meant a long trip, breaking into whatever work was being done at home. So ten stations were set up at different points on the Reservation, with a blacksmith's shop there for repairing farm tools and shoeing horses, a white farmer whose work was to teach the Indians around him how to farm and to care for livestock, and a corral for the beef cattle that were to be issued. After that, nobody had more than a few miles to go.

Issue days were big times for all of us. The men who were to do the killing painted their faces and rode their fastest horses and brought along their best bows and arrows, or their guns. The women followed along, usually with a pony travois to carry the smallest children and to bring home the beef. People all put on some of their finery, and braided some colored cloth into the manes and tails of their horses, and made a holiday out of the work they had to do. All across the prairies, on Monday mornings, people in bright colors and high spirits came riding to the issue station. There were visiting and excitement and work and feasting ahead for everyone. One by one, as the clerk stamped the ration tickets of the heads of families, the men in the corral drove a beef from the pen and sent it down the chute. Yelling and racing his pony and with his family coming along behind as close as they could manage to do, the man rode after his wohaw as it bellowed and plunged and tore across the prairie, trying to escape. Wohaw could run almost as fast and bellow and turn almost as wildly as the buffalo once did. For a few hours, the Arapaho knew once more some of the excitement of the old buffalo hunt. And when at last the beef was shot down, the women moved in with their knives and kettles, skinning the hide off and cutting up the meat to take back to their lodges. Everybody had a piece of the raw liver, fresh and warm, before the families set out for home. Then, in the tipis or outside, fires were kindled; some of the beef was cooked, and the feasting began. Lodge walls were lifted at the sides if the weather was good, and the skins at the entrance were propped up overhead, so that several lodges could be thrown together during the feast. It was a time of plenty and of hospitality for everyone.

Next day the women were busy outside the tipi, cutting into strips whatever meat was left and hanging it from poles to dry. We had never heard of refrigerators in those days, but the sun and the wind soon cured the meat so that it did not spoil. The cattlemen who leased pastures on our Reservation called this jerked meat, or jerky. But usually there was little left of our wohaw for drying. When there was anything to feast on in our villages, we feasted well.

After 1896, the method of issuing beef was changed. To shorten the time required for the issue, and to do away with the celebrating that went with it, live beeves were no longer given out. Instead the cattle were slaughtered, and issued from the block. At first all the men objected to the change, and the chiefs protested to the Agent. Many a Cheyenne family went hungry until the proud chiefs of that tribe decided they must bow to authority and accept slaughtered beef. The sport that had been as important as the feasting on issue days was ended with that change from beef on the hoof to beef on the block. Progress was catching up with us.

NOTES

[1] Red Cloud to anthropologist Warren Moorehead, quoted in James C. Olson, *Red Cloud and the Sioux Problem* (Lincoln: University of Nebraska Press, 1965), 336–37.

[2] John G. Neihardt, *Black Elk Speaks: Being the Life Story of a Holy Man of the Oglala Sioux* (Lincoln: University of Nebraska Press, 1988 ed.), 213–14.

[3] Frank B. Linderman, *Plenty Coups, Chief of the Crows* (Lincoln: University of Nebraska Press, 1962), 311.

[4] Peter Nabokov, *Two Leggings: The Making of a Crow Warrior* (New York: Thomas Y. Crowell, 1967), 197.

[5] Charles Eastman, *From the Deep Woods to Civilization: Chapters in the Autobiography of an Indian* (Lincoln: University of Nebraska Press, 1977 ed.), 165.

6 Frank B. Linderman, *Pretty-shield: Medicine Woman of the Crows* (Lincoln: University of Nebraska Press, 1972 ed.), 86, 252–53.

7 Quoted in Olson, *Red Cloud and the Sioux Problem*, 266.

8 Red Cloud probably refers to the 1851 Treaty of Fort Laramie.

9 Eastman, *From the Deep Woods to Civilization*, 185.

10 William T. Hagan, *Quanah Parker, Comanche Chief* (Norman: University of Oklahoma Press, 1993), 40–49.

12

Attending the White Man's Schools

Indian children bore the brunt of the United States government's campaign of cultural genocide. Many non-Indian reformers threw up their hands in despair at the cultural conservatism of Indian adults but believed that children could be changed, and thereby "saved." Children represented the future and, in the eyes of American reformers and educators, the only hope for Indian people to adapt and survive into the twentieth century. Educating Indian children in the white man's ways was nothing new — several colonial colleges had attempted it — but in the late nineteenth century, the United States launched a sustained campaign to rid Indian children of their tribal heritage and reeducate them in the skills and values they deemed necessary for life in modern America.

Indian children had always received an education, of course, although not in the things white teachers deemed important, and not by the methods employed in nineteenth-century schools: "We never struck a child," said Pretty Shield, "never." Through stories and rituals, children learned to be good relatives. Through play, experience, and the example of older relatives, they learned the skills they needed to be productive members of their societies. Boys learned to hunt and fight, girls to cultivate food and family. Pretty Shield recalled how Crow women "had our children to care for, meat to cook, and to dry, robes to dress, skins to tan, lodges, and moccasins to make."[1] A Southern Cheyenne woman recalled how children played games that "imitated the customs and ways of grown-up people. . . . The boys would go out hunting. . . . We girls would pitch our tipis and make ready everything as if it were a real camp life."[2] Buffalo Bird Woman, a Hidatsa, wondered, "How can any child grow up without play?" She remembered her girlhood, learning to cook and sew from elder female relatives, as "the happiest time of my life."[3] Luther Standing Bear wrote that in Lakota society all elders were teachers, and children learned by example. "Native education was not a class education but one that strengthened and encouraged the individual to grow," he said.[4]

While the work of undermining tribal culture proceeded on the reservations, thousands of Indian children were taken from their homes and families and shipped off to boarding schools (Figure 23). There, they experienced an education that was very different from the kind enjoyed by Pretty Shield and Buffalo Bird Woman.

Following his experimental program of educating and "civilizing" Plains Indian prisoners at Fort Marion in Florida, Captain Richard Henry Pratt sought and received governmental approval to embark on an ambitious new project: educating Indian children. In 1879, Pratt established Carlisle Industrial School at a disused army barracks in Carlisle, Pennsylvania, as a boarding school for Indian children. There, Indian students from across the country could be educated far from the contaminating influences of family and tribal society. In time, Carlisle became a model for other Indian boarding schools and the flagship of the United States' assault on the hearts and minds of America's Indian youth.

For many Indian students, the boarding school experience was traumatic and final. The cemetery at Carlisle is filled with the graves of children who died far from home — of tuberculosis, suicide, and heartbreak. The regimen, racism, and culture shock the children experienced left an imprint on impressionable minds and personalities from which some students never recovered. The military-style discipline, forced use of English, and mental abuse that were commonplace in such places appalls our twentieth-century sensibilities. Charles Eastman, who believed his college days to be generally positive, recalled how, at Dr. Alfred Riggs Santee Training School in Nebraska, "we youthful warriors were held up and harassed with words of three letters . . . rat, cat, and so forth . . . until not a semblance of our native dignity and self-respect was left."[5] Luther Standing Bear never forgot being "cowed and humiliated *for the first time in my life*" by a teacher in a reading class at Carlisle.[6] Buffalo Bird Woman said simply: "It is a very hard thing for us to have to let our children be taken away from us and sent away to school where we cannot see them." But she also had concerns about what the children learned in schools closer to home. "In the old days, mothers watched their daughters very carefully; and girls did not give birth to babies before marriage," she asserted. "But after schools were started on this reservation, then our daughters began to have babies before marriage, for they now learned English ways."[7]

Jim Whitewolf, a Kiowa Apache from Oklahoma, went to school in 1891. "The first thing they did was to cut my hair." Shorn of his braids and wearing "school clothes," Whitewolf found himself in an institution where life was dictated by the ringing of bells. He ran away three times.

Figure 23.   U.S. Indian Agent and Chief of Police Take a Child to School
Charles H. Barstow, a clerk in the Bureau of Indian Affairs at the Crow reservation from 1878 to 1898, collected this drawing, made in 1891 by "boys from Carlisle Indian School." Barstow's notation on the drawing reads: "Major Wyman, U.S. Ind. Agent at Crow Agency Mont. with his chief of Police 'Boy that Grabs' trying to get Indian children for the school. A Crow Indian squaw leading her little girl by the hand to deliver her to the Capt. of Police." Clearly, however, there is more going on here than Barstow explains. The leering expression of the overweight, cigar-smoking agent suggests the Indians' view of the people to whom they were being asked to deliver their children, and the angry gesture of the mother indicates defiance and confrontation rather than willing compliance.[8]

When measles broke out at his school and students started dying, he and other boys were sent home. They took the disease with them and more children died, including Whitewolf's younger brother.[9] Many Indian people, then and now, felt anger and bitterness at what was done to them and their children.

And yet, surprisingly, some former students remembered their school days with a certain amount of happiness and derived benefit from the training they received. For some, life at the boarding school, however harsh, offered a haven from the hunger and the breakdown of families and social values they had seen on the reservation. Others were able to use what they learned to return to their reservation: Carl Sweezy said he was glad "that as a boy and a young man I had the kind of schooling I had. It brought me back to the Reservation again, each time after I had been away, and gave me employment at one place or another among my own people."[10] The selections in this chapter illustrate the agony of the boarding school experience for many people and the cultural limbo in which many graduates found themselves; the narrative of Luther Standing Bear also demonstrates an individual's capacity to make the best of a bad situation and remain true to himself even under an oppressive system.

EARLY DAYS AT CARLISLE

Plenty Kill, the son of Standing Bear, was one of a group of Sioux boys and girls who volunteered to leave their homes in South Dakota and enroll in Richard Pratt's new school at Carlisle "to learn the ways of the white man." At eleven years of age in 1879, Plenty Kill was the first student to enter the school, where he received a new name: Luther Standing Bear. In later life, he recalled those first days at Carlisle, which began with a fifty-mile wagon trip from the Rosebud reservation, embarking on a steamboat, and boarding a train for the East. It was just three years after Little Big Horn and, as the train stopped at stations en route, crowds of curious onlookers gathered to stare at the children and see what the killers of Custer looked like. Some of the older boys sang their death songs, expecting to be killed. Luther did not think he was going away to learn the ways of the white man. Instead, like a young warrior of old, he thought of himself going away to perform a brave deed: "I had come to this school merely to show my people that I was brave enough to leave the reservation and go East, not knowing what it meant and not caring," he wrote later. Likewise, Charles Eastman's father sent him off to school with the words, "Remember, my boy, it is the same as if I sent you on your first war-path. I shall expect you to conquer."[11]

LUTHER STANDING BEAR

Life at Boarding School
1879

At last the train arrived at a junction where we were told we were at the end of our journey. Here we left the train and walked about two miles to the Carlisle Barracks. Soon we came to a big gate in a great high wall. The gate was locked, but after quite a long wait, it was unlocked and we marched in through it. I was the first boy inside. At that time I thought nothing of it, but now I realize that I was the first Indian boy to step inside the Carlisle Indian School grounds.

Here the girls were all called to one side by Louise McCoz, the girls' interpreter. She took them into one of the big buildings, which was very brilliantly lighted, and it looked good to us from the outside.

When our interpreter told us to go to a certain building which he pointed out to us, we ran very fast, expecting to find nice little beds like those the white people had. We were so tired and worn out from the long trip that we wanted a good long sleep. From Springfield, Dakota, to Carlisle, Pennsylvania, riding in day coaches all the way, with no chance to sleep, is an exhausting journey for a bunch of little Indians.

But the first room we entered was empty. A cast-iron stove stood in the middle of the room, on which was placed a coal-oil lamp. There was no fire in the stove. We ran through all the rooms, but they were all the same — no fire, no beds. This was a two-story building, but we were all herded into two rooms on the upper floor.

Well, we had to make the best of the situation, so we took off our leggins and rolled them up for a pillow. All the covering we had was the blanket which each had brought. We went to sleep on the hard floor, and it was so cold! We had been used to sleeping on the ground, but the floor was so much colder.

Next morning we were called downstairs for breakfast. All we were given was bread and water. How disappointed we were! At noon we had some meat, bread, and coffee, so we felt a little better. But how lonesome the big boys and girls were for their far-away Dakota homes where there was plenty to eat! The big boys seemed to take it worse than we smaller chaps did. I guess we little fellows did not know any better. The big boys would sing brave songs, and that would start the girls to crying. They did

Luther Standing Bear, *My People the Sioux* (Boston: Houghton Mifflin, 1928), 133–49.

this for several nights. The girls' quarters were about a hundred and fifty yards from ours, so we could hear them crying. After some time the food began to get better; but it was far from being what we had been used to receiving back home. . . .

One day when we came to school there was a lot of writing on one of the blackboards. We did not know what it meant, but our interpreter came into the room and said, "Do you see all these marks on the blackboard? Well, each word is a white man's name. They are going to give each one of you one of these names by which you will hereafter be known." None of the names were read or explained to us, so of course we did not know the sound or meaning of any of them.

The teacher had a long pointed stick in her hand, and the interpreter told the boy in the front seat to come up. The teacher handed the stick to him, and the interpreter then told him to pick out any name he wanted. The boy had gone up with his blanket on. When the long stick was handed to him, he turned to us as much as to say, "Shall I — or will you help me — to take one of these names? Is it right for me to take a white man's name?" He did not know what to do for a time, not uttering a single word but he acted a lot and was doing a lot of thinking.

Finally he pointed out one of the names written on the blackboard. Then the teacher took a piece of white tape and wrote the name on it. Then she cut off a length of the tape and sewed it on the back of the boy's shirt. Then that name was erased from the board. There was no duplication of names in the first class at Carlisle School!

Then the next boy took the pointer and selected a name. He was also labeled in the same manner as Number One. When my turn came, I took the pointer and acted as if I were about to touch an enemy. Soon we all had the names of white men sewed on our backs. When we went to school, we knew enough to take our proper places in the class, but that was all. When the teacher called the roll, no one answered his name. Then she would walk around and look at the back of the boys' shirts. When she had the right name located, she made the boy stand up and say "Present." She kept this up for about a week before we knew what the sound of our new names was.

I was one of the "bright fellows" to learn my name quickly. How proud I was to answer when the teachers called the roll! I would put my blanket down and half raise myself in my seat, all ready to answer my new name. I had selected the name "Luther" — not "Lutheran" as many people call me. "Lutheran" is the name of a church denomination, not a person.

Next we had to learn to write our names. Our good teacher had a lot of patience with us. She is now living in Los Angeles, California, and I still like to go and ask her any question which may come up in my mind. She first wrote my name on the slate for me, and then, by motions, indicated that I was to write it just like that. She held the pencil in her hand just so, then made first one stroke, then another, and by signs I was given to understand that I was to follow in exactly the same way.

The first few times I wrote my new name, it was scratched so deeply into the slate that I was never able to erase it. But I copied my name all over both sides of the slate until there was no more room to write. Then I took my slate up to show it to the teacher, and she indicated, by the expression of her face, that it was very good. I soon learned to write it very well; then I took a piece of chalk downstairs and wrote "Luther" all over everything I could copy it on.

Next the teacher wrote out the alphabet on my slate and indicated to me that I was to take the slate to my room and study. I was pleased to do this, as I expected to have a lot of fun. I went up on the second floor, to the end of the building, where I thought nobody would bother me. There I sat down and looked at those queer letters, trying hard to figure out what they meant. No one was there to tell me that the first letter was "A" the next "B" and so on. This was the first time in my life that I was really disgusted. It was something I could not decipher, and all this study business was not what I had come East for anyhow — so I thought.

How lonesome I felt for my father and mother! I stayed upstairs all by myself, thinking of the good times I might be having if I were only back home, where I could ride my ponies, go wherever I wanted to and do as I pleased, and, when it came night, could lie down and sleep well. Right then and there I learned that no matter how humble your home is, it is yet home. . . .

One day we had a strange experience. We were all called together by the interpreter and told that we were to have our hair cut off. We listened to what he had to say, but we did not reply. This was something that would require some thought, so that evening the big boys held a council, and I recall very distinctly that Nakpa Kesela, or Robert American Horse, made a serious speech. Said he, "If I am to learn the ways of the white people, I can do it just as well with my hair on." To this we all exclaimed "Hau!" — meaning that we agreed with him.

In spite of this meeting, a few days later we saw some white men come inside the school grounds carrying big chairs. The interpreter told us these were the men who had come to cut our hair. We did not watch to see where the chairs were carried, as it was school time, and we went to our classroom. One of the big boys named Ya Slo, or Whistler, was missing. In a short time he came in with his hair cut off. They then called another boy out, and when he returned, he also wore short hair. In this way we were called out one by one.

When I saw most of them with short hair, I began to feel anxious to be "in style" and wanted mine cut, too. Finally I was called out of the schoolroom, and when I went into the next room, the barber was waiting for me. He motioned for me to sit down, and then he commenced work. But when my hair was cut short, it hurt my feelings to such an extent that the tears came into my eyes. I do not recall whether the barber noticed my agitation or not, nor did I care. All I was thinking about was that hair he had taken away from me.

Right here I must state how this hair-cutting affected me in various ways. I have recounted that I always wanted to please my father in every way possible. All his instructions to me had been along this line: "Son, be brave and get killed." This expression had been moulded into my brain to such an extent that I knew nothing else.

But my father had made a mistake. He should have told me, upon leaving home, to go and learn all I could of the white man's ways, and be like them. That would have given a new idea from a different slant; but Father did not advise me along that line. I had come away from home with the intention of never returning alive unless I had done something very brave.

Now, after having had my hair cut, a new thought came into my head. I felt that I was no more Indian, but would be an imitation of a white man. And we are still imitations of white men, and the white men are imitations of the Americans.

We all looked so funny with short hair. It had been cut with a machine and was cropped very close. We still had our Indian clothes, but were all "bald-headed." None of us slept well that night; we felt so queer. I wanted to feel my head all the time. But in a short time I became anxious to learn all I could.

Next we heard that we were soon to have white men's clothes. We were all very excited and anxious when this was announced to us. One day some wagons came in, loaded with big boxes, which were unloaded in front of the office. Of course we were all very curious, and gathered around to watch the proceedings and see all we could.

Here, one at a time, we were "sized up" and a whole suit handed to each of us. The clothes were some sort of dark heavy gray goods, consisting of coat, pants, and vest. We were also given a dark woolen shirt, a cap, a pair of suspenders, socks, and heavy farmer's boots.

Up to this time we had all been wearing our thin shirts, leggins, and a blanket. Now we had received new outfits of white men's clothes, and to us it seemed a whole lot of clothing to wear at once, but even at that, we had not yet received any underwear.

As soon as we had received our outfits, we ran to our rooms to dress up. The Indian prisoners were kept busy helping us put the clothes on. Although the suits were too big for many of us, we did not know the difference. I remember that my boots were far too large, but as long as they were "screechy" or squeaky, I didn't worry about the size! I liked the noise they made when I walked, and the other boys were likewise pleased.

How proud we were with clothes that had pockets and with boots that squeaked! We walked the floor nearly all the night. Many of the boys even went to bed with their clothes all on. But in the morning, the boys who had taken off their pants had a most terrible time. They did not know whether they were to button up in front or behind. Some of the boys said the open part went in front; others said, "No, it goes at the back." There is where the boys who had kept all their clothes on came in handy to look at. They showed the others that the pants buttoned up in front and not at the back. So here we learned something again. . . .

I now began to realize that I would have to learn the ways of the white man. With that idea in mind, the thought also came to me that I must please my father as well. So my little brain began to work hard. I thought that some day I might be able to become an interpreter for my father, as he could not speak English. Or I thought I might be able to keep books for him if he again started a store. So I worked very hard.

One day they selected a few boys and told us we were to learn trades. I was to be a tinsmith. I did not care for this, but I tried my best to learn this trade. Mr. Walker was our instructor. I was getting along very well. I made hundreds of tin cups, coffee pots, and buckets. These were sent away and issued to the Indians on various reservations.

After I had left the school and returned home, this trade did not benefit me any, as the Indians had plenty of tinware that I had made at school.

Mornings I went to the tin shop, and in the afternoon attended school. I tried several times to drop this trade and go to school the entire day, but Captain Pratt said, "No, you must go to the tin shop — that is all there is to it," so I had to go. Half school and half work took away a great deal of study time. I figure that I spent only about a year and a half in school, while the rest of the time was wasted, as the school was not started properly to begin with. Possibly you wonder why I did not remain longer, but the Government had made an agreement with our parents as to the length of time we were to be away.

A short time later, some boys, myself among the number, were called into one of the schoolrooms. There we found a little white woman. There was a long table in front of her, on which were many packages tied in paper. She opened up one package and it contained a bright, shining horn. Other packages disclosed more horns, but they seemed to be different sizes.

The little white woman picked up a horn and then looked the boys over. Finally she handed it to a boy who she thought might be able to use it. Then she picked out a shorter horn and gave it to me. I learned afterward that it was a B-flat cornet. When she had finished, all the boys had horns in their hands. We were to be taught how to play on them and form a band.

The little woman had a black case with her, which she opened. It held a beautiful horn, and when she blew on it it sounded beautiful. Then she motioned to us that we were to blow our horns. Some of the boys tried to blow from the large end. Although we tried our best, we could not produce a sound from them. She then tried to talk to us, but we did not understand her. Then she showed us how to wet the end of the mouth-piece. We thought she wanted us to spit into the horns, so we did. She finally got so discouraged with us that she started crying.

We just stood there and waited for her to get through, then we all tried again. Finally, some of the boys managed to make a noise through their horns. But if you could have heard it! It was terrible! But we thought we were doing fine.

So now I had more to occupy my attention. In the morning I had one hour to practice for the band. Then I must run to my room and change my clothes and go to work in the tin shop. From there I had to run again to my room and change my clothes and get ready for dinner. After that, I had a little time to study my lessons.

Then the school bell would ring and it was time for school. After that, we played and studied our music. Then we went to bed. All lights had to be out at nine o'clock. The first piece of music our band was able to play was the alphabet, from "a" to "z." It was a great day for us when we were able to play this simple little thing in public. But it was a good thing we were not asked to give an encore, for that was all we knew!

After I learned to play a little, I was chosen to give all the bugle calls. I had to get up in the morning before the others and arouse everybody by blowing the morning call. Evenings at ten minutes before nine o'clock I blew again. Then all the boys would run for their rooms. At nine o'clock the second call was given, when all lights were turned out and we were supposed to be in bed. Later on I learned the mess call, and eventually I could blow all the calls of the regular army.

I did these duties all the time I was at Carlisle School, so in the early part of 1880, although I was a young boy of but twelve, I was busy learning everything my instructors handed me.

One Sunday morning we were busy getting ready to get to Sunday School in town. Suddenly there was great excitement among some of the boys on the floor below. One of the boys came running upstairs shouting, "Luther Standing Bear's father is here!" Everybody ran downstairs to see my father. We had several tribes at the school now, many of whom had heard of my father, and they were anxious to see him.

When I got downstairs, my father was in the center of a large crowd of the boys, who were all shaking hands with him. I had to fight my way through to reach him. He was so glad to see me, and I was delighted to see him. But our rules were that we were not to speak the Indian language under any consideration. And here was my father, and he could not talk English!

My first act was to write a note to Captain Pratt, asking if he would permit me to speak to my father in the Sioux tongue. I said, "My father is here. Please allow me to speak to him in Indian." Captain Pratt answered, "Yes, my boy; bring your father over to my house."

This was another happy day for me. I took my father over to meet Captain Pratt, who was so glad to see him, and was very respectful to him. Father was so well dressed. He wore a gray suit, nice shoes, and a derby hat. But he wore his hair long. He looked very nice in white men's clothes. He even sported a gold watch and chain. Captain Pratt gave father a room with Robert American Horse, in the boys' quarters. He allowed the boys to talk to him in the Indian tongue, and that pleased the boys very much. Here Father remained for a time with us.

Not all visiting parents received a reception as warm as that accorded to Standing Bear; nor did they share Standing Bear's positive reactions. The Brulé Sioux chief, Spotted Tail, sent three sons, one daughter, and a granddaughter to the school, but when he visited Carlisle he was so appalled by what he saw that he gathered his children together, loaded them on a train, and took them home to South Dakota.[12]

WOHAW IN TWO WORLDS

Many Indian students left Carlisle and other schools without adequate training or preparation for working and living in modern American society. Nor did most Americans expect, or want, Indians to become fully participating citizens. As reformers and politicians lost faith in the Indians' ability to be totally assimilated, they settled instead for assigning Indians to the kind of inferior status shared by other nonwhite minorities in the United States.[13] When Indian students did return home, they did not usually fulfill their teachers' expectations and reject their parents' ways. Nevertheless, education in the white man's schools and ways changed many Indian students sufficiently that they did not feel they fully belonged among their own people either. Many returning students were considered suspect by other Indians, who charged them with having become too white. Students who returned home often faced painful, and sometimes tragic, periods of readjustment and doubt about their identity. Some committed suicide; others turned to alcohol.

Wohaw, or Spotted Cow, a Kiowa Indian imprisoned in Fort Marion, produced many drawings depicting the old life he knew as a warrior-hunter as well as new scenes he witnessed as a prisoner-student. Two notebooks of Wohaw's drawings, bought by a couple from St. Louis on their honeymoon in Florida, are now in the Missouri Historical Society. The most famous of these drawings is reproduced here (Figure 24). This symmetrical pictograph metaphorically and poignantly portrays the dilemma of a person who, like most Plains Indians in the late nineteenth century, but especially those who had been away at school, was caught between two cultures and faced an uncertain future. Wohaw depicts himself in traditional dress but identifies himself by printing his name above his head rather than employing a traditional name symbol. Under the sun, the moon, and a flaming meteor, he stands on the plains but between two worlds. On his righthand side is his Indian way of life, represented by the buffalo, tepee, and woods; on his left, the cow, church, and plowed fields represent the new way of life. He offers a pipe to both in a traditional gesture of respect and both animals blow clouds, signifying power, toward him. But his placing his foot on the farmlands and his facing the cow suggest he is being pulled toward the new way.[14]

Wohaw, who knew that Pratt and other like-minded whites would see his drawing, may have been deliberately ambiguous in his autobiographical sketch, suggesting that, despite being a target of Pratt's aggressive program of assimilation, he remained a Kiowa in many ways even as he ventured down new paths.[15]

Other Indians who returned home from school wrestled with their dilemma in different ways. In 1890, during the time of the Ghost Dance troubles on the Pine Ridge reservation, a young Sioux by the name of Plenty Horses shot and killed an army officer. Plenty Horses was a graduate of Carlisle and, at his trial for murder, he explained his motives:

Figure 24. Wohaw's Self-Portrait
Drawn by the Kiowa artist after his release from Fort Marion in 1878.

"I am an Indian. Five years I attended Carlisle and was educated in the ways of the white man. . . . I was lonely. I shot the lieutenant so I might make a place for myself among my people. Now I am one of them. I shall be hung and the Indians will bury me as a warrior. They will be proud of me. I am satisfied." But Plenty Horses did not get his wish. The federal court acquitted him of murder. After all, if his was an act of murder, then the mass slaying of Sioux women and children by U.S. troops at Wounded Knee surely constituted murder. Instead, the court decided that a state of war existed, thereby vindicating the Army and allowing Plenty Horses to go free. Denied the chance to make a place for himself among his people, Plenty Horses lived out a life of poverty and despondency.[16]

NOTES

[1] Frank B. Linderman, *Pretty-shield, Medicine Woman of the Crows* (Lincoln: University of Nebraska Press, 1972), 24, 134.

[2] Truman Michelson, ed., "Narrative of a Southern Cheyenne Woman," *Smithsonian Miscellaneous Collections* 87, no. 5 (1932), 3, quoted in Margaret Connell Szasz, *Indian Education in the American Colonies, 1607–1783* (Albuquerque: University of New Mexico Press, 1988), 23.

[3] *Waheenee: An Indian Girl's Story.* Told by Herself to Gilbert L. Wilson (1921; reprint Lincoln: University of Nebraska Press, 1981), 54, 117.

[4] Luther Standing Bear, *Land of the Spotted Eagle* (Lincoln: University of Nebraska Press, 1978) 13–16.

[5] Charles Eastman, *From the Deep Woods to Civilization* (Lincoln: University of Nebraska Press, 1977 ed.), 46.

[6] Standing Bear, *Land of the Spotted Eagle*, 17.

[7] Carolyn Gilman and Mary Jane Scheider, *The Way to Independence: Memories of a Hidatsa Family, 1840–1920* (St. Paul: Minnesota Historical Society Press, 1987), 233.

[8] Evan M. Maurer, et al., *Visions of the People: A Pictorial History of Plains Indian Life* (Minneapolis: The Minneapolis Institute of Arts, 1992), 284.

[9] Charles S. Brant, ed., *The Autobiography of a Kiowa Apache Indian* (New York: Dover Publications, 1991 ed.), 83–97.

[10] Althea Bass, *The Arapaho Way: A Memoir of an Indian Boyhood* (New York: Clarkson N. Potter, 1966), 40.

[11] Luther Standing Bear, *My People the Sioux* (Boston: Houghton Mifflin, 1928), 128–31, 135; Eastman, *From the Deep Woods to Civilization*, 31–32.

[12] Luther Standing Bear, *My People the Sioux*, 157.

[13] Frederick E. Hoxie, *A Final Promise: The Campaign to Assimilate the Indians, 1880–1920* (Lincoln: University of Nebraska Press, 1984).

[14] Janet Catherine Berlo, "Wo-Haw's Notebooks: 19th Century Kiowa Indian Drawings in the Collections of the Missouri Historical Society," *Gateway Heritage* 3 (Fall 1982), 5–13.

[15] Louise Lincoln, "The Social Construction of Plains Art, 1875–1915," in Maurer et al., *Visions of the People*, 49–51.

[16] Robert M. Utley, *The Indian Frontier of the American West 1846–1890* (Albuquerque: University of New Mexico Press, 1984), 227–28, 245.

13

The Life and Death
of Sitting Bull

Tatanka-Iyotanka, or Sitting Bull, is best known to non-Indians as the Hunkpapa Sioux chief who masterminded Custer's defeat at the Battle of the Little Big Horn. In fact, as befitted a man in his mid-forties, whose arms were still swollen from the sacrifices made in the sun dance, Sitting Bull directed most of his energies that day to protecting the women and children. His major influence on the battle was exerted before the conflict began, in his vision of the soldiers falling into camp.

Sitting Bull's fame among his own people rested on his spirituality as much as his military reputation. He was both a war chief and Wichasha Wakan ("holy man").[1] Born in the early 1830s, he counted his first coup at age fourteen; he had accumulated more than sixty coups by 1870, and he fought against both Indian and American enemies. He displayed the virtues his people admired most — courage, fortitude, generosity, and wisdom — and attained the unprecedented position of supreme chief. Wooden Leg, whose Northern Cheyenne people joined Sitting Bull prior to the Little Big Horn, explained the sources of the Hunkpapa's influence. Sitting Bull was "the most consistent advocate of the idea of living out of all touch with white people," he said:

> He had come into admiration by all Indians as a man whose medicine was good — that is, as a man having a kind heart and good judgment as to the best course of conduct. He was considered as being altogether brave, but peaceable. He was strong in religion — the Indian religion. He made medicine many times. He prayed and fasted and whipped his flesh into submission to the will of the Great Medicine.[2]

As American pressure on Sioux lands and culture intensified, Sitting Bull came to personify his people's struggle for freedom. After the Little Big Horn, he led his followers to Canada rather than submit to life on the reservation. Driven by hunger to return to the United States, he surrendered at Fort Buford, Dakota Territory, in 1881, expressing his wish that he be remembered as "the last man of my tribe to surrender my rifle."

Almost two years as a prisoner of war did nothing to alter Sitting Bull's devotion to the way of life he had fought to defend:

> White men like to dig in the ground for their food. My people prefer to hunt buffalo as their fathers did. White men like to stay in one place. My people want to move their tepees here and there to different hunting grounds. The life of white men is slavery. They are prisoners in towns or farms. The life my people want is a life of freedom. I have seen nothing that a white man has, houses or railways or clothing or food, that is as good as the right to move in open country, and live in our own fashion.[3]

At the Standing Rock agency, Sitting Bull continued to resist assimilation. A stint of touring eastern cities with Buffalo Bill Cody's Wild West Show in 1884–85 seems only to have confirmed his conviction that he "would rather die an Indian than live a white man." He argued forcefully against allotment. The agent at Standing Rock, James McLaughlin, portrayed him as an obstinate troublemaker and worked to undermine his authority among his people. But when the Ghost Dance religion took hold among the Sioux in 1890, it was natural that the people should look to Sitting Bull as their spiritual leader, whether or not he himself embraced the new religion. It was equally natural that the authorities should identify him as a ringleader who had to be removed.

The selections in this chapter illustrate Sitting Bull's record as a warrior, his continuing defense of Sioux interests even after his defeat, and his death at the hands of men who had once fought beside him.

SCENES FROM A WARRIOR'S LIFE

Sitting Bull drew many pictographic representations of the coups he had counted, following the traditional conventions of pictographic composition even though he used paper and pencils rather than paint on hide. The drawings reprinted here (Figure 25) are taken from a series done by Sitting Bull in 1870. He gave them to his adopted brother, Jumping Bull, who added some of his own. Another Lakota artist, Four Horns, copied the drawings, and they were eventually purchased by Assistant Surgeon James Kimball at Fort Buford. From there they were

transferred to the Army Medical Museum in Washington, D.C., and finally to the archives of the Bureau of American Ethnology. In some of his drawings, Sitting Bull signed his name in English, but Four Horns used the more traditional name glyph, a drawing of a seated buffalo, to identify the hero.[4] The four drawings testify to Sitting Bull's prowess as a warrior, but each one also records an event that affected the course of his life in some way.

Figure 25 (pp. 184–185).   Sitting Bull's Drawings of Scenes from His Life as a Warrior (1870)

(p. 184, top)
In a fight with Crow Indians, the fourteen-year-old Hunkpapa counts his first coup. The eagle on the shield represents his war medicine and identifies his spirit helper. In recognition of his son's first coup, his father gave him his own name, Sitting Bull, and presented him with a lance and a shield.

(p. 184, bottom)
Sitting Bull's drawings record more than a dozen fights with Crows and Assiniboines in the 1850s. This one, which occurred in 1856, left Sitting Bull limping for life. Early in his career, Sitting Bull became a member of the Strong Heart warrior society. He achieved such prominence that he became one of only two bonnet wearers, or sash bearers. The sash bearers were expected to stand their ground, pinned by the sash, until released by a comrade or killed. In this exchange of gunfire, Sitting Bull, wearing the Strong Heart headdress and sash, shoots a Crow through the belly but is wounded in the foot.

(p. 185, top)
The next year, wearing his Strong Heart bonnet and a white blanket coat, Sitting Bull strikes an Assiniboine youth with his lance, counting coup. Impressed with the boy's courage, Sitting Bull adopted him as his brother, naming him Jumping Bull.

(p. 185, bottom)
Near Fort Totten, in Devil's Lake country, Sitting Bull, wearing a red blanket, pursues a white man in a fringed buckskin jacket and shoots him in the back. This was Sitting Bull's first white victim. It would not be his last.[5]

SITTING BULL'S SURRENDER SONG

Following his surrender at Fort Buford in 1881, Sitting Bull composed a song that illustrated how he felt as he confronted the transition from warrior and chief to prisoner and ward of the government.

I - ki - ĉi - ze   wa - on   kon   *he*   wa - na   he - na - la   ye - lo

he   i - yo - ti - ye   ki - ya   wa - on

A warrior / I have been / Now / It is all over / A hard time / I have.

"IT IS YOUR OWN DOING THAT I AM HERE."

In 1883, the United States Senate sent a select committee of five men, chaired by Henry Dawes, the future proponent of the Allotment Act, "to investigate the condition of the Indian tribes of Montana and Dakota." When the committee met with the Sioux, the Indians bombarded them with complaints, but the committee members seemed uninterested in hearing grievances. The committee and agent McLaughlin accorded Sitting Bull (Figure 26) no special recognition as chief, but he still exerted considerable influence. "You have conducted yourselves like men who have been drinking whiskey," he told the committee, and with a wave of his hand he led the Indians out of the room. The next day, however, Sitting Bull thought better of his actions and took the opportunity to report on his people's condition.

Figure 26.   Sitting Bull
This photograph was taken about the time of Sitting Bull's meeting with the Senate select committee in 1883.

SITTING BULL

Report to the Senate Committee

1883

If a man loses anything, and goes back and looks carefully for it he will find it, and that is what the Indians are doing now when they ask you to give them the things they were promised them in the past. And I do not consider that they should be treated like beasts, and that is the reason I have grown up with the feelings I have.

Whatever you wanted of me I have obeyed, and I have come when you called me. The Great Father sent me word that what ever he had against me in the past had been forgiven and thrown aside, and he would have nothing against me in the future, and I accepted his promises and came in. And he told me not to step aside from the white man's path, and I told him I would not, and I am doing my best to travel in that path.

I feel that my country has gotten a bad name, and I want it to have a good name. It used to have a good name, and I sit sometimes and wonder who it is that has given it a bad name. You are the only people now who can give it a good name, and I want you to take care of my country and respect it.

When we sold the Black Hills we got a very small price for it, and not what we ought to have received. I used to think that the size of the payments would remain the same all the time, but they are growing smaller all the time.

I want you to tell the Great Father everything I have said, and that we want some benefits from the promises he has made to us. And I don't think I should be tormented with anything about giving up any part of my land until those promises are fulfilled. I would rather wait until that time, when I will be ready to transact any business he may desire.

I consider that my country takes in the Black Hills, and runs from the Powder River to the Missouri, and that all of this land belongs to me. Our reservation is not as large as we want it to be, and I suppose the Great Father owes us money now for land he has taken from us in the past.

You white men advise us to follow your ways, and therefore I talk as I do. When you have a piece of land, and anything trespasses on it, you catch it and keep it until you get damages, and I am doing the same thing now. And I want you to tell this to the Great Father for me. I am looking

48th Congress, 1st Session, Senate Rep. No. 283, Serial 2164, 80–81.

into the future for the benefit of my children, and that is what I mean, when I say I want my country taken care of for me.

My children will grow up here, and I am looking ahead for their benefit and for the benefit of my children's children, too; and even beyond that again. I sit here and look around me now, and I see my people starving, and I want the Great Father to make an increase in the amount of food that is allowed us now, so that they may be able to live. We want cattle to butcher — I want you to kill 300 head of cattle at a time. That is the way you live and we want to live the same way. This is what I want you to tell the Great Father when you go back home.

If we get the things we want, our children will be raised like the white children. When the Great Father told me to live like his people I told him to send me six teams of mules, because that is the way white people make a living, and I wanted my children to have these things to help them to make a living. I also told him to send me two spans of horses with wagons, and everything else my children would need. I also asked for a horse and buggy for my children. I was advised to follow the ways of the white man, and that is why I asked for those things.

I never ask for anything that is not needed. I also asked for a cow and a bull for each family, so that they can raise cattle of their own. I asked for four yokes of oxen and wagons with them. Also a yoke of oxen and a wagon for each of my children to haul wood with.

It is your own doing that I am here. You sent me here, and advised me to live as you do, and it is not right for me to live in poverty. I asked the Great Father for hogs, male and female, and for male and female sheep for my children to raise from. I did not leave out anything in the way of animals that the white men have; I asked for every one of them. I want you to tell the Great Father to send me some agricultural implements, so that I will not be obliged to work bare-handed.

Whatever he sends to this agency our agent will take care of for us, and we will be satisfied because we know he will keep everything right. Whatever is sent here for us he will be pleased to take care of for us. I want to tell you that our rations have been reduced to almost nothing, and many of the people have starved to death.

Now I beg of you to have the amount of rations increased so that our children will not starve, but will live better than they do now. I want clothing, too, and I will ask for that, too. We want all kinds of clothing for our people. Look at the men around here and see how poorly dressed they are. We want some clothing this month, and when it gets cold we want more to protect us from the weather.

That is all I have to say.

"LIEUT. BULLHEAD FIRED INTO SITTING BULL."

On December 14, 1890, the Indian police at Standing Rock agency were ordered to report to Lieutenant Henry Bullhead's home and proceed to Sitting Bull's cabin to arrest the chief. There are many accounts of what took place the next day, but one of the best is that of Lone Man, or John Loneman, as translated and recorded by his relative, Robert Higheagle, who was home from school at the time. Lone Man had fought with Sitting Bull against Custer and had accompanied him to Canada, but now was "trying the new way of living" and regarded the Ghost Dance religion as a threat. He was once a strong supporter of Sitting Bull but "had adopted new ways and had discarded all superstitions and other old-time customs and practices."[6] On being alerted to his impending arrest, Sitting Bull apparently said: "If the white men want me to die, they ought not to put up the Indians to kill me. I don't want confusion among my own people. Let the soldiers come and take me away and kill me, whenever they like. I am not afraid. I was born a warrior. I have followed the war path ever since I was able to draw a bow."[7] But it was in the government's interest to have resistive Indian leaders removed by other Indians, and Sitting Bull's arrest turned into a shoot-out between former comrades-in-arms. Sitting Bull's favorite son, Crow Foot, who handed over his father's rifle at Fort Buford, was shot down by Indian policemen with tears streaming down their cheeks.[8] According to Lone Man, Crow Foot had taunted his father into resisting arrest. "It was like Crow Foot to do that," he said.[9]

LONE MAN

The Death of Sitting Bull

1890

Daybreak was drawing near and Lieut. Bullhead asked that we offer up a prayer before starting out and without waiting or calling upon anyone else, led us in prayer. After this, order was issued to saddle up our horses. When everyone was ready we took our places by two and at the command "hopo" we started.

Stanley Vestal, ed., *New Sources of Indian History, 1850–1891* (Norman: University of Oklahoma Press, 1934), 49–55.

We had to go through rough places and the roads were slippery. As we went through the Grand River bottoms it seemed as if the owls were hooting at us and the coyotes were howling all around us that one of the police remarked that the owls and the coyotes were giving us a warning — "so beware" he said.

Before we started, Bullhead assigned Red Bear and White Bird to have the favorite white horse of Sitting Bull's (which was always kept in the shed or in the corral at nights) caught and saddled up and be in readiness for the Chief to ride to the Agency upon his arrest. The rest of the force were ordered to station themselves all around Sitting Bull's cabin for the purpose of keeping order while the officers went into the cabin and cause the arrest. Bullhead said to me "now you used to belong to this outfit and was always on the good side of the Chief. I wish you would use your influence to keep order among the leaders who are going to become hostile."

We rode in a dogtrot gait till we got about a mile from the camp, then we galloped along and when we were about a quarter of a mile, we rode up as if we attacked the camp. Upon our arrival at Sitting Bull's cabin, we quickly dismounted and while the officers went inside we all scattered round the cabin. I followed the police officers and as per orders, I took my place at the door. It was still dark and everybody was asleep and only dogs which were quite numerous, greeted us upon our arrival and no doubt by their greetings had aroused and awaken the ghost dancers.

Bullhead, followed by Red Tomahawk and Shavehead, knocked at the door and the Chief answered "How, timahel hiyu wo," "all right come in." The door was opened and Bullhead said "I come after you to take you to the Agency. You are under arrest." Sitting Bull said, "How," "Let me put on my clothes and go with you." He told one of his wives to get his clothes which was complied with. After he was dressed, arose to go and ordered his son to saddle up his horse. The police told him that it was already outside waiting for him. When Sitting Bull started to go with the police that, according to the custom of Indian wives and other women relatives, instead of bidding him good bye, the way it was done by the civilized people, one of Sitting Bull's wives burst into a loud cry which drew attention. No sooner had this started, when several leaders were rapidly making their way toward Sitting Bull's cabin making all sorts of complaints about the actions of the Indian police. Mato wawoyuspa, the Bear that Catches, particularly came up close saying "Now, here are the 'ceska maza' — 'metal breasts' (meaning police badges) just as we had expected all the time. You think you are going to take him. You shall not do it." Addressing the leaders. "Come on now, let us protect our Chief." Just about this time, Crow Foot got up, moved by the wailing of his mother and the complaining remarks of Bear that Catches, said to Sitting Bull: "Well — You always called yourself a brave chief. Now you are allowing yourself to be taken by the Ceska maza." Sitting Bull then changed his mind and in response to Crow Foot's remark said, "Ho ca mni kte sni yelo." "Then I will not go." By this time the ghost dancers were trying to get close to the Chief in every possible manner, trying to protect him and the police did their best, begging in their way, not to cause any trouble but they would not listen, instead they said "You shall not take away our Chief."

Lieut. Bullhead said to the Chief: "Come, now, do not listen to any one." I said to Sitting Bull in an imploring way: "Uncle, nobody is going to harm you. The Agent wants to see you and then you are to come back, — so please do not let others lead you into any trouble." But the Chief's mind was made up not to go so the three head officers laid their hands on him. Lieut. Bullhead got a hold on the Chief's right arm, Shavehead on the left arm, and Red Tomahawk back of the Chief — pulling him outside. By this time the whole camp was in commotion — women and children crying while the men gathered all round us — said everything mean imaginable but had not done anything to hurt us. The police tried to keep order but was useless — it was like trying to extinguish a treacherous prairie fire. Bear that Catches in the heat of the excitement, pulled out a gun, from under his blanket, and fired into Lieut. Bullhead and wounded him. Seeing that one of my dearest relatives and my superior, shot, I ran up toward where they were holding the Chief, when Bear that Catches raised his gun — pointed and fired at me, but it snapped. Being so close to him I scuffled with him and without any great effort overcame him, jerked the gun away from his hands and with the butt of the gun, I struck him somewhere and laid him out. It was about this moment that Lieut. Bullhead fired into Sitting Bull while still holding him and Red Tomahawk followed with another shot which finished the Chief.

The rest of the police now seeing nothing else for them to do but to defend themselves became engaged in a bitter encounter with the ghost dancers. It was day-break and the ghost dancers fled to the timber and some already started running away into the breaks south of the Grand River. The police took refuge behind the sheds and corrals adjoining the Chief's residence, knocked the chinks out, firing in the direction of the fleeing ghost dancers. One of our police was lying on the ground behind a shed when some ghost dancer shot him in the head and killed him instantly. This was my brother-in-law John Strong Arms, who came with me from our camp.

Finally, there was no more firing and we proceeded gathering up our dead and the wounded.

Hawkman, another relative of mine, a cousin, who hailed from same camp I came from, was sent to carry the news of the fight to the Military Forces. We brought them to the cabin and cared for them. While we were doing this, my friend, Running Hawk, said to the police: "Say, my friends, it seems there is something moving behind the curtain in the corner of the cabin." The cabin, instead of being plastered, the walls were covered with strips of sheeting, sewed together and tacked on the walls making quite a bright appearance within. All eyes were directed to the corner mentioned and without waiting for any orders I raised the curtain. There stood Crow Foot and as soon as he was exposed to view, he cried out, "My uncles, do not kill me. I do not wish to die." The police asked the officers what to do. Lieut. Bullhead, seeing what was up, said, "Do what you like with him. He is one of them that has caused this trouble." I do not remember who really fired the shot that killed Crow Foot — several fired at once.

It was about this time that the soldiers appeared on the top of high hills toward the Agency. According to the instructions received we were expecting them but they did not show up in our critical moment. Maybe it was just as well they did not for they would have made things worse as heretofore they generally did this. Immediately they fired a cannon toward where we were. Being ordered to display a "flag of truce" I tore off a piece of the white curtain, tied it on a long pole, ran out where they could see me, thinking they would cease firing but all was of no avail. They continued firing and the cannon balls came very close to where I was that at times I dodged. Finally, they stopped firing and made a bee-line toward us. They arrived and upon learning what had happened the officer ranking highest proceeded to where Sitting Bull's corpse was and with a (branch/brush) took the third *coup* and said: "Sitting Bull — big chief, you brought this disaster upon yourself and your people." Louis Primeau was interpreting.

The soldiers having dismounted rushed to the camp — ransacking anything worth keeping. Red Tomahawk took charge of the police force and after everything was prepared to take the dead and the wounded Indian police as well as Sitting Bull's corpse, discharged us from this campaign, and having complimented us for doing our duty as we did, asked us to attend the funeral of our comrades, killed in the fight. Strong Arm, Hawkman, Little Eagle, and Akicita were killed. Bullhead, Shave-head, and Middle were wounded seriously. Seven ghost-dancers besides Sitting Bull were killed on the Sitting Bull's side.

About this time, some of the relatives of the police killed arrived and such lamenting over the dead was seldom known in the history of my race. Taking a last look on my dead friends and relatives, I, in company with Charles Afraid of Hawk, started for home. On the way, we passed several deserted homes of the ghost dancers and felt sorry that such a big mistake was made by listening to outsiders who generally cause us nothing but trouble.

I reached home and before our reunion I asked my wife, brothers, sisters, and mother to prepare a sweat bath for me, that I may cleanse myself for participating in a bloody fight with my fellow men. After doing this, new or clean clothes were brought to me and the clothes I wore at the fight were burned up. I then, was reunited with my family. God spared my life for their sake.

The next day I took my family into the Agency. I reported to Major McLaughlin. He laid his hand on my shoulders, shook hands with me and said: "He alone is a Man, I feel proud of you for the very brave way you have carried out your part in the fight with the Ghost Dancers." I was not very brave right at that moment. His comment nearly set me a crying.

NOTES

[1] The discussion of Sitting Bull's life is based on Robert M. Utley, *The Lance and the Shield: The Life and Times of Sitting Bull* (New York: Henry Holt and Co., 1993).

[2] Thomas B. Marquis, *Wooden Leg: A Warrior Who Fought Custer* (Minneapolis: The Midwest Co., 1931), 178–79.

[3] Quoted in Utley, *The Lance and the Shield*, 247.

[4] M. W. Stirling, "Three Pictographic Autobiographies of Sitting Bull," *Smithsonian Miscellaneous Collections* 95, no. 5 (Washington, D.C.: U.S. Govt. Printing Office, 1938). Thirty-two of the drawings, together with interpretations, are reproduced in Stanley Vestal, *Sitting Bull, Champion of the Sioux* (Norman: University of Oklahoma Press, 1957). According to Vestal (p. 324), the interpretations of the exploits given in the Smithsonian collections "do not tally with the information given me by Indians who were present in the fights portrayed."

[5] Vestal, *Sitting Bull*, 316–18.

[6] Stanley Vestal, ed., *New Sources of Indian History, 1850–1891* (Norman: University of Oklahoma Press, 1934), 42, 45–47.

[7] Ibid., 309–10.

[8] Utley, *The Lance and the Shield*, 302.

[9] Vestal, ed., *New Sources of Indian History*, 56.

14

Killing the Dream

Killing Sitting Bull did not stop trouble on the Sioux reservations; instead, it proved to be only a prelude to greater tragedy. Two weeks later, amid continuing tensions occasioned by the spread of the Ghost Dance religion, soldiers of the Seventh Cavalry slaughtered some two hundred Miniconjou people at Wounded Knee. The event marked the end of the armed conflict between Plains Indians and the United States Army and came to symbolize the end of a way of life.

Around 1889 a Paiute Indian named Wovoka, known to whites as Jack Wilson, had a visionary experience. He began to preach a new religion that promised a return to former times when buffalo were plenty and no whites existed in North America. In anticipation of the end of the present world, Wovoka taught his followers to live in harmony and to perform a ritual circle dance that would hasten the coming of the new age (Figure 27). Among some tribes the dance involved falling into a trance-like state. The Ghost Dance spread rapidly across the plains, taking hold among the Lakotas, the Cheyennes, and the Arapahos. "The people were hungry and in despair, and many believed in the good new world that was coming," said Black Elk.[1] The promise of a rejuvenated world had tremendous appeal to people who looked about them and saw poverty, chaos, and confusion. Believing that the buffalo had originated within the earth and had been driven back there by white men, many Indians believed that the buffalo could be induced to return by practicing the proper ceremonies. For the Lakotas, the Ghost Dance was a means of renewing their world through ritual and a spiritual response to their ills, but whites interpreted the Indians' "frenzied" dancing as a sign of impending war. As it had done with the Sun Dance and other religious ceremonies, the government moved to suppress the Ghost Dance. "The white people made war on the Lakotas to keep them from practicing their religion," said Short Bull, one of the Lakota religious leaders. Ultimately, a movement that began with a vision of a new world of peace and harmony ended in carnage at Wounded Knee.[2]

196

Figure 27. The Ghost Dance
Yellow Nose, a Ute artist living among the Cheyennes, produced the hide painting of the Ghost Dance for James Mooney in 1891. A circle of dancers surrounds a group of figures. Cheyenne women (with braided hair) and Arapaho women (with loose hair) participate; two women carry babies on their backs. Several dancers wear belts decorated with disks of German silver; others wave handkerchiefs, and some, lying on the ground at the center, have fallen into a trance. A woman at lower center holds a stuffed crow; a man at left holds a shinny stick; another holds a hoop. One woman at the upper right has raised her arms in trance and dropped her spotted shawl. A medicine man at the far right extends his arms, helping a dancer to achieve a trance.[3]

THE MESSIAH'S LETTER

As news of Wovoka's teachings spread in 1889–90, delegates from northern plains tribes traveled to see and hear the messiah. On their return, they related their experiences and conveyed the message they received to their own people.[4] The anthropologist James Mooney recorded some of these accounts in a report on the Ghost Dance religion that he prepared for the government in 1891–92, but he also included what he described as "the genuine official statement of the Ghost-dance doctrine as given by the messiah himself to his disciples." What follows is a statement delivered by Wovoka to the Cheyenne and Arapaho delegates. The message was written down "in broken English" by Casper Edson, a young Arapaho who had attended the Carlisle Indian School. The daughter of Black Short Nose, one of the Cheyenne delegates, wrote out another version in somewhat better English and tried, unsuccessfully, to erase the clause about concealing the message from whites. Black Short Nose gave the message to Mooney in 1891 because "the Cheyenne and Arapaho were now convinced that I would tell the truth about their religion . . . and they were anxious to have the whites know it was all good and contained nothing bad or hostile." Mooney reproduced both the original Cheyenne and Arapaho versions and the following "translation for the benefit of those not accustomed to Carlisle English."[5]

WOVOKA

Message to the Cheyennes and Arapahos

ca. 1890

When you get home you must make a dance to continue five days. Dance four successive nights, and the last night keep up the dance until the morning of the fifth day, when all must bathe in the river and then disperse to their homes. You must all do in the same way.

I, Jack Wilson, love you all, and my heart is full of gladness for the gifts you have brought me. When you get home I shall give you a good cloud [rain?] which will make you feel good. I give you a good spirit and give you all good paint. I want you to come again in three months, some from each tribe there [the Indian Territory].

There will be a good deal of snow this year and some rain. In the fall there will be such a rain as I have never given you before.

James Mooney, "The Ghost-Dance Religion and the Sioux Outbreak of 1890," *14th Annual Report of the Bureau of American Ethnology, 1892–93,* part 2 (Washington, D.C.: U.S. Govt. Printing Office, 1896), 781.

Grandfather [a universal title of reverence among Indians and here meaning the messiah] says, when your friends die you must not cry. You must not hurt anybody or do harm to anyone. You must not fight. Do right always. It will give you satisfaction in life. This young man has a good father and mother. [Possibly this refers to Casper Edson, the young Arapaho who wrote down this message of Wovoka for the delegation]. Do not tell the white people about this. Jesus is now upon the earth. He appears like a cloud. The dead are all alive again. I do not know when they will be here; maybe this fall or in the spring. When the time comes there will be no more sickness and everyone will be young again.

Do not refuse to work for the whites and do not make any trouble with them until you leave them. When the earth shakes [at the coming of the new world] do not be afraid. It will not hurt you.

I want you to dance every six weeks. Make a feast at the dance and have food that everybody may eat. Then bathe in the water. That is all. You will receive good words again from me some time. Do not tell lies.

"SOMETHING TERRIBLE HAPPENED."

As Wovoka's pacifist message reached the Sioux reservations it appeared to the whites to assume a militant twist: Dancers began to wear "ghost shirts," which they believed would render them invulnerable to the white man's bullets, and they expressed growing defiance of the authorities. The dancing unnerved Indian agents and Army officers. Lakotas on Pine Ridge ignored the orders to stop dancing issued by their agent, Daniel Royer. Black Elk recalled that "we got more lies than cattle, and we could not eat lies. When the agent told the people to quit dancing, their hearts were bad."[6] They ridiculed Royer as Young Man Afraid of Indians.[7] Taking steps to quell the uprising before it started, General Nelson Miles concentrated some five thousand troops in western South Dakota. The Seventh Cavalry went to round up Big Foot and some 350 Miniconjous who had left the Cheyenne River reservation. Sick with pneumonia, Big Foot offered no trouble when the cavalry found him and he agreed to accompany the soldiers to their camp in the valley of Wounded Knee Creek. There, on the morning of December 29, with soldiers and hotchkiss guns surrounding the Indian tepees, Colonel James Forsyth ordered Big Foot's band disarmed. Tempers flared, a shot rang out, and the soldiers opened fire. The mêlée degenerated into a massacre. Some two hundred people died, many freezing to death in a blizzard that hit the area that night.

Charles Eastman, who had been educated at Dartmouth College and Boston University, was working as a doctor on Pine Ridge at the time. He tended the wounded but "lost the greater part of them." "Fully three miles from the scene of the massacre we found the body of a woman completely covered with a blanket of snow," he wrote, "and from this point on we found them scattered along as they had been relentlessly hunted down and slaughtered while fleeing for their lives." Most of the dead were old men, women, and children. "It took all of my nerve to keep my composure in the face of this spectacle," said Eastman; it was "a severe ordeal for one who had so lately put all his faith in the Christian love and lofty ideals of the white man."[8] Others who had embraced "civilization" experienced similar revulsion and questioning when they saw dead babies clinging to their dead mothers' breasts: An Indian called American Horse told Mooney, "I stood very loyal to the government all through these troublesome days," but felt "a very great blame on my heart."[9]

The Oglala holy man Black Elk, a young man at the time, responded to the massacre with fury. In his old age he reflected on how much more had ended at Wounded Knee.

BLACK ELK

Massacre at Wounded Knee

1890

It was now near the end of the Moon of Popping Trees, and I was twenty-seven years old (December, 1890). We heard that Big Foot was coming down from the Badlands with nearly four hundred people. Some of these were from Sitting Bull's band. They had run away when Sitting Bull was killed, and joined Big Foot on Good River. There were only about a hundred warriors in this band, and all the others were women and children and some old men. They were all starving and freezing, and Big Foot was so sick that they had to bring him along in a pony drag. They had all run away to hide in the Badlands, and they were coming in now because they were starving and freezing. When they crossed Smoky

John G. Neihardt, *Black Elk Speaks: Being the Life Story of a Holy Man of the Oglala Sioux* (Lincoln: University of Nebraska Press, 1988 ed.), 253–62, 270.

Earth River, they followed up Medicine Root Creek to its head. Soldiers were over there looking for them. The soldiers had everything and were not freezing and starving. Near Porcupine Butte the soldiers came up to the Big Foots, and they surrendered and went along with the soldiers to Wounded Knee Creek where the Brenan store is now.

It was in the evening when we heard that the Big Foots were camped over there with the soldiers, about fifteen miles by the old road from where we were. It was the next morning (December 29, 1890) that something terrible happened.

That evening before it happened, I went in to Pine Ridge and heard these things, and while I was there, soldiers started for where the Big Foots were. These made about five hundred soldiers that were there next morning. When I saw them starting I felt that something terrible was going to happen. That night I could hardly sleep at all. I walked around most of the night.

In the morning I went out after my horses, and while I was out I heard shooting off toward the east, and I knew from the sound that it must be wagon-guns (cannon) going off. The sounds went right through my body, and I felt that something terrible would happen. . . .

[Black Elk and his companions rode toward the sound of the shooting.]

In a little while we had come to the top of the ridge where, looking to the east, you can see for the first time the monument and the burying ground on the little hill where the church is. That is where the terrible thing started. Just south of the burying ground on the little hill a deep dry gluch runs about east and west, very crooked, and it rises westward to nearly the top of the ridge where we were. It had no name, but the Wasichus sometimes call it Battle Creek now. We stopped on the ridge not far from the head of the dry gulch. Wagon guns were still going off over there on the little hill, and they were going off again where they hit along the gulch. There was much shooting down yonder, and there were many cries, and we could see cavalrymen scattered over the hills ahead of us. Cavalrymen were riding along the gulch and shooting into it, where the women and children were running away and trying to hide in the gullies and the stunted pines. . . .

By now many other Lakotas, who had heard the shooting, were coming up from Pine Ridge, and we all charged on the soldiers. They ran eastward toward where the trouble began. We followed down along the dry gulch, and what we saw was terrible. Dead and wounded women and children and little babies were scattered all along there where they had been trying to run away. The soldiers had followed along the gulch, as they ran, and murdered them in there. Sometimes they were in heaps because they had huddled together, and some were scattered all along. Sometimes bunches of them had been killed and torn to pieces where the wagon guns hit them. I saw a little baby trying to suck its mother, but she was bloody and dead.

There were two little boys at one place in this gulch. They had guns and they had been killing soldiers all by themselves. We could see the soldiers they had killed. The boys were all alone there, and they were not hurt. These were very brave little boys.

When we drove the soldiers back, they dug themselves in, and we were not enough people to drive them out from there. In the evening they marched off up Wounded Knee Creek, and then we saw all that they had done there.

Men and women and children were heaped and scattered all over the flat at the bottom of the little hill where the soldiers had their wagon-guns, and westward up the dry gulch all the way to the high ridge, the dead women and children and babies were scattered.

When I saw this I wished that I had died too, but I was not sorry for the women and children. It was better for them to be happy in the other world, and I wanted to be there too. But before I went there I wanted to have revenge. I thought there might be a day, and we should have revenge.

After the soldiers marched away, I heard from my friend, Dog Chief, how the trouble started, and he was right there by Yellow Bird when it happened. This is the way it was:

In the morning the soldiers began to take all the guns away from the Big Foots, who were camped in the flat below the little hill where the monument and burying ground are now. The people had stacked most of their guns, and even their knives, by the tepee where Big Foot was lying sick. Soldiers were on the little hill and all around, and there were soldiers across the dry gulch to the south and over east along Wounded Knee Creek too. The people were nearly surrounded, and the wagon-guns were pointing at them.

Some had not yet given up their guns, and so the soldiers were searching all the tepees, throwing things around and poking into everything. There was a man called Yellow Bird, and he and another man were standing in front of the tepee where Big Foot was lying sick. They had white sheets around and over them, with eyeholes to look through, and they had guns under these. An officer came to search them. He took the other man's gun, and then started to take Yellow Bird's. But Yellow Bird would not let go. He wrestled with the officer, and while they were wrestling, the gun went off and killed the officer. Wasichus and some others have said he meant to do this, but Dog Chief was standing right there, and he told me it was not so. As soon as the gun went off, Dog Chief told me, an officer shot and killed Big Foot who was lying sick inside the tepee.

Then suddenly nobody knew what was happening, except that the soldiers were all shooting and the wagon-guns began going off right in among the people.

Many were shot down right there. The women and children ran into the gulch and up west, dropping all the time, for the soldiers shot them as they ran. There were only about a hundred warriors and there were nearly five hundred soldiers. The warriors rushed to where they had piled their guns and knives. They fought soldiers with only their hands until they got their guns.

Dog Chief saw Yellow Bird run into a tepee with his gun, and from there he killed soldiers until the tepee caught fire. Then he died full of bullets.

It was a good winter day when all this happened. The sun was shining. But after the soldiers marched away from their dirty work, a heavy snow began to fall. The wind came up in the night. There was a big blizzard, and it grew very cold. The snow drifted deep in the crooked gulch, and it was one long grave of butchered women and children and babies, who had never done any harm and were only trying to run away. . . .

[Black Elk and other warriors wanted to fight the soldiers, but Red Cloud persuaded them to think of the women and children and submit.]
And so it was all over.

I did not know then how much was ended. When I look back now from this high hill of my old age, I can still see the butchered women and children lying heaped and scattered all along the crooked gulch as plain as when I saw them with eyes still young. And I can see that something else died there in the bloody mud, and was buried in the blizzard. A people's dream died there. It was a beautiful dream.

And I, to whom so great a vision was given in my youth, — you see me now a pitiful old man who has done nothing, for the nation's hoop is broken and scattered. There is no center any longer, and the sacred tree is dead.

NOTES

[1] John G. Neihardt, *Black Elk Speaks: Being the Life Story of a Holy Man of the Oglala Sioux* (Lincoln: University of Nebraska Press, 1988 ed.), 249.

[2] The classic study of the movement, conducted immediately after the Wounded Knee massacre, is James Mooney, "The Ghost-Dance Religion and the Sioux Outbreak of 1890," *14th Annual Report of the Bureau of American Ethnology, 1892–93,* part 2 (Washington, D.C.: U.S. Govt. Printing Office, 1896). See also Raymond J. DeMallie, "The Lakota Ghost Dance: An Ethnohistorical Account," *Pacific Historical Review* 51 (1982), 385–405. Short Bull's quote is from James R. Walker, *Lakota Belief and Ritual,* ed. Raymond J. DeMallie and Elaine A. Jahner (Lincoln: University of Nebraska Press, 1980), 141.

[3] Evan M. Maurer, et al., *Visions of the People: A Pictorial History of Plains Indian Life* (Minneapolis: Institute of Arts, 1992), 168.

[4] See, for example, "Porcupine's Account of the Messiah," in Mooney, "The Ghost-Dance Religion," 793–96; One Bull's account in James McLaughlin, *My Friend the Indian* (Boston: Houghton Mifflin, 1910), 185–89.

[5] Mooney, "The Ghost-Dance Religion," 780.

[6] Neihardt, *Black Elk Speaks,* 249.

[7] Robert M. Utley, *The Indian Frontier of the American West, 1846–1890* (Albuquerque: University of New Mexico Press, 1984), 254.

[8] Charles Eastman, *From the Deep Woods to Civilization: Chapters in the Autobiography of an Indian* (Lincoln: University of Nebraska Press, 1977 ed.), 110–14.

[9] Mooney, "The Ghost-Dance Religion," 886.

Epilogue

The conquest of the American West left Indian people with a bitter legacy: searching for a place and a purpose in the new world. But some Indian people maintain that the West never really was lost. Pointing to their ancient presence in this country, they remind us that the history of the United States is relatively brief and suggest that Indian peoples can outlast the United States just as they outlasted other periods of hardship and misfortune.

Indian peoples survived the policies of forced acculturation that were supposed to eradicate Indian cultures and values. Ironically, in some ways forced assimilation brought Indian people closer together as boarding schools and compulsory education in the English language gave Indian students a common experience and a common means of communication. In the early twentieth century, a new generation of Indians, schooled in the white men's ways, took the first steps toward pan-Indian unity and founded the Society of American Indians in 1911. "Red Progressives" such as Charles Eastman, the Sioux writer Gertrude Bonin, Henry Standing Bear, and the Reverend Sherman Coolidge, an Arapaho Episcopalian who had been raised by an Army captain and lived many years in New York City, sometimes disagreed on strategy and on what was an acceptable measure of acculturation, but they worked to improve the conditions of all Indian people.

Plains Indians endured continuing acculturation policies in the twentieth century. Some benefited from John Collier's "Indian New Deal" in the 1930s, although the new styles of tribal government established under the Indian Reorganization Act of 1934 created problems and aggravated divisions on some reservations.[1] After World War II, in which Indians fought, the United States in the late 1940s and 1950s turned again to dismantling tribal governments and cultures in an effort to assimilate Indians into American society. Many tribes were targeted for termination. Individuals and families were encouraged to leave the reservations and move to the cities, where government policymakers hoped they would be swallowed up by mainstream America. However, city life produced new sources of common Indian identity and protest, culminating in the creation of the American Indian Movement (AIM) in Minneapolis in 1968. AIM drew together Indians from across the country and pursued tactics that focused national attention on Indian demands. After an escalation of tensions, Indians once again confronted the armed forces of the United States in a seventy-day seige at Wounded Knee, South Dakota, in 1973.

Having lost most of their lands in the nineteenth century, Indians in the twentieth century experienced a renewed assault on what remained of their homelands as the U.S. government and energy companies sought to gain access to the energy resources to be found on Indian reservations.[2] As the twenty-first century approaches, Indian people wage recurring battles over water rights, oil and gas revenues, sacred sites, religious freedom, sovereignty, and the repatriation of skeletal remains and cultural artifacts. After five hundred years of contact, Indians and whites are still trying to work out their relations, and Indians continue to fight to hold on to things they deem essential to their survival as a people.

Indian cultures have changed as all cultures change, and Plains Indians today can be found throughout the United States in virtually all walks of life. But Indian people and Indian culture remain very much a part of the Great Plains.[3] Many Indians have become successful cattle ranchers, and Indian cowboys and white cowboys today face many common problems.[4] In some areas of the plains, Indian reservations are growing in population as neighboring ranching communities decline.[5] Some tribes have opened gambling casinos in the hope of bringing income and employment to their reservations.

In all of their struggles, Indian peoples have drawn on the traditions of the past to help guide them in the present and future. In some ways, Plains Indian societies never recovered from the slaughter of the buffalo herds in the late nineteenth century. Just as the disappearance of the buffalo symbolized the collapse of a traditional way of life, so, for many Indian people, a return of the buffalo would symbolize a revival of that life.

At the end of his novel *Fools Crow,* Blackfeet/Gros Ventre author James Welch conveys the importance of the buffalo to the Piegan Indians in the old days:

> Far from the fires of the camps, out on the rain-dark prairies, in the swales and washes, on the rolling hills, the rivers of great animals moved. Their backs were dark with rain and the rain gathered and trickled down their shaggy heads. Some grazed, some slept. Some had begun to molt. Their horns glistened in the rain as they stood guard over the sleeping calves. The blackhorns had returned and, all around, it was as it should be.[6]

Today, things are less simple. Bringing back the buffalo offers no panacea for the problems confronting Indian communities on the plains. Nevertheless, helping the buffalo come back carries great symbolic and spiritual significance. In the early 1990s, some thirty tribes joined forces to form the Inter-tribal Bison Cooperative, centered in Rapid City, South Dakota. The cooperative works to help the tribes rebuild buffalo herds on their reservations. Buffalo meat offers a source of food, of course, but as Fred DuBray, chair and one of the founders of the cooperative, put it, "our spiritual connection with these buffalo is our No. 1 priority."[7] In Sioux belief, long ago White Buffalo Woman was sent by the Buffalo People to establish relations with humans, so that ever after human beings would have food. The relationship of buffalo and people became an integral part of the fixed order of the universe. When whites came and drove away the buffalo, the world was thrown into disorder.[8] Indian people who want to see the buffalo return do not intend to go back to living in tepees and hunting for a living; they live in the twentieth century and are preparing for the twenty-first. But the buffalo stands as an important cultural guidepost as Plains Indian peoples face the present and future. Rebuilding the herds means restoring some order to a world that, as Luther Standing Bear said, was made wild when hairy men arrived from the East.[9]

NOTES

[1] For example, Thomas Biolsi, *Organizing the Lakota: The Political Economy of the New Deal on the Pine Ridge and Rosebud Reservations* (Tucson: University of Arizona Press, 1992).

[2] Marjane Ambler, *Breaking the Iron Bonds: Indian Control of Energy Development* (Lawrence: University of Kansas Press, 1990).

[3] See, for example, Peter Iverson, ed., *The Plains Indians of the Twentieth Century* (Norman: University of Oklahoma Press, 1985); Donald L. Parman, *Indians and the American West in the Twentieth Century* (Bloomington: Indiana University Press, 1994).

[4] Peter Iverson, *When Indians Became Cowboys: Native Peoples and Cattle Ranching in the American West* (Norman: University of Oklahoma Press, 1994).

[5] Thomas Biolsi, "The Political Economy of Lakota Consciousness," in John H. Moore, ed., *The Political Economy of North American Indians* (Norman: University of Oklahoma Press, 1993), 20–42.

[6] James Welch, *Fools Crow* (New York: Penguin, 1987), 390–91.

[7] Quoted in the *Billings Gazette* (Montana), Jan. 6, 1995, and the *Casper Star Tribune* (Wyoming), Jan. 5, 1995. DuBray was referring to buffalo that wandered from Yellowstone National Park onto private land and that were being killed by park rangers and game wardens lest they infect cattle. The cooperative asked that they be allowed to take the buffalo, keep them in quarantine, and then distribute them among the tribes.

[8] Raymond J. DeMallie and Douglas R. Parks, eds., *Sioux Indian Religion* (Norman: University of Oklahoma Press, 1987), 31.

[9] In Wisconsin in the summer of 1994 a sign of hope for Indian people across America came to life when a white buffalo calf was born, the first birth of this kind to occur in fifty years.

Chronology of How the West Was Lost

1540: Coronado leads Spanish expedition on to southern plains.

1600–1700: Horses spread from the Southwest across the plains.

1779–83: Major smallpox epidemic from Mexico to Canada.

1801–02: Smallpox epidemic.

1804–06: Lewis and Clark expedition.

1830: Indian Removal Act: Tribes from the Southeast and Great Lakes forced west to Oklahoma and Arkansas.

1837: Smallpox breaks out on upper Missouri and spreads across the plains.

1846–48: War between the United States and Mexico.

1848–49: California Gold Rush.

1851: Treaty of Fort Laramie with northern plains tribes.

1854: Sioux annihilate Lieutenant John Grattan's command.

1861–65: American Civil War.

1862: Sioux "uprising" in Minnesota.

1864: Colorado militia massacres Southern Cheyennes at Sand Creek.

1866–67: "Red Cloud War": Sioux fight to close Bozeman Trail.

1867: Treaty of Medicine Lodge with southern plains tribes.

1867–83: Buffalo herds exterminated.

1868: United States Army campaigns against southern plains tribes; George Custer destroys Southern Cheyenne village on the Washita River. Treaty of Fort Laramie with the Sioux.

1869: Transcontinental railroad completed.

1869–70: Smallpox on the northern plains.

1870: United States Army destroys Piegan village on the Marias River.

1871: U.S. Congress ceases to make treaties with Indian tribes.

1874–75: Red River War on the southern plains.

1875: Seventy-two southern plains warriors sent as prisoners of war to Fort Marion, Florida.

1876–77: "The Great Sioux War": Sioux and Cheyennes annihilate Custer's command at the Little Big Horn.

1877: Crazy Horse killed.

1879: Captain Richard H. Pratt opens Carlisle Indian School in Carlisle, Pennsylvania.

1881: Sitting Bull surrenders.

1881: U.S. Supreme Court decides *Ex Parte Crow Dog.*

1883: Courts of Indian Offenses established.

1887: Congress passes Dawes Allotment Act.

1889–90: Ghost Dance spreads from Nevada to the plains.

1890: Sitting Bull killed. Wounded Knee massacre at Pine Ridge reservation, South Dakota.

1903: U.S. Supreme Court rules Congress has power to abrogate treaties with Indian tribes in *Lone Wolf v. Hitchcock.*

Questions for Consideration

1. What are the advantages and disadvantages of the documents and drawings reproduced in this book as sources for understanding or reconsidering Plains Indian history and the history of the American West?
2. What do the sources in this book tell us about the lives and experiences of Plains Indians? What do they omit?
3. Which, if any, of the sources appear (a) to be of dubious authenticity; (b) to betray the influence of non-Indian editors or interpreters; or (c) to have been created consciously for a white audience?
4. The Great Plains region in the early nineteenth century has been described as "a world in flux." To what extent do the sources justify this description?
5. Account for the relatively rapid defeat of the Plains Indians by the United States in the second half of the nineteenth century.
6. What do the sources in this book reveal about the different ways in which Indian people responded to the demands and pressures imposed by the United States government in the late nineteenth century?
7. In what ways did the lives of Plains Indian people change between 1800 and 1900? In what ways, if any, did their lives display continuity and resilience?
8. Two Leggings said that "nothing happened" after his people were confined to the reservation. What evidence do the sources in this book provide to help us (a) understand this reaction and (b) refute this statement?

Selected Bibliography

The literature on the history and culture of the Plains Indians is voluminous. This bibliography lists only a selection of the sources used in preparing this book. Students should refer to the notes for additional works.

PRIMARY SOURCES

Annual Reports of the Board of Indian Commissioners 1870–1880 (Washington, D.C.: U.S. Govt. Printing Office, 1871–81).

Gary Clayton Anderson and Alan R. Woolworth, eds., *Through Dakota Eyes: Narrative Accounts of the Minnesota Indian War of 1862* (St. Paul: Minnesota Historical Society Press, 1988).

Althea Bass, *The Arapaho Way: A Memoir of an Indian Boyhood* (New York: Clarkson N. Potter, 1966).

George Catlin, *Letters and Notes on the Manners, Customs, and Conditions of North American Indians.* 2 vols. (London: Author, 1844).

Raymond J. DeMallie, ed., *The Sixth Grandfather: The Teachings of Black Elk Given to John G. Neihardt* (Lincoln: University of Nebraska Press, 1984).

Charles Eastman, *From the Deep Woods to Civilization: Chapters in the Autobiography of an Indian* (Lincoln: University of Nebraska Press, 1977 ed.).

Jerome A. Greene, comp. and ed., *Lakota and Cheyenne: Indian Views of the Great Sioux War* (Norman: University of Oklahoma Press, 1994).

Charles J. Kappler, ed., *Indian Affairs: Laws and Treaties.* 2 vols. (Washington, D.C.: U.S. Govt. Printing Office, 1904).

Arnold Krupat, ed., *Native American Autobiography: An Anthology* (Madison: University of Wisconsin Press, 1994).

O. G. Libby, ed., "The Arikara Narrative of the Campaign Against the Hostile Dakotas," *Collections of the North Dakota State Historical Society* 6 (1920).

Frank B. Linderman, *Plenty Coups, Chief of the Crows* (Lincoln: University of Nebraska Press, 1962).

Frank B. Linderman, *Pretty-shield, Medicine Woman of the Crows* (Lincoln: University of Nebraska Press, 1972).

Garrick Mallery, "Picture Writing of the American Indians," *10th Annual Report of the Bureau of American Ethnology, 1888–89* (Washington, D.C.: U.S. Govt. Printing Office, 1893), 266–328.

Thomas B. Marquis, interpreter, *Wooden Leg: A Warrior Who Fought Custer* (Minneapolis: The Midwest Co., 1931).

James Mooney, "Calendar History of the Kiowa Indians," *17th Annual Report of the Bureau of American Ethnology 1895–96*, part 1 (Washington, D.C.: U.S. Govt. Printing Office, 1898), 129–445.

James Mooney, "The Ghost-Dance Religion and the Sioux Outbreak of 1890," *14th Annual Report of the Bureau of American Ethnology, 1892–93*, part 2 (Washington, D.C.: U.S. Govt. Printing Office, 1896).

Peter Nabokov, *Two Leggings: The Making of a Crow Warrior* (New York: Thomas Y. Crowell, 1967).

John G. Neihardt, *Black Elk Speaks: Being the Life Story of a Holy Man of the Oglala Sioux* (Lincoln: University of Nebraska Press, 1988 ed.).

"Prince Maximilian of Wied's Travels in the Interior of North America, 1832–1834," in Reuben G. Thwaites, ed., *Early Western Travels, 1748–1846*, vols. 22–25 (Cleveland: The Arthur H. Clark Co., 1906).

Report of the Joint Special Committee on the Condition of the Indian Tribes. [Doolittle Report] 39th Congress, 2nd session (1866–67) Senate Report No. 156. Serial 1279.

James Willard Schultz, *Blackfeet and Buffalo: Memories of Life among the Indians* (Norman: University of Oklahoma Press, 1962).

Luther Standing Bear, *My People the Sioux* (Boston: Houghton Mifflin, 1928).

M. W. Stirling, "Three Pictographic Autobiographies of Sitting Bull," *Smithsonian Miscellaneous Collections*, vol. 95, no. 5 (Washington: U.S. Govt. Printing Office, 1938).

Stanley Vestal, ed., *New Sources of Indian History, 1850–1891* (Norman: University of Oklahoma Press, 1934).

W. Raymond Wood and Thomas D. Thiessen, eds., *Early Fur Trade on the Northern Plains: Canadian Traders among the Mandan and Hidatsa Indians, 1738–1818* (Norman: University of Oklahoma Press, 1985).

SECONDARY SOURCES

Janet Catherine Berlo, "Wo-Haw's Notebooks: 19th Century Kiowa Indian Drawings in the Collections of the Missouri Historical Society," *Gateway Heritage* 3 (Fall 1982), 5–13.

Alfred W. Bowers, "Hidatsa Social and Ceremonial Organization," *Bureau of American Ethnology Bulletin* 194 (Washington, D.C.: U.S. Govt. Printing Office, 1965).

H. David Brumble, III, *American Indian Autobiography* (Berkeley: University of California Press, 1988).

Colin G. Calloway, "'The Only Way Open to Us': The Crow Struggle for Survival in the Nineteenth Century," *North Dakota History* 53 (Summer 1986), 25–34.

John C. Ewers, *The Blackfeet: Raiders on the Northwestern Plains* (Norman: University of Oklahoma Press, 1958).

Dan Flores, "Bison Ecology and Bison Diplomacy: The Southern Plains, 1800–1850," *Journal of American History* 78 (1991), 465–85.

Carolyn Gilman and Mary Jane Schneider, *The Way to Independence: Memories of a Hidatsa Indian Family, 1840–1920* (St. Paul: Minnesota Historical Society Press, 1987).

Frederick E. Hoxie, *Parading Through History: The Making of the Crow Nation in America, 1805–1935* (New York: Cambridge University Press, 1995).

Joseph Jablow, "The Cheyenne in Plains Indian Trade Relations, 1795–1840," *Monographs of the American Ethnological Society* 19 (1966; reprinted Lincoln: University of Nebraska Press, 1994).

Douglas C. Jones, *The Treaty of Medicine Lodge: The Story of the Great Treaty Council as Told by Eyewitnesses* (Norman: University of Oklahoma Press, 1966).

Evan M. Maurer, et al. *Visions of the People: A Pictorial History of Plains Indian Life* (Minneapolis Institute of Arts, 1992).

James C. Olson, *Red Cloud and the Sioux Problem* (Lincoln: University of Nebraska Press, 1965).

Karen Daniels Peterson, *Howling Wolf: A Cheyenne Warrior's Graphic Interpretation of His People* (Palo Alto, Cal.: American West Publishing, 1968).

James P. Ronda, *Lewis and Clark among the Indians* (Lincoln: University of Nebraska Press, 1984).

Frank R. Secoy, "Changing Military Patterns on the Great Plains," *Monographs of the American Ethnological Society* 21 (1953; reprinted Lincoln: University of Nebraska Press, 1992).

Joyce M. Szabo, *Howling Wolf and the History of Ledger Art* (Albuquerque: University of New Mexico Press, 1994.)

Russell Thornton, *American Indian Holocaust and Survival: A Population History since 1492* (Norman: University of Oklahoma Press, 1987).

Robert M. Utley, *The Indian Frontier of the American West 1846–1890* (Albuquerque: University of New Mexico Press, 1984).

Robert M. Utley, *The Lance and the Shield: The Life and Times of Sitting Bull* (New York: Henry Holt and Co., 1993).

James Welch, *Fools Crow* (New York: Penguin, 1987).

Richard White, "The Winning of the West: The Expansion of the Western Sioux in the Eighteenth and Nineteenth Centuries," *Journal of American History* 65 (1978), 319–43.

216

ACKNOWLEDGMENTS

(Continued from page ii)

Little Bear, "The Sand Creek Massacre, 1864." From *Life of George Bent: Written from His Letters*, by George E. Hyde. Copyright © 1968 by the University of Oklahoma Press.

Lone Man, "The Death of Sitting Bull, 1890." From *New Sources of Indian History, 1850–1891: A Miscellany*, by Stanley Vestal. Copyright © 1934 by the University of Oklahoma Press.

Old Lady Horse, "The Last Buffalo Herd." From *American Indian Mythology*, by Alice Marriot and Carol K. Rachlin, pp. 173–77. Copyright © 1968 by Alice Marriot and Carol K. Rachlin. Reprinted with permission of HarperCollins Publishers, Inc.

Saukamappee, "Memories of War and Smallpox, 1787–1788." From *David Thompson's Narrative, 1784–1812*, edited by Richard Glover. Toronto: The Champlain Society, 1962, pp. 240–47.

Sweezy, Carl, "Learning the White Man's Ways" and "On Taking 'the New Road.'" From *The Arapaho Way*, by Althea Bass. Copyright © 1966 by Althea Bass. Reprinted by permission of Crown Publishers, Inc.

Two Leggings, "The Dream and Reality of a Raid." From *Two Leggings: The Making of a Crow Warrior*, by Peter Nabokov, pp. 122–26. Copyright © 1967 by Peter Nabokov. Reprinted by permission of HarperCollins Publishers, Inc.

Wooden Leg, "A Cheyenne Account of the Battle" and "Serving as Judge." From *Wooden Leg, A Warrior Who Fought Custer*, by Thomas B. Marquis. Minneapolis: Midwest Co., 1931, pp. 217–21, 366–69. Reprinted by permission of the University of Nebraska Press.

ILLUSTRATIONS

Figure 2. A Great Battle. Courtesy of the Southwest Museum, Los Angeles. Photo N.34650.

Figure 3. Lone Dog's Buffalo Robe. Courtesy of the National Museum of the American Indian, Smithsonian Institution, New York.

Figure 5. Trading Guns for Horses. Courtesy of Joslyn Art Museum, Omaha, Nebraska.

Figure 7. Four Bears, as Painted by Karl Bodmer in 1834. Courtesy of Joslyn Art Museum, Omaha, Nebraska.

Figure 8. Buffalo Robe. Courtesy of the Bernisches Historisches Museum, Bern, Switzerland.

Figure 9. Four Bears's Drawing Depicting His Killing of a Cheyenne Chief. Courtesy of Joslyn Art Museum, Omaha, Nebraska.

Figure 10. Crow Indians Pursue Sioux in a Running Battle. Courtesy of Montana State University, Billings, Montana.

Figure 11. Piegan Artist George Bull Child's Hide Painting of the Massacre on the Marias (ca. 1930). Courtesy of the Denver Art Museum, 1985.106.

Figure 12. Council with Army Officers. Courtesy of the Yale Collection of Western Americana, Beinecke Rare Book and Manuscript Library, Yale University, New Haven, Connecticut.

Figure 13. A Drawing of Buffalo Hunting in the Old Days by Howling Wolf and Soaring Eagle. Courtesy of Allen Memorial Art Museum, Oberlin College, Oberlin, Ohio.

Figure 14. Seizing a Soldier's Gun at the Battle of the Little Big Horn. Courtesy of the Southwest Parks and Monuments Association, Crow Agency, Montana.

Figure 15. The Indian Village in the Valley of the Little Big Horn. Courtesy of the National Anthropological Archives, Smithsonian Institution, Washington, D.C.

Figure 16. Soldiers Charging the Indian Village. Courtesy of the National Anthropological Archives, Smithsonian Institution, Washington, D.C.

Figure 17. Repulsing Reno's Attack, as Indicated by the Cavalry Being Forced Back Over Their Own Hoofprints. Courtesy of the National Anthropological Archives, Smithsonian Institution, Washington, D.C.

Figure 18. The Sioux Fighting Custer's Command. Courtesy of the National Anthropological Archives, Smithsonian Institution, Washington, D.C.
Figure 19. The Dead Soldiers and Indians. Courtesy of the National Anthropological Archives, Smithsonian Institution, Washington, D.C.
Figure 20. The Indians Leaving the Battlefield as They Hear that Relief Columns of Infantry Are Approaching. Courtesy of the National Anthropological Archives, Smithsonian Institution, Washington, D.C.
Figure 22. Kiowa Husbands and Wives Going to a Dance. Courtesy of the Morning Star Gallery, Santa Fe, New Mexico.
Figure 23. U.S. Indian Agent and Chief of Police Take a Child to School. Courtesy of Montana State University, Billings, Montana.
Figure 24. Wohaw's Self-Portrait. Courtesy of the Missouri Historical Society, St. Louis, Missouri.
Figure 25. Sitting Bull's Drawings of Scenes from His Life as a Warrior (1870). Courtesy of the National Anthropological Archives, Smithsonian Institution, Washington, D.C.
Figure 26. Sitting Bull. Courtesy of the Montana Historical Society, Helena, Montana.
Figure 27. The Ghost Dance. Courtesy of the National Museum of Natural History, Department of Anthropology, Smithsonian Institution, Washington, D.C.

Index

218

Made in the USA
Las Vegas, NV
16 January 2024

84438074R00134